Dutch Colonialism and Indonesian Islam

Contacts and Conflicts 1596-1950

Karel Steenbrink

Translated by
Jan Steenbrink and Henry Jansen

Rodopi

Amsterdam - New York, NY 2006

Cover photo: Dutch Resident W. de Vogel with the Muslim ruler of Surakarta, Susuhunan Pakubuwana X ca. 1897

Cover design: AartJan Bergshoeff

The paper on which this book is printed meets the requirements of "ISO 9706:1994, Information and documentation - Paper for documents - Requirements for permanence".

Second Revised Edition.
ISBN-10: 90-420-2071-7
ISBN-13: 978-90-420-2071-9
©Editions Rodopi B.V., Amsterdam - New York, NY 2006
Printed in the Netherlands

Contents

FORWARD BY DR. H. ABDUL MUKTI ALI   7

1. STARTING-POINTS AND EXPLORATIONS   11

2. THE FIRST ENCOUNTERS:
   MUSLIMS AS RESPECTED HERETICS   25

3. THE THEOLOGICAL HOMEFRONT:
   MUSLIMS AS DETESTABLE HERETICS   43

4. COMPANY DIRECTORS IN "NATURAL HOSTILITY"
   TOWARDS "UNTRUSTWORTHY AND FANATIC MUSLIMS"   60

5. THE ADVISORS HOLLE, HURGHRONJE AND HAZEU:
   TUTORS TO "MEMBERS OF A BACKWARD RELIGION"   76

6. THE AGE OF MISSION (1850-1940) AND THE MUSLIMS:
   BETWEEN ANTICIPATION AND ACCOMMODATION   98

7. INDONESIAN REACTIONS
   TO THE CHRISTIANS' ARRIVAL   124

8. MUSLIMS AND CHRISTIANS
   IN INDEPENDENT INDONESIA 1945-2005   140

BIBLIOGRAPHY   155

INDEX   169

Subscripts to the photographs:

Procession to the mosque of Ternate for prayer on Idul Adha. In commemoration Abraham who was willing to offer his son, a goat will be slaughtered (front of the procession). he sultan is walking at the back, accompanied by a servant who holds the ceremonial umbrella (payung). From Keuning, 1938 III:125.

Forward

Karel Steenbrink began his study of Indonesian Islam as a student and researcher at the *pesantren* of Gontor, one of the most modern islamic colleges in Indonesia. This *pesantren* is an islamic boarding school that still teaches the old traditions but at the same time attempts to keep up with modern developments. During his stay in Indonesia Dr. Steenbrink lived among the more than 1200 moslem students and their teachers. After completing his study here (about 1970) he wrote his dissertation on these schools.

I myself became acquainted with Dr. Steenbrink at a later date, when my studies took me in the opposite direction - from Indonesia to The Netherlands. From 1978-79 I attended the University of Leiden as a Ph.D. fellow to work on my dissertation on the Dutch colonial government's policy toward Islam, particularly from 1889 onwards - thus from the time of Snouck Hurgronje. I was a member of a group of nine fellows from islamic institutions in Indonesia, five of whom completed our dissertations: Dr. M. Chatib Quzwain (IAIN Jami), Dr. Chalidjah Hasanuddin (IAIN Bandung), Dr. Burhan Daya (IAIN Yogyakarta), Dr. Alfani Daud (IAIN Banjarmasin) and myself.

As the director of the program and tutor, Dr. Steenbrink was of great assistance in my studies and those of my colleagues in The Netherlands. This program was special in that it also aimed at increasing interest in Indonesian Islam in The Netherlands, which had decreased significantly since the end of the colonial period. Consequently, there were only a few very old retired experts in the field whose studies had been done when Indonesia was still a Dutch colony. The younger generation, to which Dr. Steenbrink belonged, had had no personal experience with the colonial period and thus were precisely in the position to reevaluate that past and, among other things, to pass on the scholarship that had been done during that period to the Indonesians themselves. In addition, they themselves wished to form a post-colonial conception of the history of Indonesian Islam and its relations with The Netherlands. Dr. Steenbrink was able to realize this in an extended way when he accepted a teaching position in Indonesia from 1981 to 1988. It was then that I came to know him with him as a critical and willing colleague, especially in the period 1981-83 when he was working in Jakarta.

We should be pleased that this academic cooperation between The Netherlands and Indonesia is being carried on, so that not only Indonesians but the Dutch as well are continuing to investigate the past of Indonesian Islam and colonial history. This is apparent in, among other things, the broadening of the collaboration through the INIS (Indonesian Netherlands Cooperation in Islamic Studies) which provides an extensive program of cooperation for 1989-93. I am also very appreciative of the fact that a number of Dutch sources have been translated into Indonesian through this program and therefore are now available to Indonesian moslems.

During the period of his employment in Indonesia, Dr. Steenbrink published at least five books in Indonesian, mostly on the history of Islam in Indonesia: *Beberapa Aspek tentang Islam di Indonesia, Abad ke-19* (Aspects of Indonesian Islam in the 19th Century), with a preface by Prof. Dr. H.M. Rasjidi, Jakarta , Bulan Bintang; *Pesantren, madrasa, sekolah: Pendidikan Islam dalam kurun moderen* (Pesantren, Madrasah, Sekolah: Islamic Education in Modern Indonesia), Jakarta LP3ES; *Perkembangen Teologi dalam Dunia Kristen Modern*, (An Introduction to Modern Christian Theology), with a preface by Prof. Dr. Abdul Mukti Ali, Yoghyakarta, Sunan Kalijaga Press; *Kitab Suci atau Kertas Toilet, Nuruddin ar-Raniri dan Agama Kristen* (Holy Scripture or Toilet Paper? Nuruddin ar-Raniri and the Christian Religion), Yogyakarta, IAIN Kalijaga Press; *Mencari Tuhan dengan Kacamata Barat Vol I: Penelitian Agama di Indonesia* (A Critical Survey of Western Studies on Religion in Indonesia, Vol. I., The Quest for God through Western Eyes) Yogyakarta Sunan Kalijaga Press.

I am glad that this book gives primary attention to the perceptions of the Dutch in their dealings with Indonesians. I believe that it gives a fair and honest picture of the colonial relations - also where the Indonesians are concerned. I would like to add the observation that during the colonial period the great Islam societies, which have been founded since the beginning of the twentieth century have always shown an open mind towards the West. Their political opposition to the colonial system was accompanied by a pronounced openness to the many achievements of Western society. Also, these organisations made a clear distinction between Western society and Christian culture, so that they were able to retain their islamic identity while studying Western culture. This openness has ultimately contributed to the modern character of Indonesian Islam in this respect.

I hope that this book will be received well and that we may expect more publications by Dr. Steenbrink.

Prof. Dr. H. Aqib Suminot, Jakarta, February, 1992
National Institute of Islamic Studies IAIN Syarif Hijdayatullah
Faculty of Da'wah

(Map of Indonesia)

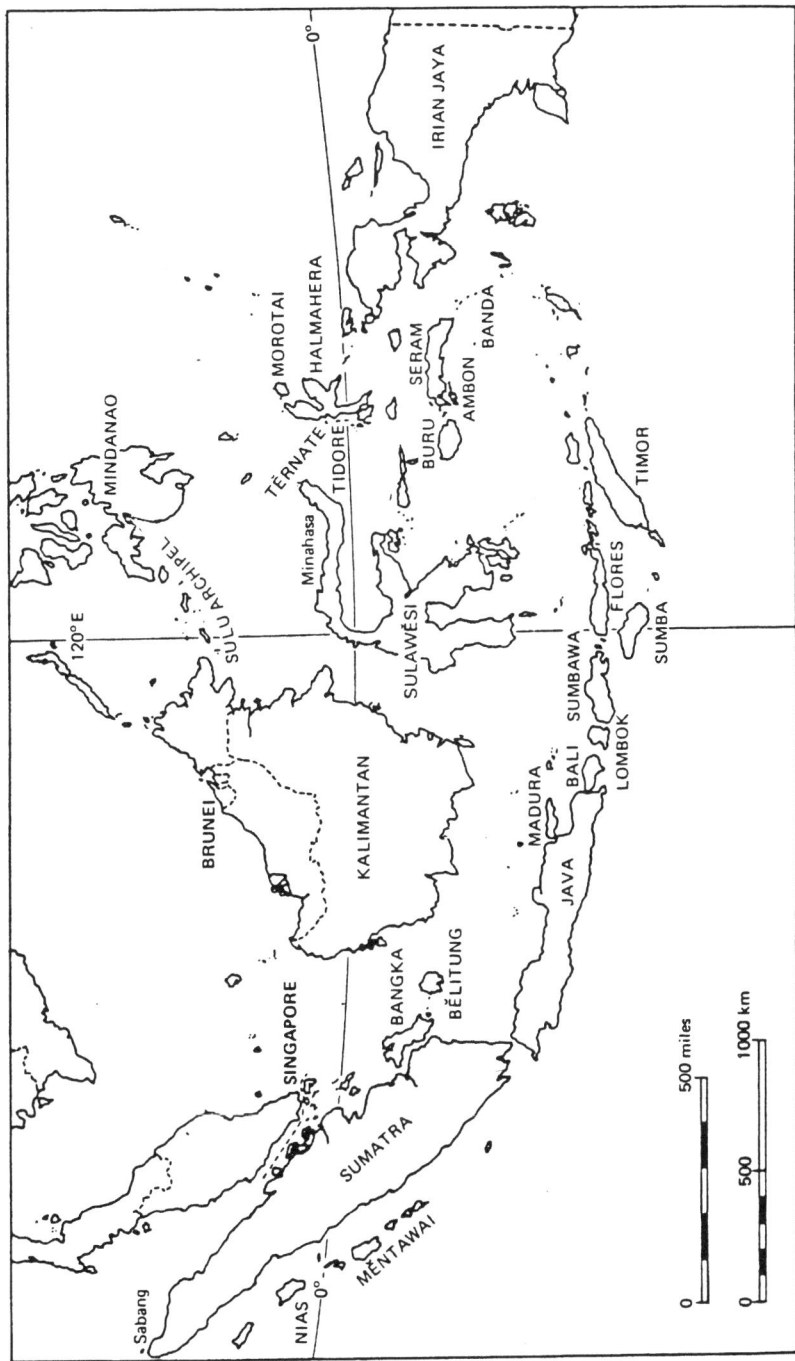

CHAPTER 1

Starting-points
and Explorations

The best introduction to this book is provided by the experiences of two colourful personalities in Dutch colonial history. The first is Frederik de Houtman (1571-1627), adventurer, trader and a participant in the first Dutch voyage to the Dutch East Indies (1595-1597). This voyage was the start of De Houtman's turbulent but very successful career in the Dutch East Indies. The other figure is Dr. Jan van Baal, who was born in 1909 and in 1934 began his career as an official in the Home Government of the Dutch East Indies. He ended his career in 1958 as the Governor of New Guinea.

The first voyage to the Dutch East Indies, organised by the *Compagnie van Verre*, was expensive. Of the four ships that left Amsterdam on 2 April 1595 only three returned after a voyage of more than two years. Only 87 of the 247 crew members survived the trip and the company made no profit whatsoever. Nonetheless, the fact that the voyage had been completed opened up prospects of profit and subsequently more fleets were sent out. On 25 March 1598 one such fleet left with Frederik and Cornelis de Houtman on board, two brothers who had already played important parts in the first voyage. The fleet consisted of only two ships with a crew of 223 hands. It was not a particularly fast voyage: on 8 June they crossed the equator; on 10 November they sighted The Cape of Good Hope and on 17 January 1599 the island of Madagascar. At the beginning of June they entered the labyrinth of the Maldives, countless small, mostly uninhabited islands situated in a shallow coral sea. While visiting one of these islands, the crew at first found only

> a crippled man who was unable to walk. However, when the [native] people saw that the cripple was not harmed, they reappeared. Our people inspected the little town, which was of no particular interest, and went into its miskit or church, where they found a large metal lamp hanging in the middle of the church. They were also shown books and writings lying in a chest in the church. Here they have the law of Mahomet, written in Arabic.[1]

---

[1] *Cort Verhael vant' gene wedervaren is Frederick de Houtman tot Atchein* (Gouda, 1880). This report has also been published in W.S. Unger, *De Oudste reizen van de Zeeuwen naar Oost-Indië*, pp. 64-111. Translators' note: The majority of the Dutch primary and secondary sources quoted

The ships arrived in the bay of Achin on 24 June. The traders first of all paid their respects to the king and they were given a house on the shore and treated to feasts in the palace. In the meantime, negotiations regarding the delivery of pepper were not making any progress: the king had taken effective measures to retain his monopoly on this condiment. One of the visits to the king coincided with the celebration of the Muslim "New Year". Frederik de Houtman's *Cort Verhael* describes in detail how the king rode to the mosque with his retinue. His description of the celebration does not strike the reader as being reflective of Islam in its strict or modern forms: its atmosphere breathes rather that of the oriental harem. Frederik went

> before the king ..., where a great deal of food had been prepared; there [the king] ordered two damsels to dance, who were very gracefully attired with gold chains, gold jewels set with stones, gold bracelets and anklets. Afterwards the king gave me a garment made in the style of the country along with a kris or poniard. After that I went with the king into the river and stood there in the water with all his nobles. And there was an abundant variety of food and drink, including very strong brandy. In the evening, moreover, I was taken home on an elephant; this is always the honour and respect paid to foreigners.[2]

According to De Houtman's report, the king did not appear much interested in trade but wanted to enlist the Dutch ships and weapons in his plans for attacking Johore. A succession of events, complicated even more by the intrigues of Portuguese traders, gave rise to misunderstanding and conflict. A number of Dutchmen were killed, including Frederik's brother, Cornelis. The other leader of the expedition, Le Fort, managed to escape with the two ships, while some thirty members of the crew, including Frederik, were held prisoner from 11 September 1599 until 25 August 1601. Sometimes Frederik was treated harshly and then again leniently. The king suggested several times that Frederik become a Muslim and thus attain a high position in the royal court. These conversion attempts began already on 19 September 1599:

> [S]ince it was one of their feasts of Machmet, the king therefore summoned me to come to him where he was in the river. Upon arrival, [I] discovered the Portuguese ambassador, Symon Nunes, to be there. After I had been there for some time, the king apologized to me through the Portuguese interpreter, explaining that the sa-

---

in this book have not been translated into English. Except where indicated, all material that is translated into English from Dutch is the translators' own. In some cases, such as De Houtman, we have attempted to retain the style of writing peculiar to the writer. De Houtman's style of writing is often that which one will find in entries in journals and diaries. At the expense of smooth English, the translator have attempted to retain De Houtman's peculiar style.

[2] *Cort Verhael*, pp. 8-9.

bander[3] was to blame [for what had happened] and that he [himself] had not ordered our people to be killed. When he had thus apologized, the king had me promise that I would not cause any difficulty and said he wanted to make me master of more than I was, in regard to which he wished me to take a wife, whom he at once ordered into the water with him. Replied that His Majesty must excuse me from this, since I already had a wife in our country and could not marry another woman .... At this the king, although not very satisfied, no longer bothered me about the woman but continued to pressure me at various times into becoming a moor. But God - who is a comforter of all distressed and afflicted hearts and a protector of all Christians who trust in him - did not allow this to occur.[4]

Not all the members of the crew were so brave and steadfast. At least five of Frederik's companions chose the new religion and new wives and from that time on Frederik always referred to them as 'renegades'. Frederik spent much of his time in chains, studying astronomy and Malay. He used this knowledge later to draft the first Dutch-Malay dictionary and to describe the night skies of the Southern Hemisphere.

After some time the occasional attempts at persuading De Houtman to become a Muslim were replaced by a more systematic endeavour to convert him. On 22 January 1601, some envoys of the king asked Frederik once more if he wished to become a 'moor'. When he replied in the negative, he was

brought before the judges, in a place where all justice is administered. [These judges] were to instruct me in the faith, and if I could not be converted to the faith of Mahomet I would be put to death. Such was the king's order to the judges. And since a great many people had gathered to witness this, [one of the judges] spoke in Malay as follows: 'Since His Royal Majesty has sent you here to us as His Majesty's judges, his order is that you accept the faith of Mahomet, since it is the only one that leads to salvation' and then said: 'what is your answer to this?' And because God strengthened my heart, as it says in Luke 12:11 [...], I replied in the same Malay tongue in this way: 'God, who is the God of all Gods, does not incline this way in my heart.'[5]

In De Houtman's account this scene is followed by an extensive religious debate, the first point consisted of a comparison of Jesus and Mohammed. De Houtman had heard his jailers speak of Moses, David and Jesus, also revered by Muslims:

I told them that I had often heard them say '*Isa Rohalla*,' and asked them what this meant. They replied that in our language it meant 'Christ, the Spirit of God.' On the other hand, I had often heard them say 'Mahomet *Resoulalla*'- what did that mean?

---

[3] 'harbour master', who at the same time was often the most important intermediary in the relations between foreigners and the local court.

[4] *Cort Verhael*, pp. 18-19.

[5] *Cort Verhael*, p. 34.

They said that it meant 'Mahomet, the Beloved of God'. To that I answered, 'If you admit that it is so, then you acknowledge by your words that Christ is older and greater than Mahomet or any other prophet.' They asked, 'How so?', to which I said: 'Is there anyone greater and older than the Spirit of God? For when God was, his Spirit existed also and existed before the world and will also continue to exist eternally. According to our scriptures and sayings, God sent his Spirit into the world and covered it with flesh and bone, equal at the same time to both God and man. So you admit that no one is nearer [to God] than Christ, for the Spirit is greater than the beloved.'[6]

The second point of debate concerned the worship of images, and of Mary in particular, which the people of Achin had observed among the Portuguese. De Houtman, a staunch Calvinist, was quick to disassociate himself from the Portuguese:

And as far as the Portuguese are concerned, I am not responsible for their actions but only for my own, because nobody should carry any burden other than his own. And if you ask whether Mary is God's wife, I say no, but I believe that Christ is God's Son, for our Scripture affirms that it was so declared from heaven by the voice of the Lord, as it is written in Matthew 3:17 ....

A third point concerned circumcision:

They asked me why we were not circumcised since our Christ himself was circumcised. I answered that circumcision was a sign of the old covenant and when God made a new covenant in Christ, Christ himself desired to be baptised after he had been circumcised and commanded all people to be baptised in the name of the Father, the Son and the Holy Spirit. So now we have baptism instead of circumcision. Then [one of the judges] again asked me whether I was willing to accept their faith or not. I answered that my God had not yet inclined me that way in my heart, but if they could teach and instruct me so that my God would incline me differently, that your faith was better, it might then occur.

In Christianity faith precedes reception into the community of believers through baptism, whereas Islam begins with the recitation of the creed, followed by further instruction in the faith and the building up of religious conviction. De Houtman was not prepared to take that first step:

They said, 'You should first lay the foundation.' When I asked what that was, they said that you should first say: la Illa Illala Mahomet Resoulalla, which in our language means: 'God of Gods and Mahomet, his Beloved'. I replied that I could not lay such a foundation nor could I repudiate my Christ ....[7]

---

[6] *Cort Verhael*, pp. 36-37.

[7] *Cort Verhael*, p. 37.

After the conclusion of this debate, more brutal forms of persuasion followed, including the threat of death. De Houtman repeatedly refused to embrace Islam while sitting in front of the executioner who stood ready with his axe. In the end, it appeared to be an empty threat. He was then threatened with having his hand cut off:

> ... they brought a piece of wood, on which I laid my left hand and set a big cleaver on my hand, and so threatened to cut off my hand. But when they saw that I was not frightened by it, they said they would fetch an elephant. After they also threatened to do this, a messenger came from the court, saying that the king had ordered me to be brought inside and taken to the castle the next day, where I would be put into a big cannon and shot out to sea - as had once been done with a Portuguese captain because of his faith; some of his companions having been killed along with him. I sat there for about three hours, suffering a great deal of mockery from the onlookers. They pulled hair out of my beard and moustache and said: 'Look here, let's braid a line from it so we can fish.'; another, taking up a kris, said: 'I'll cut his throat, if he does not wish to become a moor,' They mocked me similarly in several other ways. When evening came, I went inside the court and was put under heavy guard.[8]

After these tortures De Houtman was again treated more gently. The sheik, who held the highest religious authority, again attempted to convert De Houtman through debate but was no more successful than before. Having met with this failure, the sheik proposed:

> The King, having seen that you have been abandoned by your people, wishes to raise you to a high position, provided you are willing to embrace the faith, so that he may have somebody to trust in case more of your countrymen come. In this way he may come to an agreement with them through you, without having to use the Portuguese.

This offer of a high-ranking position in the empire of Achin also failed to convert De Houtman. At last on 25 August 1601 he was taken to a blacksmith to have his chains removed and he was able to return to the Netherlands, rejoicing

> that God had delivered me from the hands of the Moors, for which laud, praise, honour and thanks be to him from now until eternity, amen.[9]

One may wonder whether this report is one hundred percent reliable as information.[10] De Houtman greatly embellished details that were of interest

---

[8] *Cort Verhael*, p. 39.

[9] *Cort Verhael*, p. 48.

[10] 'Slave stories', while in reality accounts of the experiences of sailors who were detained by Muslims for ransom, were a literary genre in the 16th and 17th centuries. Cf. Boon, 1987, pp. 42-45 and Hardenberg, 1950, pp. 1-12, among others, for stories about the adventures of Christian

to his Dutch readers (the account was dedicated to Prince Maurice). Certainly both the colourful setting and the cruelty of his interrogators were by no means understated. In his account of the theological debates one can detect in places the Christian terminology common to the sixteenth century. For example, he uses the phrase - more Christian than Islamic - 'the law of Mahomet'. More than likely the Muslims would never have characterized their religion as the 'only one leading to salvation' - this conception does not play any part in Islamic theology. His translation of the word *rasul* for Mohammed as 'Beloved' is more suggestive of Matthew 3:17 ('This is my beloved Son'), which De Houtman quotes, than of its proper meaning of 'envoy' or 'prophet'.

However, these are rather minor details and, in spite of these small evidences of selective and altered understanding and reporting, it is clear that De Houtman also had a good grasp of some aspects of the faith of his Muslim hosts but was not willing to accept them. His account shows him to have been respectful and reasonably interested in the customs and ideas, including the religious ones, of the foreign nations with whom he comes into contact. Nowhere does he display any missionary zeal: the expression "To you your religion, and to me my religion" is Koranic (Koran 109:6), but it almost seems to have been De Houtman's personal motto. De Houtman does not show any real sympathy and understanding and obviously his opinion about the 'Moors' had already been established - he had already been immunized against them. He can be credited with a great deal of tolerance, certainly in view of the bad treatment he was given. But it is the tolerance characteristic of the businessman who, in spite of his negative experiences, still has business interests at stake. De Houtman lacks genuine empathy and openness, but then he was neither a theologian nor a profound thinker; he was a young man in his late twenties who had chosen to lead a life of adventure. Indeed, by means of his greater sensitivity in diplomatic and political affairs, he was able to live this sort of life longer than his impetuous brother.

Jan van Baal was born at Scheveningen in 1909 and studied Indology from 1927-1934. Having grown up in Reformed (*gereformeerd*)[11] surroundings, he was always greatly interested in religion but in the Dutch East Indies he

---

slaves in Algeria.

[11] Various kinds of 'Reformed' churches exist in the Netherlands. One of the most distinctions is that between the *Hervormd* and *gereformeerd*. In reference to churches, the former refers exclusively to the Dutch state church, which dates back to the period of the Reformation, and the latter refers to a movement that grew out of the opposition to the modernist tendencies in the *Hervormde Kerk* in the first half of the nineteenth century. The distinction between *Hervormd* and *gereformeerd* is virtually impossible to translate clearly, concisely, and smoothly into English. For that reason, the translators have left the Dutch terms in parentheses in the text. Translators' note.

developed a more liberal attitude. He has written a number of important works on religious anthropology, a field of study which he took up because of ethnology. When he had to make a choice about his field of study during his years as a student, he abandoned Islam

> ... for in order to study Islam a wide knowledge of Arabic was required and by then I knew enough of it to realise that I would have to spend three days a week for more than two years studying the language in order to acquire that knowledge".[12]

From 1934 until halfway through 1936 Van Baal gained his first experience of the Dutch East Indies in Kediri (East Java), Madura and Jember (again East Java). He stayed only a short time in each place and occupied himself mainly with police and judicial matters, besides handling business transactions for large commercial interests. His knowledge of these areas was so limited that in reference to Madura he could only repeat the commonplace that the population there was 'strictly Islamic, candid and warlike'.[13] He did, however, have to admit that he remained on the fringe of Madura's indigenous culture. He remarks in connection with bullracing, the most prominent type of popular entertainment on the island:

> As a spectator, I was little more than a tourist, just as I also remained an outsider to the religious experience that occurred right behind our garden every night. There was a *langgar*, where the members of the I-don't-know-what (oh, for shame! - I should have known) *tarekat* (brotherhood) gathered to recite the Koran and sing the creed at the top of their voices. It began at six o'clock in the evening and lasted until late in the night. But I was too busy with other things at the time to try to establish contact.[14]

After an initial period in New Guinea (1936-1938) Van Baal was again posted in Islamic areas. He was first posted to Banyumas (on Central Java), where he describes the Christmas party organized by the Resident's Prussian wife:

> After the first drink everybody was pressed into singing Christmas carols in various places in the house and especially at the back near the servants' quarters. The fact that those servants were Muslims did not seem to make any difference. When we finally returned to the reception hall behind her, she flopped down into a big chair with a loud 'goddamnit, I sure could use a drink now!'[15]

---

[12] J. van Baal, *Ontglipt Verleden*, I, Franeker, p. 51.

[13] *Verleden*, p.74.

[14] *Verleden*, p. 77.

[15] *Verleden*, p. 326.

After Banyumas Van Baal was posted to neighbouring Purwokerto and in 1941 to the island of Lombok, where he mentions the strict and pious Muslims more often in his autobiography. Nevertheless, because Van Baal's job was to research the structure of the desa (village), he mainly paid attention to pre-Islamic customs and institutions.

Van Baal has become known primarily as an expert in Papuan culture. During his first period in that region he already had much closer contact with the population than was the case on Java, Madura or Lombok. He wrote a major work on the Marind Anim culture that was published in 1966. These people had suffered from a venereal disease introduced in 1910, which had spread rapidly because of the sexual promiscuity which occurred at several traditional feasts. This disease also caused infertility. In an article published in 1939, Van Baal wrote,

> Where are the Marind going? ... For the Marind as a people there is only one way out - that of the complete adoption of Christianity, in this case Roman Catholicism. The road to paganism is closed for them: first, because of the depravity and nature of their culture which is incapable of improvement and secondly, because of what happened to them after 1910."[16]

A survey of the history of New Guinea (now the Indonesian province of Irian Jaya) in the fifty years since Van Baal wrote his article gives rise to the question: why did Van Baal mention only the two alternatives of paganism and Christianity? Why did he not consider Islam - surely as safe a choice in the area of sexual morality as Christianity - to be a viable option? About 88% of Indonesia is now Muslim. The Reformed (gereformeerd) Van Baal had certainly moved beyond his own background by 1939, but was Catholicism, in his eyes, such an obviously better choice than Islam?[17] He spent a number of years among a predominantly Islamic community, yet seems to have remained immune to it. Or was it purely practical motives that prompted him to this view of the future? At the same time Van Baal stands in a long tradition of the Dutch and Indian colonials who did not attack Islam and often treated those who professed that religion with the necessary respect. They governed

---

[16] J. van Baal, "De bevolking van Zuid-Nieuw-Guinea onder Nederlandsch Bestuur: 36 Jaren," (The population of South New Guinea under Dutch rule: 36 years), TBG, 79 (1939): 309-414. The quote is found on p. 407.

[17] 'Better Papist than Muslim' ('Liever Paaps dan Turks') was used at first as a working title for this book. It ultimately came to light that there was not enough positive feeling towards Roman Catholicism in the Dutch colonial world after all to justify that title. Van Baal himself was not uncritical of the Catholic Mission either. In the second part of his autobiography Ontglipt Verleden he categorically refuses to regard the government as an ancilla ecclesiae and especially rejects the use of force in religious matters and related customs. Cf. J. van Baal, 1989, pp. 408-410.

and traded in this atmosphere of tolerance but could not consider Islam as an definite partner *in religiosis*. In the following pages we will meet this sort of tolerance - silent and fleeting - often.

In more than one respect this study forms a sequel to the work of Norman Daniel and R.W. Southern. In 1960 Norman Daniel published *Islam and the West: The Making of an Image*[18], which has been reprinted several times and has become a classic. In this book Daniel discusses how an image of Islam originated in the European sources between 1100 and 1350 and since then has not undergone any essential change.[19] Before the twelfth century there were hardly any contacts between Western Europe and the Islamic world and in those areas where contacts were possible, such as the caliphate of Cordoba, spiritual contacts between the various religious groups were completely or almost completely non-existent. According to Daniel, the western image of Islam arose at the time of the crusades and since that time has only laboriously and slowly changed. Daniel gives a rather static description of a large number of aspects of this image: the view of the Koran, the life of Mohammed, holy war, women and the harem, Islamic morality, attitudes towards other religions and their adherents. It was during the crusades that a deficient knowledge of the facts arose, mingled with fabrications, slander and malicious invention, - a conglomeration of judgements and prejudices about Islam that has generally persisted since that time. Across the dividing lines that have since arisen between Catholic and Protestant, the believer and atheist, a common image has been preserved that to a great extent is still decisive in the Western image of Islam.[20]

Southern gives a more dynamic picture of the developments. In three lectures delivered at Harvard in 1961, he discussed the Western views of Islam in roughly the same period as that treated by Daniel.[21] He subdivides this era into three periods: a) a "Time of Ignorance" prior to 1140, during which the image of Islam was based not on a knowledge of the facts but on fantasy, fear and distorted information; b) The period from 1140-1250 was an "Age of Reason and Hope", in which the reports on Islam became more and more objective and based on solid information; c) after 1250 distortions of Islam

---

[18] Norman Daniel, *Islam and the West: The Making of an Image* (Edinburgh: University Press, 1960). Here I have used the fourth edition (1980).

[19] Daniel, *Making of an Image*, p. 1: "The European West has long had its own characteristic view, which was formed in the two centuries or so after 1100 and which has been modified only slowly since ...."

[20] Daniel, *Making of an Image*, p. 271.

[21] R.W. Southern, *Western Views of Islam in the Middle Ages* (Cambridge, Massachusetts: Harvard University Press, 1962).

and negative reports were predominant, only rarely countered by "Moments of Vision". Within a virtually continuous stream of prejudice, here and there we come across those who combined a hopeful expectation for the future in respect to Christian-Muslim relations with more positive and factual information. To these "Moments of Vision" belong the activities of individual scholars like John Bacon, John of Segovia and Nicholas of Cusa. At the end of his study Southern wonders if any progress can be detected during this process in which the image of Islam was formed. Very cautiously he indicates some positive points: the phrasing of the questions about Islam have become more detailed and nuanced, whereas the information about Islam has also become more comprehensive.[22]

The period treated in this study begins 400 years later than that which was the object of investigation by Daniel and Southern, namely 1600-1950.[23] Our subject has shifted from theirs geographically as well: we will concentrate on the southeastern part of the Islamic world, an area where there were hardly any adherents of Islam in the year 1100 and the Islamising process was still in full swing in 1600. Nonetheless, we will discover that the formation of the image, as outlined by Daniel, continued. We will also encounter "Moments of Vision" and progress, so cautiously described by Southern, but not any more stronger, more frequent or more evident than those to which he points.

The encounter between Muslims of the Dutch East Indies and the Dutch colonialists differs from the relations described by Daniel and Southern primarily because of the greater number of straightforward and friendly contacts, direct encounters for the sake of trade. Because of this our study has much in common with the study of colonial history. Current studies of colonial history emphasize the economic rather than the political aspects. In addition, a number of studies emphasize the social aspect: important for our purpose here are the studies done by Leonard Blussé and Jean Gelman Taylor on the social structure of the city of Batavia. In various studies Heather Sutherland has also given a penetrating picture of the complex society which arose around the trading centres of the Dutch East India Company (VOC), especially in and around Makassar. Knaap's dissertation gives a fascinating description of the

---

[22] Southern, *Western Views*, p. 108-109.

[23] Daniel himself wrote a continuation of his successful *Islam and the West* with the publication of *Islam, Europe and Empire* in 1966. Here he discusses the contacts between colonialism and Islam in the 19th century. But without offering any reason for it, he neglects the largest Islamic country, known then as the Dutch Indies. The more than 600 pages of this work offer a large quantity of factual material, but from his residence in Khartoum at the time this medievalist was apparently unable to develop a coherent view of Islam and 19th century imperialism.

Moluccas. While we will certainly include all these aspects of colonial history in our study, we will concentrate on the history of religion and mission insofar as this can be considered an encounter or missed opportunity for encounter between the Dutch Christians and the Muslims of the Indonesia.

Academic studies of Islam, including those that relate to Indonesia, will, for the most part, be left out of consideration here. Insofar as such studies were undertaken on the basis of historical sources, manuscripts and published books, they can hardly be considered as falling under the aspect of encounter. Moreover, since this kind of contact has already been extensively treated several times, there is no need for us to go into this matter in detail.[24]

In 1596 the first Dutch fleet entered the Indian Ocean. At the time this was an Islamic inland sea or 'a Muslim Mediterranean',[25] From Madagascar by way of the Arab peninsula to Persia, to the ports on the west and east coast of India and from there by way of the Malaysian archipelago as far as the sultanate of the Sulu archipelago to the south of what are now called the Philippines, the coastal areas of this great ocean had largely converted to Islam. Many of the inland areas, especially in the centre and east of the Indian Ocean, had not yet embraced the new faith. When Marco Polo visited a part of North Sumatra in 1292, he wrote, "Muslim traders visit this kingdom so frequently that they have converted the merchants of the town; but the people in the interior still live like animals, eat human flesh and all other kinds of meat, clean or unclean."[26] Since then Islam has continued to expand.

In 1600 these areas were not at all in political or economic decline - in fact, the opposite was true. Three great empires had just reached the height of their development. After conquering Istanbul in 1453, the Ottoman empire had extended to the south as well and reached Aden in 1530, which made the entire Red Sea an Ottoman inland sea. The great Safawid Shah Abbas I (1558-1629) ruled Persia and brought this dynasty, which dated back to 1501, to its peak. The Mogul empire in Northern India had just expanded in 1570 as far as the peninsula of Gujarat in northeast India. At that time they also conquered Surat, "the home port of what was undoubtedly the largest mer-

---

[24] Cf. B.J. Boland and I. Farjon, *Islam in Indonesia, A Bibliographical Survey, 1600-1942*, Leiden, KITLV, 1983, Juynboll, 1931 and Brugman, 1979. Cf. Steenbrink, 1988, for a study of this type on Indonesia.

[25] Chaudhuri, 1985; Johns, 1984, p. 116.

[26] Cf. also Kern, 1938, p. 309.

chant fleet of that time in the Indian Ocean".[27] Within these Islamic trading networks the Portuguese and later on the Dutch, English and others as well at first were only small competitors. Only after the collapse of the three great Islamic empires shortly after 1700 could these colonial powers greatly increase their share in trade and in direct government.

Aside from present-day Indonesia, the Dutch were also heavily involved in Sri Lanka, where they exercised administrative control over all aspects of life, especially in the coastal areas. From 1650 onwards they were engaged in the attempt to prohibit trade in which the 'Moors' were involved, for which purpose various discriminatory and restrictive measures with respect to the Muslims were taken. In his *Memorie* of 1663 Rijkloff van Goens, who established the Dutch government on Ceylon, provided his successor with a survey of this policy. Attempts were made in the principal trading centres to exclude the Muslims from trade, their main source of income. Additional duties were imposed on the import of rice and textiles, while Muslims were strictly forbidden to do retail business in textile goods. Nor were they allowed to live in Colombo, the most important port city, or to own property there. When they died, a third of their inheritance went to the Dutch East India Company. In 1675, after a later term in office, Van Goens once more gave a concise summary of the policy towards Muslim traders: "How much the Moors on these Islands hinder us daily is shown by their activity, certainly nothing else than a cancer in the Company's advantages and the chief corruptors of morals".[28] For Ceylon, now Sri Lanka, and some parts of southern India this policy also meant in the long run that Islamic influence could not be extended. In the second half of the eighteenth century especially the Dutch East India Company resigned itself to the established position that the Muslims had acquired in retail trade.[29] In 1796 this region came under British control and the Dutch subsequently concentrated more and more on the Dutch East Indies, now Indonesia. For that reason we will also concentrate on this area.

This book was written as part of a research project on concrete examples of encounter (whether successful or not) between Christians and adherents of non-Christian religions. In this book we chose as our starting-point the perspective of the Dutch. In some respects we were limited by the source material: our access to direct information was restricted to only those Dutch people

---

[27] A. Das Gupta, "De VOC en Suratte in de 17e en 18de eeuw," in M.A.P. Meilink-Roelfs (ed.), *De V.O.C. in Azië*, Bussum, 1976, pp. 64-84. The quote is taken from p. 78.

[28] The text of these memoirs was published in Reimers, 1932, from which the quote is taken (p. 86). Cf. also pp. 61, 65-66 and 69 for the restrictive regulations with regard to Muslim trade. See also Das Gupta, 1976a and 1976b, Arasaratnam, 1976 and s'Jacob, 1976 for these areas.

[29] Van Goor, 1978, pp. 13-14.

who wrote, which implies a restriction to a very important but at the same time also very select group. The majority of the people on board the ships of the Dutch East India Company, those in the Company settlements, the people of the KNIL (Royal Dutch East Indian Army) and other groups, consisted of those who wrote little or not at all. In addition, we were not able to consult all the material available: the colonial archives alone already contain some thirty kilometres of material![30] As with all histories which deal with attitudes, the primary task was not to elaborate on the quantitative aspect, to give a complete description of the entire development, but to emphasize the variety of encounters as they occurred.

As a supplement to studies which we published elsewhere, the seventh chapter gives a short outline of the reactions of the "other side" to the arrival of traders and other visitors from the West. Although these reactions are not the main subject of this study, they form a transition to the concluding eighth chapter, in which we make some connections to present-day Indonesia. We also sketch some patterns in this chapter that could be useful with respect to developments in Europe since the sixties, when large numbers of Muslims emigrated to Europe and established an Islamic minority.

The encounter between Dutch Christians and Indonesian Muslims has gone through several stages. Generally speaking, we can distinguish four main patterns with reference to the Dutch. We use the term 'pattern' because it indicates a complexity of attitudes in which different themes are interwoven. In the first pattern we see a mixture of caution, curiosity and selective admiration, but, on the other hand, a significant and clear distancing is immediately noticeable from the start. The first Dutch traders lacked a strong basis for negotiation and were often more shrewd and less biased in their outlook than their successors. Their ideas had not yet become fixed. This pattern offers a number of 'signs of hope', but its effects were quite superficial. These traders often express appreciation especially for the behaviour of Muslims, with respect to both their religious rituals as such and morality. On the other hand, they speak disapprovingly of the content of their religious doctrines, with which they had already become familiar in their native country, while the Muslims' actual conduct in both respects mentioned above provided new experiences. The second chapter will deal with this pattern under the title *Muslims as Respected Heretics*.

The first travellers setting out for the Dutch East Indies already had opinions about Islam when they left the Netherlands. The second pattern concerns these prejudices, rooted in dogma, with regard to *Muslims as Detestable Heretics*. In connection with this, special attention is paid to seventeenth-

---

[30] F. Jacquet, "Mutiny en Hadji-ordonnantie: ervaringen met 19e eeuwse bronnen," *BKI* 136 (1980): 283-312. Cf. also Jaquet, 1983. Coolhaas, 1980, provides an important guide to the published sources.

century theology in the Netherlands. These theologians assessed Islam in terms of unbelief, superstition or heresy. It was often the case that the theological description did not correspond to actual Muslims in far away countries but to erroneous forms of Christian belief in its own environment, such as lax behaviour, dissension and inclinations toward Arianism or other dogmatic errors. In the third chapter some theoretical expositions of this pattern are discussed. This pattern also influences the other patterns and is the legacy of the Middle Ages and the sixteenth century: it combines crusader ideals with Luther's politically biased rejection of Islam in connection with the expansion of the Ottoman empire. The pirates of the African northern coast also play an important role. In order to be able to emphasize the concrete encounters in the Dutch East Indies for the sake of structure, we did not wish to place this third chapter immediately after the introductory chapter.

After the first traders had settled in the East Indies, they built a wall around themselves in most places, figuratively but often also literally, as a defence against undesired contact with the native population. It is for this reason that the Company's trading stations were fortresses. As a religion, Islam was viewed primarily as dynamite, as the greatest danger to the Europeans' security. This provides the third pattern of attitudes and response. After a somewhat more hopeful and positive initial phase we see nothing but negative attitudes in this period. Wherever the Company was able to exercise significant power, Muslims were forbidden to participate in trade. This applied to Sri Lanka, as seen above, and we will see it again in the case of the Moluccas and parts of Java. Where the Company had less power they had no choice but to live and trade *with untrustworthy and fanatic Muslims "in natural hostility"*.

A fourth and final pattern emerged when colonial rule had established itself so definitely that fear was no longer required. It is only then that a clear feeling of superiority gained the upper hand and a patronising attitude developed. The Dutch began to consider themselves teachers or even as guardians of the still uneducated people. This was manifested in two ways: secular ideas of development, centred mainly on education, and Christian missions. The two cannot finally be separated, however. Perhaps it is not coincidental that the flourishing of the great missionary activity took place precisely during the period of the extension of the colonial system of education. Indeed, many missionary activities were conducted by way of that system of education. Islam was then primarily regarded not so much a worthy, although heretical, partner of the Christian faith *as a backward and superstitious religion*.

In the final two chapters of the book we will look at the reverse side: the reaction of the Indonesian Muslims to the Christians' arrival and finally the question as to what can be learned from this history, especially since so many Muslims have emigrated to Europe and America since 1960.

CHAPTER 2

The First Encounters:
Muslims as Respected Heretics

When the Dutch traders first arrived in the East Indies in 1596, they exercised hardly any military or political influence in the region. Because the expedition was essentially exploratory, their reports included information of a much wider variety than later, when the Dutch were an established power in the region and trade and government officials were mainly interested in continuing those relations which were already in existence. In this later period as well, travellers who stayed in certain places for a short time often described these places in a much different way than those who remained for longer periods of time. These short-term visitors were quite often interested in religious customs and described them, whereas the trader or military official could hardly find any space for them among the figures and surveys of cargoes and contracts in their 'matter-of-fact' reports. In this chapter we will look at this varied picture of that first encounter.

The Portuguese were the first Europeans to arrive in the East Indies, where they subsequently built up a basis for trade. In 1511 Albuquerque, the great pioneer in this area, captured Malacca in order to use it as a centre for further expansion. While Goa on India's west coast remained the principal Portuguese administrative base in the East, Malacca became the centre of Portuguese power in the more remote areas until the Dutch conquered it in 1641. The Portuguese were quite sparing with information about this area, because their trading advantage was due to the fact that their knowledge of this area was much more extensive than other Europeans'. A Dutchman, Jan Huygen van Linschoten (1563-1611), however, was employed by various Portuguese officials, including the archbishop of Goa, from 1579 until 1589. He collected a great deal of information on the Portuguese empire and published it in his *Itinerario* in 1596, which was quite useful to the Dutch in their first expedition. While his work contains no mention of Muslims in the East Indies,[1] it does include information on them in other countries such as Persia

---

[1] Jan Huygen van Linschoten, *Itinerario*, I, pp. 81-88.

and India. His account of a visit to a mosque just outside Goa is characteristic of the difference in approach between Dutch Calvinists and Portuguese Catholics. In Goa itself the Portuguese did not allow Muslim worship services "nor any Indian [Hindu] services, although they live in the city with their families and own their own houses." They were only allowed 'to practise their ceremonies and superstitions freely" outside the city limits,[2] where the Muslims had

> their *meskytas*, where they have their prayers and there are several lofts and galleries above the sanctuary where they teach catechism to the children. Before they enter the church they wash their feet - there always being a watertank beside the church for that purpose. They always leave their *alparcos*, or shoes, outside the church door before they go inside. Upon entering, they immediately fall flat on their faces and make several futile gestures with uplifted arms and hands. They are also circumcised like the Jews and eat no pork. When they die, they are buried and they have no statues or images whatsoever in their church other than erected stones or tombstones engraved with Chaldee letters from their Al Koran. Once, when I happened to pass by with a Portuguese, I was seized by an extraordinary desire to see this Machometist church and their method of prayer. The doorkeeper, however, stopped us and told us to take off our shoes. When we refused to do so, he said that we were not allowed to enter the church with them on, but he allowed us to stand in the doorway so that we could watch, and opened some windows from the inside, so that we could clearly see what was going on. Then the Portuguese asked him where their god and saints they worshipped were, since, as already noted, he saw that the church was devoid [of images]. The Moor answered that they did not pray to wood and stone but to the living God who is in heaven. Then he said, "You Portuguese Christians and heathens are all the same: you worship statues which you yourselves have made and you show them the honour only belongs to the living God almighty." This answer made the Portuguese fly into such a rage that he began to rail at him harshly, so that a large crowd of Moors and Indians gathered. This might have caused a great deal of trouble if I had not apologized and pulled him away from there. And so we left and that was all there was to report.[3]

This account displays some ambiguity towards Muslims. On the one hand, Van Linschoten, in keeping with the general tendency of people like himself, makes negative and derogatory remarks. He refers, for instance, to Muslim customs as 'superstitions' and caricatures their gestures during prayer. The comparison to Jews with respect to circumcision and their refusal to eat pork could also be intended in a negative way. On the other hand, there is also some indication of his appreciation for Muslims, as in his comparison of the mosque to a church and catechetical instruction. Here one should especially note the rejection of images and the classification of Portuguese Catholics under the same category as pagans.

---

[2] *Itinerario*, II, p. 41.

[3] *Itinerario*, II, pp. 42-43.

Van Linschoten combines his own observations with information he received from other sources - including, possibly, written ones. He emphasizes the differences between Muslims and Hindus and contrasts the Islamic funeral with the Hindu cremation as an example of these differences. Van Linschoten reports that the people in the coastal areas under Portuguese control were quite tolerant of one another. According to his account, Jews lived alongside Hindus and Muslims: "These three nationalities each observe their own laws and ceremonies and live together peacefully, observing good laws and justice, and all three are employed in the King's Council with his *naires*."[4] This could not be said of all places in this region. The term *shi'ite* was as yet unknown but Van Linschoten does refer to the rise of a *shi'ite* government under the Safawides in what is now Iran. Shah Ismael, who was crowned in 1501, is cited as the main leader of the sect. In relation to the issue of tolerance in Iran he comments: "Because those Turks adhere to the old Law of Machomet and stand by it heart and soul on every minute detail, there is constant hostility and bloody conflict between these two nations".[5] Van Linschoten's information in regard to this, however, is quite fragmentary.

Certainly not all the Portuguese were as negative towards Muslims and their belief as Van Linschoten's guide when he visited the mosque. A more varied and positive image comes to the fore again and again in the two most important sixteenth-century accounts dealing with the East Indies. Because a comparison with these two Portuguese authors will result in a clearer view of the observations of the Dutch, we will look at them here briefly.

Tomé Pires, a pharmacist by profession, settled in Malacca shortly after the Portuguese conquered the city in 1511. He then entered the Portuguese service as an envoy to different locales in the East Indies and elsewhere. He had almost finished his *Suma Oriental* already before he was sent to China in 1515. In this book Pires gives a full account of the political relations in the East Indies and in areas more to the north such as Siam (Thailand) and China. He also discusses trade goods in elaborate detail, paying close attention to the basic ingredients of medicines, scents and perfumes. He describes accurately which areas had already been Islamized and which had not and quite often also expresses his views on which conditions were favourable or not for Islamization. In his opinion, it was due mainly to the prestige of Islamic traders that inhabitants of the port cities became Muslims.

Pires reported on Muslim doctrines and religious practices only if they deviated from what he considered to be properly Islamic. In his section on Java, for instance, he describes in great detail the system of hermits "divided

---

[4] *Itinerario*, I, pp. 50-51.

[5] *Itinerario*, I, p. 118.

into three or four orders" all of which observed the vow of chastity. These hermits were also honoured by the Muslims "who put great faith in them, give alms to them and greatly value the opportunity to welcome them into their houses."[6] Pires writes, in a tone suggestive of the Inquisition, that in his opinion the Lord of Tuban, the grandson of a pagan who was converted, did "... not seem to have a firm belief in Mohammed."[7] He relates a story about the kingdom of Pasai, the oldest Islamic centre of Islam in the East Indies, which may have appeared to deviate from the Islamic traditions with which he was familiar. According to his account, the local ruler had been deposed by an Islamic Bengalese trader 160 years earlier. From that time on, anyone who staged a *coup d'état* and killed the king could become king himself if he was a Muslim. So intense was this desire to become king and die as a king that at one time there were seven successive kings in one day - each of whom became king by killing his predecessor. Bodyguards were "out of the question, for, according to them, [what happened] was predestined by God."[8] Pires dedicated his book to the king of Portugal who is honourably mentioned in the introduction as one "who does not cease to fight against the name of Mohammed".[9] When Pires wrote this first and important survey of a new area of Portuguese influence, he obviously did not see any necessity to dwell on Muslims at length. We may safely assume that he thought that his readers to be sufficiently familiar with Islam and were interested only in local variations.

The second important Portuguese source is *A Treatise on the Moluccas*, which may have been written by Antonio Galvao, the seventh Portuguese governor of the Moluccas (1536-1539). Even though Portugal had already been established in the region for sometime, the author patterns his description completely on that most often used by the first explorers. The writer of travel accounts often has much in common with the writer of history: both have a reader in mind who is unacquainted with the matter in question. Thus, in this *Treatise on the Moluccas*, one sees surprise first of all, mixed with disapproval and admiration. To the category of disapproval belongs the description of people who uninhibitedly attend to their natural needs in public places, such as the beach: "If one comments on this, he receives the answer that this is the Moluccan *tjara* or local custom."[10] He is surprised that girls from sixteen to twenty years old walk about practically naked until they are married: "Even though they walk like that among the men, they remain chaste and decent,

---

[6] Tomé Pires, *Suma Oriental*, ed. Armando Cortesao (London: Hakluyt Society, 1944), p. 177.

[7] *Suma Oriental*, p. 191.

[8] *Suma Oriental*, p. 143.

[9] *Suma Oriental*, p. 2.

[10] H. Jacobs, *A Treatise on the Moluccas* (Rome: Jesuit Historical Centre, 1971), p. 70.

which seems quite impossible among such a depraved people. These women are much to be praised and are a good example for us."[11] He directs such small sermonettes to his fellow countrymen more than once in his account. The author explicitly denies that homosexuality existed among the Moluccan Muslims but at the same time he taunts the Spanish whose centuries-long domination by the Muslims was supposedly due to this "horrible sin".[12]

Generally speaking, the account of Islam given in this work is not derived from the author's own experience but from other written material with which he was familiar. A case in point is the view that the main points of Muslim faith derive from the Old and New Testaments and from idolatry (*da velha he nova he da idolatria*). Elsewhere, however, he does write about matters which were based on his personal experiences, such as the observation that there were large drums in the mosques for calling the worshippers to "Matins and other hours of prayer".[13] To provide examples to his readers, he even relates three edifying stories about women from Ternate, Tidore and Panarukan (northeast Java) to illustrate in detail the great value these oriental peoples placed on chastity.

Thus, the difference between the Portuguese and the Dutch with regard to their approach to foreign peoples is merely relative: we encounter the same patterns of surprise and admiration, as well as disapproval, in Portuguese as well as in Dutch writers. In colonial politics, however, after the Portuguese had become firmly established, they proved far less inclined to tolerate other religions within the sphere of their influence and power.

As we noted in the first chapter, Frederick de Houtman invented the first method for learning Malay during his imprisonment. This method consisted of twelve conversations or 'chats' between different persons. One should certainly not consider everything in these 'chats' to be a *verbatim* reproduction of De Houtman's conversations with the Achinese. Much of the conversation in his examples has to do with liquor. *Tuak* and *arak* are of course used most often, but when he uses the example "is there any beer in your mug?" - employing the Malay variant of the word 'beer'- it is clear that he did not derive from his conversations with the Achinese people.[14] The names for God and

---

[11] *Treatise*, p. 88.

[12] *Treatise*, p. 119. The author refers here to Islamic rule in Spain between the eighth and fifteenth centuries.

[13] *Treatise*, p. 86, "*che chamo as matinas he oras ordinarias.*"

[14] The Englishman John Davies also took part in the same voyage. In his travel account he also repeatedly mentions drinking customs in Achin. Cf. his account in W.S. Unger, *De Oudste Reizen van de Zeeuwen naar Oost-Indië 1598-1604*, p. 50, "Excessive drinking was our entertainment."

conventional religious formulas occur quite often in his dictionary: almost every conversation begins and ends with some of these formulas. Here De Houtman most often uses formulas derived from social contact and the usual Arabic greetings can be found here.[15] In the fourth conversation the 'Dutchman' Jacob speaks with the 'Indian' Gabriel. Jacob uses a Malay formula as a parting wish: "Go, God be with you".[16] While it is not always possible to determine from the characters' names whether the conversation partners are Dutch or Achinese - the names are all derived from the Bible - this formula is most certainly of Dutch Christian origin and not representative of Muslim discourse. In the tenth conversation a trader from Ghent is mentioned. When a person named David asks, "What street does he live in?", another person, designated only as A., answers, "He lives near the new church." This translates into Malay as follows: *Dya doedock ampir moskit baroe*.[17] In the Malay version, De Houtman uses the term for mosque, even though he transcribes it as *moskit* following the Portuguese. Did De Houtman not know of any Malay word for church[18] or did he consider the words for Christian and Islamic places of worship to be interchangeable? In any case, De Houtman is still quite a distance from the language policy of the present Malaysian government, which recently decided that religious terminology should be connected to a specific religion and that Christians and Muslims should not use specific terms interchangeably. Whether because he lacked the motivation to do otherwise or because it fit better within the framework of exploration, De Houtman never showed himself to be a strict and orthodox Christian in his language exercises. He had persons of both nations and religions use the same religious vocabulary.

 This interchangeability of religious terminology appears often in this period of explorers and first encounters. One may see this especially in the travel account of John Davies, an Englishman who accompanied De Houtman on his voyage to Achin. Davis describes the Muslims in Achin in the following way:

> The people boast themselves to come of Ismael and Hagar, and can reckon the genealogie of the Bible perfectly. In religion, they are Mahometists and pray with beades, as the Papists doe. They bring up their children in learning, and have many schooles. They have an archbishop and spirituall dignities. Here is a prophet in

---

[15] Denys Lombard, ed., *Le "Spraeck ende Woord-boek de Frederick de Houtman,"* (*Essalemalecom, Ibrahim*), p. 14, (*Alhemdelilla*), p. 29, (*Insi Alla*), p. 31.

[16] Lombard, p. 59, *"Pegy, Allah serta kamoe."*

[17] Lombard, p. 143.

[18] The common Malay word for church later was *gereja*, which was ultimately borrowed from the Portuguese.

Achien whom they greatly honour; they say that hee hath the spirit of prophesie as the ancients have had. He is dignified from the rest in his apperell and greatly imbraced of the King ...[19]

As happened so often - and also among the Dutch seafarers of Protestant background - Davis compares Muslims closely to Catholics in regard to such matters as the rosary and the function of a bishop. The common property of the biblical histories and the attention paid to instruction are indeed special themes here which appear to accentuate the equal status of the religions.

Not all De Houtman's companions demonstrated such perseverance with respect to the Christian faith as he himself did. He mentions five men by name who were converted to Islam. When one of them, Lenard van Wormer, later tried to contact a Dutch ship, "the king ... deprived Lenard the renegade of his wife and house, land and money".[20] As a rule, such a 'renegade' could not expect much compassion from the Dutch side either. Eventually Van Wormer did get a position as a intermediary and went to the Netherlands as a guide for the Achinese delegation which visited Middelburg in 1602. At the end of this visit he was sent back with a new mission:

[It h]as been arranged with Lenardt van Wormer, the renegade, that he will be employed by the commissioner of the king of Achin and always be at his service without leave to go where he chooses. He will receive nine guilders a month, for which the new company will be liable.[21]

Van Wormer was known as the 'renegade' for the duration of his life. As so often happens, however, the sources give no further information about the religious aspects.[22]

During the time that De Houtman was imprisoned in Achin, another expedition led by Jacob van Neck and Wybrant Warwijck made the first voyage to the Moluccas. In the Netherlands itself a great deal of interest was taken in the results of this expedition and the account of this voyage was reprinted

---

[19] *The Voyage of Captaine John Davis to the Easterne India, Pilot in a Dutch Ship, written by Himselfe*, in Unger, *De Oudste Reizen van de Zeeuwen*, pp. 56-57. For the complete account see pp. 45-63. Nieuwenhuijze (1945, p. 18) comments on Davis' account. For another English account of religious officials at the court of Achin, cf. Lancaster, 1877, p. 96.

[20] Unger, *De Oudste Reizen van de Zeeuwen*, p. 87.

[21] Unger, *De Oudste Reizen van de Zeeuwen*, p. 183.

[22] Cf. also Wap, 1862, p. 17, who describes Van Wormer in this way: "the delegation's translator from Luxembourg, whom they appeared to have called Pusque Camis" (tolk der Ambassade, een Luxemburger, dien zij Pusque Camis schijnen te hebben genoemd").

several times and supplemented in different versions. Every edition contains elaborate portrayals of the religion on the island of Banda. All the inhabitants here were

> heathens, professing the Mahometan faith,[23] to which they are greatly devoted - indeed, they will not even leave or go to their watch before they make their prayers in their temple, which they call Musquita in their language. Before they enter the church or their Musquita they always wash their feet and then enter, for there are generally always large jars in front of their Musquita, into which they put water to clean and wash themselves. They enter the church and make their prayers with crying and shrieking, so loud that one can hear it from a distance of twenty houses away, and all this with words which they usually repeat two or three times: *Stofferolla, Stofferolla, Ascehad an la, Ascehad an la, Yll la, Ascehad an la, Yll lol la, Yll lol la, Machumed die rossulla.*[24] While speaking the last word, they wipe their faces with their hands and thus show great devotion. They recite still more and different prayers as well, which they do silently and in a murmur. They do this in a very peculiar fashion: they spread a little rug on the ground to stand on and fall down on the ground two or three times. They do this often - also, as a rule, in their houses, and sometimes also in public in their *Karcolles*[25] or on the road and on the beach.[26]

Information that is solely based on one's own experience is obviously more reliable than information based on hearsay. The account includes the following description of a funeral and prayers at the gravesite:

> A piece of fine white cotton cloth lies over the corpse, which is carried on their shoulders. The deceased is followed first by the men and then the women. Immediately after the burial a censer is brought in which they burn incense all day and night. During the night there is always a lamp burning under a little house which they have made over the grave. In the morning and in the evening the people, both rich and poor, come and pray there on the grave, which they continue to do for a long time. When we asked them why they did that, they asked us in turn whether we ourselves did not do the same when any of our people had died. After that we asked them about their prayers and they told us that they prayed so that the deceased would not rise again from the dead. They believed this firmly, thinking that the deceased would

---

[23] Such placing of Muslims under the general heading of pagans occurred very seldom. Almost every writer makes a clear distinction between Muslims and pagans, as we will also see in our discussion of Valentijn below.

[24] This is surely to be read as: *Astaghfiru'llah* ('God forgive me'), *Ashadu an la ilaha illa'llah* ('I confess no god but God'), *Ashhadu anna Muhammada rasul Allah* ('I confess that Muhammad is God's messenger').

[25] These are sometimes also called *kora-kora*, boats used by the natives in the eastern part of the East Indies.

[26] J. Keuning (ed.), *De Tweede Schipvaart der Nederlanders ...*, III, pp. 82-83.

rise again from the dead if they did not pray on his grave. This is a great error among them.[27]

We know do that in several places in Indonesia native people have a great fear of the wandering spirits of the deceased, but the fear that the dead would actually rise probably existed more in the minds of the seafaring Dutch rather than among the Indonesians themselves. For the rest, the account and the observations seem accurate and reliable.

An edition of this travel account was published in 1601 in which the editor gave some general supplementary information about Islam. This consisted of an outline of a small work on the main points of Islam, called *The Book of the Thousand Questions*, which is composed in the form of a conversation between Mohammed and an interested Jewish rabbi. The complete version exists only in Persian and Malay, but an edition comprising one hundred questions had already been translated into Latin in 1114 as part of the large translation project under the direction of Peter the Venerable, abbot of Cluny.[28] Van Neck incorporated an outline of thirty-seven questions in his travel account,[29] most of which deal with the origin of the world, the heavens, sun, moon and stars. The sun, for example is spoken of in this way: "It is situated in a hot Fountain, and this Fountain is situated in a valley; the valley is situated in a meadow, and this meadow on Mount Caff; Mount Caff stands on the hand of an Angel who carries the whole world and supports it until the day of judgement ...." Some questions are more like riddles, such as the one which refers to night: "who lives and nevertheless has no spirit?" Another such question is the following: "Tell me, who was the woman who came only from a man and who was the man who only came from woman? Eve came only from Adam and Jesus Christ from the Virgin Mary ..."[30]

Two supplementary stories explain "why their law forbids them to drink wine" and why Muslims are forbidden to eat pork. Both stories originated in anti-Islamic polemics. The ban on wine was said to have originated in the desire of "a very beautiful woman" to enter heaven. To that end she enticed the prophet Mohammed and his two guardian angels into becoming drunk and afterwards "into sleeping with her on the condition that they would first teach her a prayer with which she could ascend to heaven and come back to earth again. All of this was done ...." Nevertheless, God condemned this woman to eternal punishment and then instituted a ban on wine. The ban on pork was

---

[27] J. Keuning (ed.), *De Tweede Schipvaart*, III, p. 90.

[28] Cf. Kritzeck, 1964, in connection with this translation project.

[29] J. Keuning, *De Tweede Schipvaart*, III, pp. LXXXV-XC and 123-130.

[30] *De tweede Schipvaart*, III, p. 129.

said to have been introduced because Mohammed's wife Ayesha had just prepared "a fragrant bath", when "a pig came into the house unexpectedly and
took a bath in it himself ...."[31] It seems that the editor of the 1601 edition
inserted these episodes from *The Book of the Thousand Questions* because the
first edition did not contain enough information about Islam. For this purpose
he used material from existing literature and not specifically that dealt with
the East Indies.

The leaders of the Van Neck and Warwijck expedition describe a circumcision that they themselves observed:

> First of all there are three or four pairs of men leading the way with loaded flintlocks
> and burning fuses in their hands. These were followed by two men carrying a pole on
> which they hang everything that they consider to be fine, such as a piece of tinfoil and
> other things they think to be beautiful. Next come another two men and then the wo-
> man who carries the child and she is followed by seven or eight pairs of women.
> When they reach the church or mosque, they discharge the flintlocks and when the
> circumcision has been completed according to their ceremonies, they go home again
> in the same grand way.[32]

The writers describe only the ceremonial procession preceding the circumcision but not the actual operation itself. We may assume, nevertheless, that
they were interested in the circumcision as well but did not witness it and
were therefore unable to tell us anything about it.

In the seventeenth century Dutch clergymen in Sri Lanka and India provided
two quite detailed accounts of the doctrine and rites of Hinduism. These accounts were based on their own experiences, interviews with knowledgeable
Hindus and translations of original writings.[33] It was not until the latter half
of the nineteenth century that similarly complete works on Muslims in the
East Indies appear. Usually we have to settle for a few pages or sometimes
half a page in the logs. The travel account of Van Neck's voyages is already

---

[31] *De tweede Schipvaart*, III, pp. 130-131.

[32] *De tweede Schipvaart*, p. 137.

[33]Philippus Baldaeus, *Afgoderye der Oost-Indische Heydenen* (Idolatry of the East Indian
Pagans) edited by A.J. de Jong, (The Hague: Martinus Nijhoff, 1917); Abraham Rogerius, *De
Open-deure tot het verborgen heydendom*, (The Open Door to Hidden Paganism), edited by W.
Caland (The Hague: Martinus Nijhoff, 1915). Less detailed but more clearly based on observation in a broader societal context is W. Geleynssen de Jongh, *Remonstrantie* (Remonstrance), ed.
W. Caland (The Hague: Martinus Nijhoff, 1929). Geleynssen was employed in the Moluccas from
1618-21 and as of 1623 at a Dutch East Indian Company settlement in northern India. He wrote
this portrayal of Indian society, in which he also describes Muslims (cf. pp. 55-71) in 1625. Completely following the style of travel accounts, he provides a great many concrete facts about rituals and customs but hardly any information about the religious doctrines themselves.

more extensive than was the usual practice. This was probably due to the fact that a substantial and easily accessible body of literature on Islam already existed in Europe - certainly if one compares this to the literature on Hinduism which existed at the time. To those employed by the Dutch East India Company the East Indian Muslims were closely associated with the Mediterranean 'Moors' and 'Turks'. This association was not only inspired by allusions to the Crusades or the attacks on Vienna by the Turks in the middle of the sixteenth century but even more by north African pirates, who were fierce competitors of the Dutch fleets first in the Mediterranean and later in Indian waters.

Among the accounts of these first voyages we do encounter a few which are unprejudiced and display a mixture of admiration, interest and astonishment at practices which appeared to be bewildering, but this kind of reporting did not last very long. Nicolaus de Graaff, a ship's doctor, was one of the most important and colourful writers of the following generation. He made several trips to the East Indies between 1639 and 1687 and related them with relish. De Graaff arrived in Achin in 1641 just as Sultan Iskandar Tsani was dying. He first describes the political riots which kept the Dutch East Indian Company's trading post closed for five days: "and [there was a] great confrontation among the powerful, during which many people lost their lives... for everyone wanted to be King ...."[34] He continues with an elaborate description of the funeral procession of the deceased prince:

> this consisted of a large retinue of princes, lords and noblemen, aside from 260 elephants, which were all covered with expensive silk, golden sheets and embroidered cloths. Some had their teeth covered with gold and others with silver; still others carried little square houses and costly tents on their backs, from which several banners interwoven with silver and gold hung. [There were] also some rhinoceroses and Persian horses with silver and golden bridles and covered in expensive cloths. A great number of the wives of the deceased king added to the funeral train. And thus the corpse was buried in the coffin of Tambago Soosa, that is, half gold and half brass, covered in all kinds of golden cloths, in the back court near his forefathers. He was mourned by his wives and concubines for one hundred days and was daily provided with all kinds of food, drink and tobacco, as if he was still alive. These were eagerly consumed by these women after they had completed their hours of mourning. No sooner had the king's corpse been laid to rest in the tomb than two small silver guns were fired, at which all the cannons in Achin were fired and discharged all through the night, accompanied by the constant cry: "God save the new Queen." And then everything was peaceful and quiet.[35]

This account, which was accompanied by a detailed illustration of the entire scene, does not seem to differ much from the general description of a similar

---

[34] J.C.M. Warnsinck, (ed.), *Reisen van Nicolaus de Graaff* (The Hague: 1930), p. 13.

[35] *Reisen*, pp. 13-14.

court scene in Europe. Indeed, in the eyes of someone such as De Graaff, the pomp and ceremony of the Achinese court were not at all inferior to that of European courts.

De Graaff managed to keep clear of religious issues quite well during his travels. At any rate he scarcely writes about them - no more than many of his colleagues who wrote of their travels. He ran into difficulties only once in the Ganges valley when he was travelling in India. While visiting the city of Mongeer, he made some notes about the length and thickness of the fortifications and was then brought

> before the Governor, whom he found surrounded by the Muslim Council and sitting on an beautifully canopied seat covered with fine rugs. He was clothed in royal dress and carried a shield and sword, with tobacco and a betel-box by his side. At the same time, we were surrounded by soldiers and did not have any idea of what they might do ...."

After De Graaff had been questioned about the notes he had made and about his compass and quadrant, the governor asked

> what kind of country Holland was, who our king was, what we believed and in whom we believed, whether we also believed in the Prophet Mahomet, and other similar questions. We answered through our interpreter that Holland was a powerful and rich country, full of people, trade, commercial and retail businesses. We said that it had large, rich cities and villages and that they traded all over the world with various nations and sailed everywhere. [We further stated] that they believed in Jesus Christ, not in Mahomet, and that they were governed by the lords of the states and had the Prince of Orange as their ruler.[36]

The Muslims persisted and once again asked

> Why we did not believe in Mahomet? We answered them and concluded by saying that all the inhabitants believed in Christ and nobody in Mahomet. To this [the governor], looking angry, replied, 'If you do not believe in the great Prophet Mahomet, then you are inferior to these dogs', indicating the bodyguards there present, who were jentives and heathens.[37]

From this short summary of what must have been a much longer but awkward (the more so because an interpreter was used) discussion it becomes clear that De Graaff was running into difficulties and was not able to answer to the satisfaction of the Muslims. He was detained for a few days but was then released because of some letters from the Dutch East Indian Company's trading post in Bengal.

---

[36] *Reisen*, pp. 113-14.

[37] *Reisen*, p. 115.

Some data on the Muslims of central Java is available in the reports written by Rijkloff van Goens who was the ambassador to the court of Mataram (situated quite close to what is now Yogyakarta) five times between 1648 and 1654. Van Goens was the company's most important negotiator following a war between the Company and the most important kingdom of Java from 1626-1646. His accounts actually discuss only one issue in connection with the Muslims: his attempts to have the Dutch prisoners of war released and to have their children, whom Javanese women had bore them during their imprisonment, to Batavia as well.[38] During his return journey to and furlough in the Netherlands Van Goens wrote a detailed account of his experiences in the inland areas of Java. He is quite negative in his general portrayal of the population:

> a very wicked and ungrateful people, without a doubt certainly an ancient, pure, independent and natural people, who do not originate from or have anything in common with the neighbouring islands, but drawn from one race (which I consider to be some of Ham's children because of their incredible wickedness) by the hand of God the Lord himself.

He already makes a distinction between pre-islamic stories and customs and Islam which arrived later:

> With the coming of Islam most peoples also adopted the Arabic script which the Malay, together with their ungodly sect, learned barely more than 100 years ago from the Arabs and Mohammedans, who by their trade and frequent contacts with the aforementioned islanders impressed their way of writing and and at the same time their faith on them, before which none among them had been able to write.[39]

Van Goens also pays more attention in this later account to the fate of the prisoners during the period of the war. Those who "were not circumcised or were not willing to marry women in accordance with [Muslim] practice" were treated poorly,[40] subjected to hard labour and tortured. The deputy trader, Anthonij Paulo, who had been detained already since 1631, assumed the role of spiritual guide for the prisoners for a while and attempted to keep them from abandoning their faith. He was eventually suspected of witchcraft and the sultan ordered him to be thrown to the crocodiles. The crocodiles, however, only sniffed at the body before diving and moving away. The sultan considered this to be clear proof of witchcraft and therefore gave the order

---

[38] H.J. de Graaf, *De Vijf Gezantschapsreizen van Rijklof van Goens* (The Hague: 1956), pp. 89-90.

[39] De Graaf, *Rijklof van Goens*, p. 194.

[40] De Graaf, *Rijklof van Goens*, p. 194.

to "Cut him to pieces and throw them into the water and then see how they swallow him." The crocodiles did not swallow them, however, and the pieces remained floating on the surface. The sultan realised then that he had been wrong: "The man was innocent, I had him killed in my wrath. Go, bury him and put up a notice of his innocence." Anthonij Paulo's remains were buried and an iron fence was set up around his grave as was done with graves of important and holy people.[41]

A good way to round off our discussion of the period of first encounters can be found in Rev. François Valentijn's major work *Oud en Nieuw Oost-Indien*. Valentijn (1666-1727) not only drew amply from the best sources of a whole century of colonial history but also often put his own experiences into writing as well.[42] His intention was to provide a 'history', a comprehensive and encyclopedic treatise on the entire area in the east where the Dutch were active. His work follows a geographical division: the first and most detailed discussion concerns the Moluccas, which is followed by an account of Java, the other parts of Indonesia and finally he takes up Sri Lanka (Ceylon), South Africa, India and the Far East.

In *Oud en Nieuw Oost-Indien* Valentijn includes some extensive discussions of Islam and in the section on the "Macassarese Matters" Valentijn himself indicates his source. In 1706 he worked on Java as an army chaplain and was in frequent contact with a Macassar captain, Daeng Matara, "one of the most sensible Mohammedans." This captain told him that a Malay had come from Sumatra

> at a time when the Macassarese still mostly worshipped trees and large stones as their gods. He showed them that it was impossible for such gods to help them in time of need, and he taught them that there was one God who had created everything and still ruled over everything. He had also sent various prophets such as Nabi Moesa [the Prophet Moses], Nabi Daoed [the Prophet David], Nabi Isa Maseekh [the Prophet Jesus Christ], but finally he sent Nabi Mohammed [the Prophet Mohammed] as the greatest and last of the prophets, to show them the straight path to salvation. They should set all their hopes on this God, therefore, and they should try to be accepted by him through the intercession of Mohammed.[43]

This is followed by a historical narrative concerning the coming of Islam to Macassar and the other southern regions of Sulawesi. Whoever thinks that

[41] De Graaf, *Rijklof van Goens*, p. 194.

[42] Cf. also J. Fisch, *Hollandsch Ruhm in Asien, François Valentyns Visions des niederländischen Imperiums im 18. Jahrhundert* (Stuttgart, 1986) and Sinnapah Arasaratnam, *F. Valentijn's Description of Cape of the Good Hope*, Vol. I-II (Cape Town, 1971).

[43] F. Valentijn, *Oud en Nieuw Oost-Indien* (Dordrecht: 1724-1726), III/2, p. 223.

Valentijn intended this discussion to be positive will be disappointed when he writes

> that this religion has spread quite extensively among these blind pagans so that the greater part of this island is Mohammedan. This religion is quite undemanding and particularly easy for them to observe - which is also the reason why it is so difficult for us to have an impact.

He also discusses Islam in the "Omstandig verhael van Amboina", because almost half of the population of the island of Amboyna, now usually called Ambon, were adherents of Islam when the Dutch arrived and this situation has hardly changed since. Valentijn discusses the pagan religion prior to Islam and concludes this religious triptych with a discussion of the Christian faith.[44] He especially castigates the violent spread of Islam in Ambon and its surroundings, through which many Christian villages were finally forced to become Islamized. He had a rather low opinion of the intellectual level of the Muslims. He was already familiar with the distinction between the Sunni and Shi'ite Muslims and considered the latter to be more orthodox because the Sunni's, in addition to the Koran, accepted a collection of statements by Mohammed "as an oral law or similar to the Mishna among the Jews". Valentijn included among the Sunni's the Arabs who brought Islam to the Moluccas, describing them as certainly "the most ignorant and least trained in the principles of their religion and know very little of the true content of the Koran." The distant and unknown Shi'ites rejected the oral doctrine, strictly observed the Koran and lived decently, modestly and piously. On Ambon, according to Valentijn, even the "Priests" had so little knowledge of Arabic that they were "barely capable of reading a chapter from the Koran correctly".[45]

In 1687 Valentijn was "on Hila, in their temple, where they allowed me to enter and observe their service from beginning to end, but they did not allow the Lord Governor Padbrugge's consort to enter, even though she was quite eager to do so at the time." She was allowed to sit before the open "church door" and thus watch the entire service, while a number of old women on her left were saying their prayers. Like other visitors, Valentijn was very much impressed by the respect and quiet piety,

> so that one did not hear the slightest noise or rustle, far less any conversation of one person with another in that temple, since everyone was equally attentive to what the priest was reading aloud. The second thing I saw there which pleased me very much

---

[44] Cf. Valentijn, *Oud en Nieuw Oost-Indien*, III/1, pp. 27-33 on Catholics and pp. 34-44 on Calvinists.

[45] Valentijn, *Oost-Indien*, III/1, p. 23.

was that not one of the men who were sitting on those mats turned their heads when the Governor's consort appeared, far less sprang to their feet (people always rise when a Councillor and such people enter the church on Batavia).[46]

Valentijn complimented his Muslim host and fellow chaplain on this and they replied

that the Massigit was the place where people came to honour God alone, not people and much less honour people above Him; that one should realize that God is present there, instead of neglecting to worship him, which is the reason why we have come there, or neglecting it for a moment in order to honour a human person above Him, however important such a person might be ...."

Here Valentijn uses the voice of his Muslim colleague in his struggle against the exaggerated honours paid to the civil authorities of Batavia - even in the church. He praises the Muslims for being very steadfast in the faith to the point of obstinacy[47] and speaks highly of the cleansing and washing before prayer. Valentijn, however, thought the observation of fasts peculiar because people kept a strict fast during the day but sobriety appeared to set with the sun: "I call it eating and drinking, but if that is fasting, then we fast every evening."[48]

Valentijn always distinguishes clearly between pagans and Muslims, regarding Islam as a wrong but nonetheless respectable religion, whereas pagan religions were the worst. He writes, for example, about the inland regions of Borneo: "They know nothing here of temples or pagodas and even less of priests, with the result that everyone chooses a god to his liking and serves him as he himself sees fit."[49] But then he goes on to discuss the greed of the 'Mohammedan priests' who charged large sums of money for circumcision and reception into Islam: one *ganteng* of golddust and one *ganteng* of lead burners.

Valentijn also applies this distinction between paganism and Islam to his account of Islam on Java. He describes the situation on Java as "at first completely pagan, in the profound darkness of blind paganism", This was changed in the year 1406 by the messenger Ibn Modlana "the distinguished founder and propagator of this religion". Following his account of the practi-

---

[46] Valentijn, *Oost-Indien*, III/1, p. 24.

[47] By way of exception he mentions the case of a certain Paul Papoewa who was hanged in 1643 because he had "been a Christian twice and a Muslim twice". Again, the facts are insufficient for us to examine the precise psychological processes in the case of such a person. Cf. Valentijn, *loc. cit.*

[48] Valentijn, *Oost-Indien*, III/1, p. 25.

[49] Valentijn, *Oost-Indien*, III/2, p. 252.

cal matters of Islam, for the most part based on his own observation in respect to Ambon, his chapter on Java contains some pages[50] of general information about Islam. He describes Islam as a

> hodgepodge ... [drawn] partly from the pure fountains of the Old and New Testament and partly from the muckheaps of both Judaism and the old Sabaean and Saracen religion. All this is patched together so foolishly and so roughly that there is ample occasion to wonder how it is possible that so many nations (and large ones as well), including some quite intelligent ones, should have indulged in such an unfounded error and objectionable religion. The drafter and institutor of this monstrous religion is Mohammmed.

Mohammed wrote the Koran with the assistance of a Jew and a Nestorian monk and

> what he writes in that Koran can be read by anyone who has a fancy for it, since all through the work one sees much conclusive proof of deceit, theft from other works, gross bluntness and his beastly behaviour, he himself more than once figuring in it as a filthy adulterer unashamed to turn God into an advocate of his lascivious lusts....

Here all the stops of an anti-Islamic polemic are again pulled out. One should perhaps consider this in contrast to the passages about Ambon where Valentijn speaks more from personal experience with Muslims, whom he apparently could appreciate as persons. In the passage just quoted, however, he falls back on the historical and written products of Christian polemics for an introduction to his account of Islam on Java. As his authority, he occasionally cites Voetius, whom we shall meet again in the next chapter. With respect to particular points of doctrine, Valentijn discusses the fact that God is certainly confessed to be one and unique but without including the divinity of the Son and the Spirit. Muslims believed that God was the creator but understood this in too materialistic a fashion. Mohammad wrote some "foolish things", particularly about the angels. And "however high he exalts Jesus Christ, he still only acknowledges him to be a human being ...." Many Muslims were supposed to doubt the resurrection of the dead, although it was a universal doctrine. The representation of paradise was "as filthy as one could imagine".[51]

All in all, the first generations of explorers do not produce much factual material on Muslims in the East Indies based on direct observation.[52] Some

[50] Valentijn, *Oost-Indien*, IV/2-4.

[51] Valentijn, *Oost-Indien*, IV/4.

[52] Boland, 1983, p. 3: "These snippets can hardly be said to form any sort of contribution to our knowledge of Islam in the Archipelago."

aspects of behaviour, such as devotion to prayer in particular, are sometimes mentioned appreciatively. For the rest, and especially with regard to questions of doctrine, a great many of the first travellers believed themselves to be already sufficiently informed and their judgements are quite unfavourable. These west Europeans did not encounter anything new in Islam as they did in "real" paganism or forms of Hinduism or Buddhism in Sri Lanka and in southern India. Indeed, only few of them thought these matters worth writing about and this was mostly done in a very brief and simple way. Their written accounts, therefore, are often a mixture of personal observation and the often heavily biased knowledge they brought with them from their homelands.

Theology on the Homefront:
Muslims as Detestable Heretics

The traders, workers and sailors who travelled to the Dutch East Indies arrived with preconceived opinions of Islam and its adherents. Scholarly treatises on Islam in circulation at the time voiced, shaped and strengthened these views to some extent. In the first part of this chapter, because of their association with the Dutch East India Company, we will discuss three of these scholars, who were representative of the theological views in the seventeenth century. Hugo de Groot (Grotius) was a member of the Company's delegation that went to London in 1613 to conduct negotiations about the legal grounds concerning monopolies. Antonius Walaeus was the founder and sole rector of the *Seminarium Indicum* (1622-1632) in Leiden and thus played a part in training clergymen who were to be sent to the area. Finally, Gisbertus Voetius was also involved in such training since a number of his students, with some of whom he corresponded regularly, also ended up as clergymen in the Dutch East Indies. Valentijn, among others, considered him to be the most authoritative theologian on India - not only in a general way but especially when it involved an assessment of Islam.[1] These three can be considered to be representative of the Christian defence against Islam in the period from 1600-1800.

The Arabist Relandus followed a different tack. At the beginning of the eighteenth century he wrote an apology of sorts of Islam, which was the first of a series of more positive appreciations of that religion. Similar appreciations were dominant in the literature of the Romantic period, of whom Onno Zwier van Haren and Bilderdijk are representative. This greater appreciation for Islam did gain a number of followers in the Netherlands, but it had little effect on the ideologues and strategists of mission at the time. This can be seen in Scharp's lectures on Islam, delivered to potential missionaries at the beginning of the nineteenth century.

---

[1] Valentijn, *Oost-Indien*, Vol. II, p. 60.

Hugo de Groot

During his imprisonment in Loevestijn (1619-1621) Hugo de Groot wrote a poem of some 4500 lines called *Bewijs van de Ware Godsdienst*. This poem was divided into six books, the last of which discusses Islam.[2] As is often the case with polemic literature, this book was not intended to be read by 'outsiders' (Muslims in this case) but by Christians.[3] It is obvious that De Groot was far removed from the world of Islam and its vague threat. He latched onto this vague threat, however, in order to summon Christianity to reform. His poem begins with the history of Christianity up to Constantine:

> With Constantine the world did enter in
> And to the church brought all her vice and sin;
> Thus by excessive opulence and ease
> Bit by bit God's image did decrease.

[God punished his people by means of many disasters ...]

> Since the people, however, in spite of all this
> Refused to repent, God at last the church's disgrace
> Exposed in the lands of the eastern race:
> Thus a proud, cruel law there did ascend
> Around the Red Sea by Mahomet's harsh hand.

De Groot then dutifully, as it were, works through the usual list of prejudices. In this section he often appears to have lost sight of any connection with his theme of reform:

> So as now to know which is the better guide
> The one by which their messengers first abide:
> Ours you yourself "God's wisdom, word and spirit" call,
> While Mahomet was merely human like us all;
> Ours had no human father - so you admit,
> While Mahomet began his life as we all did;

---

[2] "Proof of the True Religion." Cf. T.C.L. Wijnmalen, *Hugo de Groot als Verdediger des Christendoms Beschouwd* (Hugo de Groot as a Defender of Christianity), (Utrecht: W.F. Dannenfelser, 1869). In the Dutch edition of this present book, I used Jeronimo de Vries' edition (Amsterdam: R. Stemvers, 1844), in which the sixth book is found on pp. 152-67.

[3] One can find a similar approach, for that matter, in Islamic polemics against Christianity. Cf., for example, T. Michel, *A Muslim Theologian's Response to Christianity: Ibn Taimiyya's Al-Jawab al'Sahih* (New York: Caravan Books, 1984), p. vii: "He seemed best able to say what Islam is (or should be) by pointing up its contradiction to what Islam is not (or must not become)."

Ours, and not that Mahomet of yours, you hold
Was God's Messiah as the ancient law foretold;
Ours always lived a pure and pious life,
While Mahomet did live by robbery and vice;
And ours to God in heaven, as you say did rise,
While Mahomet still in the grave enclosèd lies.

It is difficult to imagine that any Muslim would be converted to Christianity
by such an account and one should bear in mind that this poem is intended
to stimulate fellow Christians. It is true that the poem was translated into
Arabic towards the end of the seventeenth century, but one may rightly doubt
whether this work would have been useful in the task of converting Muslims.

De Groot uses Islam to frighten Christians into repentance elsewhere as
well. He begins his *Klacht over 't verdeelde Christendom* (Lament for a divided
Christianity):

The Christian church of days gone by,
Exalted very high,
- Which by the strength unfurled
In its virtue true,
Caused the devils' rue
And the splendour of the world,

And with a sound of conquest great
Through the cross's gate
They to heaven thronged,
And over every stain
Behind the cross contained
They raised their triumph song -

Now broken lies this Christian church
In agonizing hurt,
Defiled by filthy stains,
Be yet compassionate
And pity this poor state
O Lord, of this your reign.

It was not you, O Lord, who set
The law of Mahomet
(Full of brutal wickedness)
Nor did you demand
The wicked Jews commands

As the way of righteousness ....[4]

Here De Groot preaches to the converted: the mention of non-christian religion serves chiefly as an appeal to Christians for purification of doctrine and morality and especially for unity within the divided camp. Still, this reaffirmation of the generally accepted view may well have played a role in influencing the views of readers who did have direct contact with Muslims.

Antonius Walaeus[5]

Antonius Walaeus was born into a Reformed family in Ghent in 1573, a turbulent time when it was still dangerous to be Reformed in that area. He became a minister at Middelburg and then played an important role at the Synod of Dort. In 1619 he was appointed a professor at Leiden and founded the *Seminarium Indicum.* He served as this institute's sole rector for the ten years (1622-1632) of its existence, during which it met in his home in Leiden. With a total number of 12 students, it was, of course, an unimpressive response to the foundation of the Propaganda Fide in Rome. Van Wijngaarden's description that "though small in design, it was nonetheless noble"[6] appears to be rather ill-founded. Walaeus devoted only a few pages to the Muslims and to Islam itself in his theological writings. His discussion of Islam only takes up up a page and a half of his *Opera Omnia*, which numbers about a thousand pages. We will summarize his treatment here because it is so brief. For this reason it will also be a fairly accurate rendering of the text.[7]

Walseus' discussion was written within a polemic context as part of an introduction to a discussion on the meaning of the term "messiah".[8] After dealing with the Jews' view of Christ, Walaeus focuses on the Muslims, who did believe that Christ was the Messiah promised in the Old Testament. In the Koran Mohammed also acknowledged that there was no one greater than

---

[4] *Klacht,* in De Vries' edition, pp. 277-278.

[5] J.D. de Lind van Wijngaarden, *Antonius Walaeus* (Leiden: G. Los, 1891).

[6] Van Wijngaarden, *Waleus,* p. 203. Cf. B. Koolen's Master's thesis, *De colleges van de compagnie.* The Catholic University of Nijmegen, 1967 for more information about this institute.

[7] A. Walaeus, *Opera Omnia* (Lugduni Batavorum: A. Wyngaerden, 1647) Vol. I, pp. 380-381.

[8] In Vol. I of his collected writings Walaeus not only gives a systematic treatment of theology in general but also includes twenty-nine individual treatises. No. 15, "De Christo Servatore Nostro" discusses the concept of messiah. Walaeus deals with this concept under four headings: a) On the Messiah in response to the Jews (p. 375); b) In response to the views on Christ contained in the Koran (p. 380); c) On the person of Christ (p. 381); and d) On the hypostatic union (p. 384).

Christ - Mohammed even calls him Word and Son of God. But the Muslims were not prepared to acknowledge that Christ was actually God. According to them, Christ's task lasted only until his successor, Mohammed, who succeeded him as Christ in his turn had succeeded Moses. Mohammed was called the Paraclete, the 'Comforter', and his way was broader and easier. Walaeus does not explain all the errors in doctrine - that task was best left to God's judgement.

Mohammed lived around the turn of the seventh century. He was poor and his companions were the Arian Sergius, Johannes Nestorianus and Iudaeus Thalmista. During the reign of the Emperor Heraclius he served in the army among his own people. Mohammed appointed himself leader in the struggle for independence when the Arabs revolted and was then chosen to be king of the Arabs. He also devised a New Law to separate his people from Constantinople, as Jeroboam had also done to separate his people from Solomon's kingdom.

Mohammed himself admitted that he did not perform any miracles, because Moses and Jesus had not been able to convince any one on the basis of the miracles they performed. Mohammed did use force in order to make recalcitrant people obedient but he himself was not invincible - he was wounded and even lost his teeth in battle.

Mohammed's teaching was wrong, because the Old and New Testaments proved that Christ was actually God. Luke 1:32 and 1 Cor. 15:24 also show that Christ's kingdom is eternal. Furthermore, one could demonstrate, on the basis of Matt. 28:20, 1 Cor. 11:26 and 2 Cor. 5:10, that Christ promised to assist his church, which implied that he did not recognize any successor. Mohammed's name was certainly never mentioned in the Bible; if it had been mentioned, within the context of the prophecy of the Paraclete, it must have been removed either before Mohammed's appearance (for which there was no reason) or after his appearance (which would have been impossible, because the Bible had already been circulated in several different copies and among many different peoples). Mohammed was a criminal, highwayman and fornicator. The Arabs themselves acknowledged this latter charge, but they claim that he was so because of a special divine privilege allowing him to defile any woman or virgin.

The Koran distorted Scripture and was full of opinions which clashed with them. In one such passage God was portrayed as a physical being, sitting on a chair that was carried from place to place by four strong angels. Mohammed claimed that Christ was only human and did not actually suffer. Instead, he managed to escape after the Jews took him prisoner, ascended to heaven and put another anonymous person in his place to be crucified. Mohammed told several fables and fairy tales about the Last Judgement that were entirely absurd and suitable only for children and old women. He also invented a story of an angel of death who was to kill all creatures on earth, including souls and the remaining angels, before he would kill himself. Then God would create a new angel, named Serafiel, who would blow a trumpet, the length of which was equal to the distance one could travel in 500 years. First, all the souls would emerge from the trumpet when it was blown and these souls would then search for their bones and gather them together. Forty years later the trumpet was to be blown once again and the bones would be covered with flesh. After another forty years they would enter purgatory and be released from it - not, however, by Abraham, or Moses or Christ but only by Mohammed. Then the time would come when the people would engage in carnal lusts and live like animals. Christians could not interpret this allegorically because Mohammed never offered any other interpretation or spoke of a more spiritual existence - only these bodily pleasures.

The law of the Koran contradicted not only the moral and divine laws on many points but also Christ's explicit directives. In particular, one should disapprove of the practice of having more than one wife and concubines, the custom within imperial families of killing their own brothers, divorce for any reason whatsoever, and crimes of a sexually perverse nature that remained unpunished.

To the objection that the patriarchs, Abraham, Isaac and Jacob also had several wives and that Moses permitted for divorce, Christians were to answer that these practices had been allowed only because of the hardness of the human heart. Christ revoked these practices, however, and nature had taught many nations such as the Romans, the Greeks and the Germanic peoples that such practices were wrong. Because of this, marriage in these nations was more stable and they had more numerous posterity than the Muslims with their many wives whom God did not bless with such fruitfulness.

Another objection was that Mohammed was right to prohibit wine so that drunkenness could be avoided. The answer to this objection was that no one can be wiser than God who had indeed given people wine.

Mohammed also distorted the stories of the Old and New Testaments and turned them into fairy tales. One such instance is the story about the grotesque birth of Adam, who was supposed to have been androgynous. In this story Adam had sexual intercourse with all the animals but was not satisfied until a woman was created for him. Mohammed similarly derived his material about Cain, Abel, Noah and the death of Moses from Talmudic stories, among which was the story of the angel who was sent to kill Adam. This angel, however, could not find any place in Adam's body through which he could extract the spirit of life. He finally managed to do so through the nose, to which the spirit of life was lured by means of the smell of an apple. The Koran contained many other similarly false and unbelievable stories.

Apart from the Koran itself (which he principally describes as "that book which cannot be understood allegorically, however much one tries, despite the good intentions of some of [the Muslims], because the Koran itself does not give any reason whatsoever for doing so"), Walaeus cites three contemporary writers in this section as his sources: Ludovicus Vivem, Busbequius and Clenardus.

Walaeus was not an expert in Islamic studies and there was no chair for such a discipline in any theological faculty at the time. In a compact way he gives an important overview of the theological judgements and prejudices of his time and his students probably acquired more missionary zeal than understanding from his teaching. There is nothing to indicate that he paid extensive attention to Islam in his seminary.[9]

Gisbertus Voetius

In 1634 Gisbertus Voetius (1589-1676) was appointed professor of theology at Utrecht, where he became the central figure in setting up theological studies after the *Illustere School* became a university in 1636. Voetius was active in many areas of theological studies and more than once devoted extensive attention to Islam. Already as a minister in Heusden, before he began his academic career, he began to study Arabic.[10]

Primarily due to Voetius's initiative, a new edition of *Confusio Sectae Mahometanae* by Iohannes Andrea, a Spanish convert to Christianity, appeared in 1646. Voetius devoted an introduction of eight pages to the refutation of Islam.[11] Voetius calls Islam the most formidable among the non-Christian religions (*extraneos*) because its adherents dominated such a large area of the world, which made it necessary to refute their doctrine. Although Christians had already fought several wars against them, they were now engaged in trade with them - in fact, were even making treaties with their rulers. All this could have been a splendid occasion for the proclamation of the gospel, if most of

---

[9] It is probable, although not quite certain, that Justus Heurnius studied at Leiden. In 1618, one year before Walaeus was appointed professor, Heurnius wrote a rather long-winded work on the proper way to convert people in India (*De legatione evangelica ad Indos capessenda admonitio*, Leiden). This work testifies to much idealism, good will and ardour but does not give any evidence of the slightest knowledge of Islam.

[10] Cf. Juynboll, 1931, pp. 204-05 concerning Voetius' study of Arabic.

[11] The work referred to here is the Latin translation of Iohannes Lauterbach, published with a preface by Voetius at "Traiecti ad Rhenum" in 1646. Valentijn, Vol. II, p. 60, mentions another refutation was written by Rector Spiljardus in the year 1660 but which was probably never published: "In Batavia they commended D. Spiljardus for his hard work but felt that there was no need for haste in printing his work, especially his *Verwerring der Mahommedaansche Godsdienst* (Confusion of the Mohammedan Religion), since a book by Johannes Andrea, called *Confusio Sectae Mohammedanae*, had already been published in Germany with Reverend Voetius' knowledge and approval."

these so-called Christians did not treat mammon or their bellies as their God rather than the crucified Jesus. Playing on the formula *cuius regio illius et religio* (the religion of a region being determined by its ruler) he claimed that most of these traders were only looking for new opportunities and had no use for religion: *regionem a se quaesitans fuisse non religionem*. Those few who had nonetheless acquired some knowledge of the language and culture in order to study Islam were therefore to be commended highly. Voetius valued Iohannes Andrea highly among these scholars as a man who had been a learned Muslim himself and therefore was a very special witness. The book was especially recommended to all clergymen who went to serve in the East Indies, since Islam was already firmly established in the trading areas frequented by the Dutch.[12]

Voetius himself also wrote a treatise on Islam.[13] Like many of his shorter works this was a response to a written request (in this case by one Joannes de Jonge) to which he replied on March 25, 1648. He apparently added to this treatise several times, with the result that it became somewhat confused towards the end. In the edition of the *Selectae Disputationes* this treatise is grouped with other treatises dealing with various rejections of the true faith such as atheism, paganism and Judaism. Voetius himself stated that he also wrote this *disputatio* for the specific reason that some of his former students had already left for the East Indies.[14] The treatise is classical in structure: first he explains the nature and essence of Islam, after which he considers possible remedies to the disease.

Before explaining Islam itself, Voetius begins with a definition upon which he later enlarges. He defines Islam as "a complete denial of the true God and the covenant of the gospel, a denial of the theological doctrine of redemption and the doctrine of morality". Voetius does support this rather abstract definition with some facts, but he was sometimes rather too much in a hurry and obviously had no intention of going too deeply into "objective information". His main purpose was to assess Islam theologically and to discuss missionary strategies.

---

[12] *... qui ad legationem evangelicam in Indias Orientales (ubi Muhammedismus sedes suas fixit in locis mercaturae Batavicae potissimum frequentatis).* Johannes Andrea organized his book historically. He begins with a biography of Mohammed, followed by a discussion of the Koran, the tradition of the prophet, the main developments in the field of Islamic law and its four schools. The entire work is richly interspersed with a quite polemic rejection of many aspects of Islamic doctrine and practice. In respect to factual information it is certainly more precise and correct in a great many particulars than the more general discussions of Hugo de Groot or Walaeus.

[13] "De Muhammedismo," *Selectae Disputationes Theologicae*, Vol. II (1655), pp. 659-683.

[14] *Selectae*, p. 660: *"quo jam aliquot ex hac Academia profecti."*

After explaining this definition, Voetius discusses individually the various names of Islam and displays his knowledge of linguistics by including a number of Arabic words, even though he transcribes them in Hebrew characters. He subjects the often used term 'Saracen' to a particularly minute inquiry, rejecting several explanations as unsatisfactory, and finally suggests that the term could derive from the Arabic *sharq* (east). Contrary to the general custom of his time, he uses the term 'Mahometismus' only when citing other writers, whereas he consistently uses the term 'Muhammedismus' in his own texts, a use which dated already from his introduction to Andrea's work. According to him, the word 'Moor' was derived from a North African people and then applied to all Muslims, because the people of this nation were among the most fanatic adherents of Islam.

Voetius does not provide a detailed and coherent account of Mohammed's life nor the composition and content of the Koran but concentrates on a theological assessment of Islam. He treats the Islamic creed ("There is no deity but God and Mohammed is His messenger") more extensively and compares this with John 17:3: ("Now this is eternal life: that they may know you, the only true God, and Jesus Christ whom you have sent".) Voetius does not concern himself with the Islamic name for God; despite his extensive knowledge of Arabic terminology, he uses the generic *deus* rather than *Allah* to refer to God. In his view, however, the content of the Islamic creed is completely at odds with the Christian creed and he emphasizes the differences - not the similarities - in the concept of God. Since Muslims denied the Trinity and the redemptive nature of Jesus' death, the central beliefs were thus already essentially different. In respect to other beliefs, Voetius severely criticizes the Islamic doctrine of heaven: the Muslims depicted heavenly life in rather carnal terms and their accounts of heaven were full of obscenities. As a result, they therefore did not object to animals as participants in salvation.[15] They replaced the Sabbath with Friday or *Dies Veneris* because they venerated the goddess of love in particular, just as pagans did.[16] This champion of Calvinist orthodoxy seems to be inspired by anti-Roman Catholic sentiments in his rejection of the practice of fasting and the pilgrimage to Mecca. In discussing the spread of Islam he does mention all of Africa, with the ex-

---

[15] *Selectae*, p. 664: "*immo et plusquam brutalibus spurcitiis consistente: cujus consequenter ipsae bestiae participes sint futurae ....*" One of Voetius' contemporaries, Nuruddin ar-Raniri from Gujarat, who held a high religious position in Achin from 1637 to 1644, was of the precisely opposite opinion. In his work on the last judgement and the resurrection *Akhbaru'l akhirat fi ahwalil qiyamat,* he claims that the animals will then be turned to clay again (*sekalian binatang itupun jadilah tanah*). Out of fear of hell the unbelievers ask that they may also be turned into clay but this request will not be granted. Cf. the still unpublished manuscript in the University Library at Leiden, Or. 1960, p. 226.

[16] *Selectae*, p. 665: "*Dies Veneris, ab ea enim Venus in Ethnicismo peculiariter colebatur.*"

ception of Abyssinia, and the empire of the Great Mogul and European countries such as Greece, Bulgaria and parts of Hungary as Islamic areas, but his
sources apparently did not mention the East Indies and neither does Voetius.
Voetius offers extensive bibliographical data, as in all his works. In this
treatise he quotes from more than fifty works, often including a brief general
discussion of their content and author. He criticizes some of his authors for
speaking too appreciatively of Islam. For example, he often quotes from Elmacinus's work, *Historia Saracenica*, but thinks this work to be structured too
much in line with the translated Arabic sources and thus "too Islamic".[17]
Elmacinus also emphasized Mohammed's favourable attitude towards Christians too much for Voetius' liking. Neither could Voetius entirely appreciate
Marsil Ficinus' work. Ficinus begins his discussion of Islam with the observation that Islam bore many similarities to Christianity, even though this religion
should be considered as a sect on a level with Arianism or Manichaeism. In
Voetius' view, this was a gross exaggeration.[18]

Still, in spite of this generally negative image of Muslims, Voetius also
mentions a few positive aspects, one of which was the prohibition against images. In this connection he draws the reader's attention not only to the discussion on images and icons in the eastern churches but to another form of
idolatry as well: the "deification of matter" in the Catholic conception of the
Eucharist. Voetius cites Ibn Rushd (also known as Averroes), the well-known
philosopher and physician from Cordoba, as saying that he could not imagine
a people more absurd than the Christians who ate their god.[19] Voetius does
not comment on this, but he must have taken the Muslims' side in this against
the Catholics.

In Voetius' view, Islam suffered from the significant problem of subdivi-
sion into sects and denominations but gave outsiders the impression of unity.
Voetius attributed this to the high rate of ignorance among their "priests":
people were called to the priesthood who had barely learned to recite the
Koran and did not know Arabic. Consequently, it was extremely difficult to
convert Muslims to Christianity. To illustrate this, he produces one of the few
reports that he himself received from the East Indies. Primarily in the Moluccas, in the kingdom of Ternate, it was possible to convert a substantial
number of pagans but only very few Muslims. For the rest, according to his
information, the *Bramines* in the kingdom of Siam were even more tenacious.

---

[17] *Selectae*, p. 670; "*stylo nimis Muhammedico.*"

[18] *Selectae*, p. 671: "*Hyperbolice nimis incipit: Mahumetenses Christiani quodammodo esse
videntur, quamvis haeretici Arianorum Manichaeorumque sectatores.*"

[19] *Selectae*, p. 667: "*Nullam, ajebat, se absurdiorem gentem vidisse Christianis, qui deum suum
comederent.*"

Already in vol. I of his collected works Voetius discusses the possibility that Mohammed might have suffered from epilepsy or lunacy.[20] He mentions, citing Iohannes Andrea as his authority, that Mohammed was regarded by his fellow citizens in Mecca as insane and possessed and that even his own wife suspected him of having fallen victim to the devil. According to Guadagnolo, this sickness had originated in the ascetic practices of fasting, keeping vigil and staying in caves. Voetius did not hesitate to add an attack on monastic life in general, Francis of Assisi and the Anabaptists.[21]

Voetius accounts for Islam's rise rather quickly and briefly: the moral decline of Christians and Christianity's internal divisions. He does not support this claim with any further discussion of history.[22]

More than a third of "De Muhammedismo" (pp. 674-683) is devoted to curing "this serious disease". In the first place, Christians were to find a solution to their internal division. Secondly, they were to distance themselves from unhealthy remedies to the disease, among which Voetius included the holy wars against the Turks, the Spanish Inquisition and the far too facile prophecies which suggested that the endtime was near when Christ's enemies would automatically disappear. Sound remedies included first and foremost prayer, the study of Scripture and of Arabic and the foundation of a *Collegia de Propaganda Fide*. He considered the papal institute founded in 1622 to be an example and calls on the Protestant nations to found something similar or even superior to it. The study of languages and the publishing of Islamic sources should also be promoted. He regretted that a complete Arabic edition of the Koran was not yet available[23] and commends the Utrecht manuscript as the finest. One can detect here the voice of the bibliophile who likes to describe various publications at length and at the same time envisages even more additions to his library.

In an appendix of sorts Voetius discusses a few problems of lesser importance such as the question of whether the Turks and Tartars can be seen as descendants of the ten lost tribes of Israel. He also takes up the question of whether Luther was right to propose that Protestants should go to war against

---

[20] Voetius, "De Energumenis," *Selectarum Disputationum Theologicarum Pars Prima* (Ultrajecti, 1648), pp. 1018-1059.

[21] *Selectarum*, I, p. 1058. Cf. also his *Politica Ecclesiastica*. Pars III, Liber II, p. 302 where he speaks of a Franciscasinus ('Francisc-ass').

[22] *Selectarum*, II, p. 671.

[23] A complete Arabic text of the Koran had, however, already been published in Venice in 1530. Cf. W. Montgomery Watt, *Bell's Introduction to the Qu'ran* (Edinburgh: University Press, 1970), p. 173.

the Pope sooner than the Turks.[24] Voetius words his positive reply very carefully: "I see no reason why this statement should not be opportune and correct, in view of the Pope's tyranny, his abuse of the Christian religion and the universal church and particularly his attitude towards church and society in Germany." He inquires further: "If we consider the present tolerance in the Turkish empire, are sailors and soldiers in the Netherlands not justified then in saying that they would rather live under Turkish than papal rule?". Voetius concedes that the lesser of two evils should be chosen, which in this is Islam, but he did not feel committed to any further conclusion concerning his absolute rejection of Islam.

In summary, one can consider Voetius' discussion to be an excellent introduction to the scholarly literature on Islam that was available in his time. He had various translations of the Koran and other important Islamic sources at his disposal. He acknowledged and regretted the gaps in his knowledge, especially where it concerned the practical religious life and the historical developments of Islam. Still, he was in fact unable to give any substantial information on the difference between Sunni and Shi'ite Muslims. He does not extensively summarize the literature available on Islam but uses fragments as points of departure for a theological evaluation which turns into a condemnation, practically without any 'extenuating circumstances'. It is true that he could still appreciate an occasional detail such as the prohibition of images, but for the rest he always views Muslim doctrines and practices negatively. The few authors with a milder and more positive view of Islam are severely critiqued for having been too servile in copying their Islamic sources or writing in 'too islamic' a fashion. The champion of true doctrine in the Netherlands was not by any means going to be carried away by them.

Romanticism and Enlightenment: Orientalist and Poetic Glorification of Islam

In his discussion of Islam, Voetius had recourse to expert knowledge that was circulated by Arabists such as Erpenius and Golius in the Netherlands. He even studied Arabic for a time with Erpenius, among others. Voetius was very selective in his use of works on orientalism and he rejected all those which yielded too positive an appreciation on Muslims, a practice which proved to be a theologically decisive trend until well into the nineteenth century. Already in the following generation, however, there were several significant figures who set a completely different tone. The most significant of these was Adrianus Relandus (1676-1718), who was commended by many as the first to

---

[24] *Selectae*, II, p. 682: "... *Potius in papam quam in Turcam (bellum) suscipiendo*". Cf. also Slomp, 1984, and K. Westerink, 'Better Muslim than Catholic: a Motto during the Revolt in the Netherlands,' *Topkapi en Turkomani, Turks-Nederlandse ontmoetingen sinds 1600*, ed. H. Theunissen (Amsterdam: De Bataafsche Leeuw, 1989), pp. 75-96.

give a fair account of Islam in a Western language.[25] Relandus provided the text edition and translation of an Arabic catechism on the Islamic doctrine in which the five pillars of the teaching on duty and the six pillars of the teaching on faith were concisely explained (*De Religione Mohammedica*, pp. 1-92). In the second part of this work he brought to light thirty-nine errors concerning this religion. In his opinion Hoornbeek made the most errors among the Dutch writers,[26] but Relandus occasionally ranks Voetius as well among those who spoke too excessively in a negative way of Islam.[27]

In order to safeguard himself against his critics perhaps, Relandus does speak about the "original doctrine of Islam and not about the doctrine as it is currently practised by a number of Muslims." This comment, however, introduces the prospect of an islamic orthodoxy created by a western scholar -

---

[25] See Daniel, 1960, and Brugman and Schröder, 1979, pp. 24-25. The work appeared in 1705 in Latin as *De Religione Mohammedica Libri Duo* and was subsequently translated into French, English, German, Dutch and Spanish. The Dutch translation was incorporated into Vol. VI of A. Moubach's *Naaukeurige Beschrijving der uitwendige Godsdienstplichten, Kerk-zeden en Gewoontens van alle Volkeren der Wereldt...*, (An Accurate Account of External Religious Duties, Ecclesiastical Customs and Traditions of all the Peoples of the World) (The Hague: e.c., 1717-1738 (VIB: 79-99 and 145-214). Moubach's work was a liberal adaptation of a French translation by Bernard Picard. Picard's French translation of Relandus was already quite liberal and Moubach took even more liberties. As a result, Relandus' pro-Muslim style appears even stronger, but the poor translation and the fact that the work is adorned with a variety of Latin poetry weakens its factual basis.

[26] Johannes Hoornbeek (1617-1665) wrote two works of some importance for this study. *De conversione indorum et Gentilium*, the 1669 Amsterdam edition of which I have used here, offers 265 pages of general missionary doctrine with extensive digressions on the religions of India and Sri Lanka. It also contains additional digressions on China and Japan, but the Muslims and the Dutch East Indies are excluded entirely. An outline of this book in Dutch was included in W. Hagerwaarts' *Afscheids-reden tot de gemeinte op Batavia*, (Farewell Speech to the Congregation on Batavia) (The Hague: 1732). In addition, Hoornbeek also wrote a *Summa controversiarum religionis cum infidelibus, haereticis, schismaticis* (Utrecht: 1658). In this extensive work he devotes pp. 70-192 to a discussion of and against Muslims. He speaks only briefly about paganism (pp. 56-61), and Judaism (pp. 62-70). The treatise against Islam is followed by discourses against Catholicism ("De Pagismo," pp. 192-330) and Anabaptism ("De Anabaptismo," pp. 331-377). These in turn are followed by treatises against the libertines, remonstrants, Lutherans, Greek Christians and Rosicrucians. Does the fact that Hoornbeek discusses Muslims after Jews and before Catholics mean that he considered Muslims to be closer to Reformed theology than Jews? The treatise on Islam was written more systematically than Voetius' somewhat rambling work, but one does note the same mixture of information and apologetics. History especially is treated on a wider scale. At the end of his discussion he once again condenses the main errors of Islam into eighteen theses. The sixteenth thesis suggests, particularly through its terminology, that Jews and Muslims are on the same level: it is superstitious to forbid the consumption of pork, of suffocated meat, of blood and of wine (*Superstitiosum est quod Muhammedani in cibo et potu abstinent a carne porcina, suffocato, sanguine et vino*, p. 192).

[27] Relandus, *De Religione Mohammedica*, p. 97.

a dangerous development for the oriental studies.[28] Relandus answers several questions as if he were an Islamic apologist, including such questions as: "Do they believe that God is physical? Do they worship Venus?" (Of course not, for belief in the oneness of God is their central doctrine and they reject all idols); "Do they deny Hell? What do they have to say about Paradise?" He always responds to such questions in a way that is reflects a positive attitude toward Muslims. Relandus does acknowledge that sensual descriptions of Paradise do exist, but argues that "the more educated Muslims understand all of this allegorically".[29] Relandus disclaims the notion that Mecca was the site of Mohammed's grave and that true Islamic teaching does not deny Jesus' death, for, according to Koran 19:34, the young Jesus said: "Peace was with me on the day I was born and will be with me on the day I shall die".[30] One sometimes has the impression that Relandus formulates the questions in such a sharp and exaggerated way so that he could answer them more easily in a favourable way. One instance of such formulation is the question of whether Mohammed was allowed by the Koran "to have as many wives as he could support," and when the question was posed in this way, Relandus was quite easily able to reply in the negative.

Relandus briefly refers only once to an Islamic source in an Indonesian languages, Malay. He uses this source to cite the traditional doxology in Arabic script.[31] It is true that Relandus indicates elsewhere that he devoted some time to the study of the Indonesian languages, but he made little use of it to enlarge his knowledge of Islam in those areas. His main questions reflected the theological and linguistic concerns that were subsequently to dominate eighteenth-century theology. Relandus paid a great deal of attention to the questions of the original human language and the original location of paradise. Etymologically, Relandus did see some connection between Malay and Dutch (*sama* means *samen* ('together') and *manusia* means *mens* or man in its generic use) but neglected to draw any significant conclusions from these connections. According to Van Ronkel, Relandus engaged in linguistic studies "without ever falling into the [usual] errors of comparative linguistics and follies of etymologies". Relandus did not draw any definite conclusions from these similarities and certainly did not think that the Dutch language had

---

[28] Relandus, *De Religione Mohammedica*, p. 161 "*Nota Lector, me de Mohammedanis non loqui qui hodie in diversa abeunt ....*"

[29] Relandus, *De Religione Mohammedica*, p. 149: "*Sensuales istae paradisi voluptates a sapientioribus Mohammedanis censentur allegoricae.*"

[30] Relandus, *De Religione Mohammedica*, p. 161: *Pax super me eo die, quo natus sum et die quo moriar.* Most Muslims do not, at any rate, deny Jesus' death as such but only his death on the cross - cf. Koran 4:158. Cf. also Parrinder, 1982, pp. 105-121 concerning this issue.

[31] Relandus, *De Religione Mohammedica*, p. 124.

priority: "... I do not think that one can correctly conclude from this that our language has originated from Malay."[32]

Islam in Missionary Training

Relandus' discussion is certainly one of those "Moments of Vision", which we already discussed in the first chapter, but he did not yet herald a new period in any definite way. Many later writers did not refer to his work. This was the case especially in missionary circles, a prime example of which was the versatile J. Scharp, a teacher in the training college of the *Nederlandsch Zendeling Genootschap* (Dutch Missionary Society). In the early nineteenth century Scharp gave extensive lectures which, in addition to discussing Islamic teaching, also suggested a method for fighting this false religion.[33] Scharp does not quote Relandus in his *Muhammedanismus* of 1824 but does quote earlier apologists such as Hugo de Groot, Hoornbeek, the chronicler Baronius and the Arabist Erpenius. He used both Maracci's 1698 Latin translation and Sale's 1734 English translation for the text of the Koran. Scharp also employed the same theological criterium as Voetius to evaluate his sources and especially warned against writers "who against their better knowledge colour their reports in such a way as they judge suitable to serve some political or religious party or to oppose the whole of Christianity, obstruct the missionary enterprise and promote frivolity through the elevation and white-washing of Islam (and of the Chinese as well)."[34] Scharp referred to a number of travel accounts, but these were all restricted to the Near East and none portrayed Islam in the East Indies. There is no indication that he took any heed of Relandus' effort to clear up misunderstandings. For example, he rejected entirely Relandus's suggestion of an allegorical conception of heaven and like a real clergyman lashed at the sensuality of the Muslims:

> Besides what we have already observed in passing, everybody is acquainted with the multitude of wives, slavegirls, female dancers and male prostitutes, the unbridled passion for perverse relations and the carnal expectations of a never-ending life, devoted to lascivious passions and indulgence to all kinds of lust, combined with the ever youthful *Houris* or *Heavenly Virgins*, as a reward for their faithfulness to the Prophet and the Koran.[35]

---

[32] Van Ronkel, 1919, pp. 297, 304.

[33] Enklaar, 1981, pp. 36-49. I have used the manuscript at the Hendrik Kraemer Institute in Oegstgeest which, as Enklaar has proven, is Scharp's original manuscript.

[34] Scharp, 1824, p. 353.

[35] Scharp, 1824, p. 24.

Onno Zwier van Haren and W. Bilderdijk: Two Representatives of Romanticism

Scharp probably included some Romantics as well among those who engaged in the "elevation and white-washing of Islam". A typical example is the Frisian nobleman Onno Zwier van Haren, who turned his personal tragedy into a five-act play, *Agon, Sulthan van Bantam*.[36] Van Haren saw his own misfortune reflected in that of the sultan of Banten who was robbed of his throne by his son. The sultan of Banten is portrayed as a devout believer in some vaguely defined Supreme Being and already at the beginning of the play confesses:

> O Maker of the Universe, who inspires all with awe
> Who through Mahomet gave us your eternal law,
> Who from the very dust raised Agon to the throne,
> Whose glorious might through you he calls his own,
> Receive his grateful heart! O Being without end,
> His soul at all times did you fully comprehend ....[37]

The play's setting more readily reflects the Dutch dunes and Frisian forests rather than Indian beaches with coconut trees, slaves and sultanates with which Van Haren was only vaguely acquainted through written sources. Only once in his play does he mention the variety of religions in the East Indies and refers primarily to Christian greed and intolerance. A Banten courtier speaks to Agon of possible support from other Europeans against the Dutch:

> Here are the French, the Danes, and men of England too -
> These people always seem to have your concerns in view.
> Although these Christians - all of them - on plunder are intent,
> We know that they to their belief in reverence attend;
> Perhaps it's up to us to grant a place for them to live,
> Where they due reverence to their laws and rituals can give,
> Or should we only offer them the exclusive right to trade ....[38]

Another embittered soul of sombre disposition was Willem Bilderdijk, who did not wish to renounce his oath of allegiance to the House of Orange in 1795 and was thus sent into exile. There he (once more) translated the Arabic *Treurzang van Ibn Doreid*, ("Elegy of Ibn Doreid") which was already known

---

[36] Nieuwenhuys, 1978, pp. 61-65; Du Perron, 1948, pp. 193-202; I have used De Waard's second edition published in 1978.

[37] Van Haren, 1978, p. 61.

[38] Van Haren, 1978, p. 61.

in some Latin translations. The poem is full of despair, vitality and masculinity (*murruwwa'*), displaying pre-Islamic ideals rather than the gentle strengths which Mohammed preached.[39] There are hardly any typical Islamic references in the poem and as such it is more representative of European romanticism than of Islam:

Never shall despair which sees no end oppress my breast ...
I swear by the devout who, out of zeal alone,
Will so much pain endure to kiss the sacred stone,
And come to holy Mecca, to their holy ground,
From all the farthest corners of the earth around!
Or by the warhorse, fearless, proud, would I sooner swear
That all the noise of battle and blazing fire bears ....[40]

J.C.M. Radermacher was one of the most outstanding representatives of the Enlightenment in the East Indies. In 1762 he founded the first Freemason lodge and in 1778 the *Batavian Society of Arts and Sciences*, apparently in imitation of the *Dutch Society of Sciences* of Haarlem, which nominated him in 1777 as one of its three directors in the Indies. The British Vice-Governor Sir Thomas Stamford Raffles later became one of the most prominent members of this Society. We will discuss his position on Islamic religion in chapter 4. Raffles' scientific and personal interest was much more centred on pre-Islamic art and archaeology and this was the general trend in the Batavian Society as a whole until the end of the colonial period. The society paid much more attention to the Buddhist and Hindu history of southeast Asia than the Islamic present. When they did turn their attention to the Islamic aspects of East Indian culture, they focussed mainly on history and linguistics at least until 1870. Only after 1870 did some scholars such as Van den Berg, Holle and Snouck Hurgronje pay more attention to the islamic present of East Indian culture. We will discuss their positions in the fifth chapter.[41]

---

[39] Goldziher, 1967, I, pp. 11-44, "Murruwwa and Din"; cf. also TishihikoIzutsu "From tribal code to islamic ethic" in Izutsu (1966), pp. 45-116. The pre-Islamic ideal of *murruwwa'* may also be translated as 'macho'.

[40] Bilderdijk, 1795, pp. 15-16.

[41] Cf. Lian The and Van der Veur, 1973, in connection with the Batavian Society and Boland and Farjon, 1983, in connection with the scientific study of Islam in Indonesia in general.

CHAPTER 4

Company Directors in "Natural Hostility" with "Untrustworthy and Fanatic Muslims"

After the period of the 'guesthouse', allotted to the first explorers and traders who wanted to leave the security of their ships, came the phase of the walled trading post, castle or fortress. The Dutch did not need to discover this on their own: not only did they appropriate the idea from the Portuguese but in a number of their forts as well. If it had been left to Jan Pieterszoon Coen (1587-1629), the architect and organizer of Dutch power in the East Indies, he would have immediately gone on to the next phase - that of the palace and the planter's residence: colonization by means of a large number of labourers and farmers from his native land. Although Coen proposed this plan often, it was never approved. He died in 1629 during the second siege of Batavia by the Sushunan of Mataram, the most powerful Muslim king of Java.

The View from the Fortress: Coen and the Untrustworthy Muslims

Coen wrote two quite extensive memoranda dealing with his plan to colonize the East Indies. The first was dated January 1, 1614.[1] In this first work he concentrated mainly on the Moluccas and their most powerful sultanate, Ternate, since it was the centre of the spice trade:

> Are good and evil compatible? The hostility that nature produces in different animal species, oil and water, [...] will apply to these matters as well, for only necessity has held our association together for so long; we are enemies by nature. The Ternatanes are Mahometan and we are Christians. They are deceitful and duplicitous as well, not even bound (so they claim) to keep their oaths or promises to Christians. They are proud, presumptuous, cruel and murderous. Although they are few in number, they do nothing but tyrannize the various nations nearby for they are completely preoccupied by war - and this not through their own manliness, power or warlike spirit, but through us ....[2]

Coen's description of the Ternatanes here very much resembles his own position, which was so closely intertwined with that of the Ternatanes: a small

---

[1] Colenbrander, 1934, summarizes the text on pp. 48-54 but includes the text in full on pp. 451-474 of the same volume.

[2] Colenbrander, 1934, p. 462.

group who wished to dominate a large nation primarily through superior military strength and therefore did not hesitate to use violence. In the years that followed Coen himself made ample use of such violence as well. In fact, there has been an ongoing discussion among students of history for quite some time already concerning the assessment of this important colonial figure. Most often cited as a consequence of his harsh and bloodthirsty policy is his cruel victory of the inhabitants of the Banda archipelago in 1621. More than two thousand civilians were killed in that attack, or rather, punitive measure, and after a bogus trial the forty-seven chiefs of the villages on the beach were all put to death.[3] Even Coen's admirers, such as his biographer Colenbrander, view this as "part of a policy that required a great deal of ruthlessness", a policy that should not in the first place be judged but only explained.[4]

For Coen the time was already past when one could view heretics, dissenters and superstitious people with a mixture of benevolence and disapproval. In the thousands of pages of his reports and letters to other places in Asia and to the Netherlands one comes across only one description of Islam of any length. The precise formulation of Coen's political intentions was only gradually attained, but from the very beginning, after his arrival in the East Indies in October, 1613, he excluded the Muslims from any real alliance with the Dutch. In his memorandum of January 1, 1614 he writes,

Should we try to make Christians of the Ternatanes or take what is ours by right from them - even with force, if need be? ... Say in reply that in the Moluccas at present religion should by all means be left alone. We must maintain our right to export cloves - by force even - but in respect to other matters we should turn a blind eye to a great deal.[5]

For Coen, religious differences provided the most important reason for colonization:

The Moors abhor us and therefore the Ternatanes and Bandanese do not permit anyone from their families to marry any of us for any reason whatsoever. If sexual intercourse occurs, they terminate the pregnancy (they say) and untimely destroy the fruit and the creature that is born so that the mother will not produce pagan offspring. Your Honour employs men, and not angels, here.[6]

When Coen wrote this, he was twenty-seven years old and still a bachelor himself. Not until 1626, twelve years later, did he bring a wife along to the East Indies when he returned from furlough in his native country. Already in

---

[3] Coolhaas, 1943-44, pp. 213-225.

[4] Colenbrander, 1934, p. 230.

[5] Colenbrander, 1934, p. 463.

[6] Colenbrander, 1934, p. 470.

his memorandum of 1614 he had requested the Company to "send here as many [people] as possible, both male and female"[7] and repeated the request on January 22, 1620 for the 'men, and not angels' employed by the Dutch East India Company: "In order to increase the population in Jacatra, Amboyna ... and other places and to relieve many orphanages in the United Netherlands, [I] pray Your Honour to send a great many young people here - and young girls in particular."[8] Since his great 'discourse' of 1614, Coen's main argument was not the lack of labourers in the Indies but the impossibility of any long-term cooperation with the Muslims:

> Is there anything in the world that unites and binds human hearts more than harmony in and pursuit of religion or, on the other hand, anything that divides human hearts and contributes more to increased hostility than religious differences? It is the latter that so alienates the Ternatanes, Bandanese and all Mahometans from us and causes natural hostility. One should also be aware that these southern people are much more devout in their religion than our northern people are in theirs. Therefore both Christians and Mahometans should leave things as they are for the time being. But the people who are sent here ought to be peaceful and experienced rather than coarse, uncircumcised idiots. This is mostly the case with pastors, as a result of which their name has fallen into contempt and has almost become an object of ridicule. It is a pity that only such people as one sees here are called to the office of pastor or deacon. It almost seems as if we ourselves do not ever speak of religion.[9]

The question of race is still absent in Coen; rather, in his opinion, Islam was the formidable opponent which the full attention of the Dutch. He often argued in his letters that the Dutch should set a good or 'notable' example for the Muslims[10] and did not even hesitate to request the death penalty for any European who committed adultery, in order to prevent the impression from arising that "we Christians set less value on the honour of our wives than the Turks, Moors and pagans."[11] The religious differences needed, therefore, to be taken into account in a variety of ways. First, the Dutch authorities needed to command respect by taking their religion seriously themselves. They also had to make certain that there was no doubt about their strength "for no

---

[7] Colenbrander, 1934, p. 473.

[8] Colenbrander, 1919, p. 534; cf. also 1934, p. 187.

[9] Colenbrander, 1934, p. 474.

[10] Colenbrander, 1920, pp. 437, 472: "It is a pity that such great offence should be given by the ungodly and irreverent lives of some of the married men among the Dutch."

[11] Colenbrander, 1921, p. 886. When he wrote this, Coen probably did not expect that he would be required to apply this later in the case of an offence committed in his own house by the lover of his maid Sara Specx, the daughter of his successor. Sara was "severely flogged", while her lover was beheaded. Cf. Colenbrander, (1934), p. 428 and Coolhaas (1943).

Moor can be satisfied by love and sweetness. Fear must prevail in Ambon, otherwise the situation will never improve."[12]

The religious issue is central for Coen and he does not express any racially discriminatory and derogatory opinions about the Indonesians as such. More than once he asserts that Ambonese Christians were much better workers than the Dutch labourers. Coen writes this in his own vivid way in a letter to Speult, the Company director in the Moluccas, dated December 8, 1619:

> In this respect do not give any preference to our ignorant drunkards over the native Ambonese but employ the most able ones and instruct each one as to what is to be done. I understand that there are some older Ambonese children who have gone to school for a long time, are able to read and write reasonably well, come of good Christian parents and are devoted to the Christian religion. These may be more suited to a management position [in reference to a previous mention of managers of small trading posts] than many of ours.[13]

Coen did not explicitly support plans to convert the Muslims.[14] He was certainly aware of the irritation and protests that such activities might provoke. In 1627 he ascribed the problems on Banda partly to the fact that "their children were beginning to be drawn into the schools, falling away from the Moorish religion and being brought up in the Christian religion."[15] Coen's views were based on the existing division between the religious communities and he tried to make the best of it. He almost always referred to the Muslims as untrustworthy. Sometimes he did this in the context of reporting that they

---

[12] Coen to the Company director Speult, November 20, 1617; cf. Colenbrander, (1920), p. 287.

[13] Colenbrander, 1920, p. 609. See also Colenbrander, (1922), p. 419, regarding a suggestion on Coen's part to "send four competent Indian youths of devout, respectable parents and are of good judgement and disposition" to the Netherlands to be educated for the ministry.

[14] The rare cases in which Coen speaks of spreading the faith concern mainly non-Islamic villages, the christianization of which would help in the struggle with Islam. In most cases he prefers discussing the consolidation of Christianity. Cf., for example, Colenbrander, 1921, p. 134. In 1627 Coen proposed a number of suggestions, "all of them contributing, that is, to the promotion of God's Holy Word and crushing what is left of the infidel religion of the Moors there" (Colenbrander, 1923, p. 181), but this may seem somewhat exaggerated as a summary of some disconnected remarks. Coen was not responsible for any large-scale schemes for christianizing the East Indies and certainly no concrete initiatives.

[15] Colenbrander, 1923, p. 50.

would not be bound by promises made to Christians,[16] but most often he used it only to indicate that there was no permanent basis for trust.[17]

One of the chief aims of a practical policy with regard to the Muslims was to stabilize relations. As early as 1609, and thus even before Coen's arrival, such stabilization had already been formulated in a contract with the 'Orangkayas', the village chiefs and leading citizens of Banda. In this contract the Dutch promised to send defectors back to the Bandese authorities, while in return, the other party declared itself "similarly bound to return all those persons who defect from our side to theirs into the custody of the Company director of Fort Nassau, without first circumcising, detaining or converting them to Islam."[18] This treatment of renegades, defectors and converts to Islam under one category clearly shows the overlapping of political and religious motives. Coen insisted that exile not be used as a punishment in the Indies "because living here among Moors and enemies, exiled Christians could become Muslims and thus become our bitterest enemies."[19] Information regarding these converts is lacking for the most part. Most of the time they are only mentioned in the documents when they tried to re-establish contact with the Dutch. We have already seen in the second chapter how one of them accompanied the Ambassador of Achin to Middelburg as an envoy, but this is hardly mentioned in the sources. In 1616 Coen protested against re-hiring someone "who had deserted in Surabaya a long time ago and had himself circumcised or became a Moor."[20] At other times Coen was more lenient. Anthonio Visoso was held prisoner in Ceribon in 1617, even though he had claimed to have already become a Muslim. Coen worked hard to get him released and promised him passage to the Netherlands.[21] Coen also laid great emphasis on maintaining the status quo laid down in contractual agree-

---

[16] Coen was not the only one who mentioned this. By way of introduction to discussing Coen's involvement in the war in Banda in 1621, the anonymous author of the "Verhael van eenige oorlogen van Indien" (Account of a Few Wars in the Indies) writes: "for they explicitly state that their Mahomet does not allow them to trust any Christian." Quoted in Coolhaas, 1943, p. 214.

[17] Concerning the assertion that one was "not to expect the Moors to be trustworthy" and their "lack of dependability", cf., among others, Colenbrander, 1919, p. 140; 1920, pp. 250, 287, 405, 427, 437, 608; 1921, pp. 37, 248, 250, 292, 451, 469, 470, 973; 1922, pp. 419, 583, 589, 593; 1923, pp. 47, 134, 522 ("malevolent"), 598, 629, 688, 721.

[18] De Jonge, Opkomst III, (Aug. 10, 1609), p. 316.

[19] Colenbrander, 1921, p. 887.

[20] Colenbrander, 1920, p. 80.

[21] Colenbrander, 1920, p. 271.

ments. For that reason he commended Speult for burning down a village of which a large part had become Muslim.[22]

Coen frequently underscored the political character of this policy of maintaining the status quo. His concern here was not hell or damnation because of apostasy,[23] but fear for his political authority and of the increasing number of enemies: "for as soon as anyone changes his religion, friends immediately become enemies."[24] Coen was not very content with the achievements of this policy of maintaining the status quo in his time. Islam's advance into the Moluccas had been contained for the time being, but its strength had certainly not yet been destroyed.[25] In connection with the alliance's precarious basis there was a constant fear of a mass 'murder of Europeans' and every now and then rumours and more or less reliable reports of conspiracies circulated. The trading posts, which had been built inside forts, did offer some protection, but apparently the atmosphere was such that the fear of such conspiracies was always present: the water might be poisoned, the place set on fire or the inhabitants lured further inland. This sometimes provided reasons to decline invitations from the local authorities, especially if such invitations were for meals.[26]

In his second extensive memorandum on colonization (1623) Coen depicted a prosperous colony for which the trade in Asia and with Europe are the main sources of income. The trading posts had to be defended and provided

---

[22] Colenbrander, 1921, p. 249: "Your Honour has done very well in burning down the village of Way and deporting the people of the castle, because more than half of them had become Moors ...." Concerning other cases where people changed religions or made attempts to do so, cf. Colenbrander, 1920, p. 134; 1921, pp. 26, 49, 728, 736. See also Knaap, 1987, pp. 75-83 for an well-documented picture of the relations between Christians and Muslims in the Moluccas in the second half of the seventeenth century. Knaap uses the term 'policy of containment' (p. 82) to describe the policy of the Dutch East Indian Company toward Islam and this term captures the active anti-islamic aspect of the policy especially well.

[23] Only rarely does he make a religious judgement. One such instance occurred in 1627 because of an extradition treaty through which "children who had already been baptized would fall victim to the evil Moorish religion, to which the church can not consent". Cf. Colenbrander, 1923, p. 51. Coen cites the more religious arguments of the ecclesiastical dignitaries as something special here. In later years he either replaced or supplemented the common epithet of *trouloos* ("untrustworthy") for the Moors with *heyloos* ("wicked"). Cf. Colenbrander, 1923, pp. 203, 207, 629.

[24] Colenbrander, 1922, p. 583.

[25] Colenbrander, 1922, p. 583: "... as a result of which the Moor's furtive advance has been somewhat shored up but not completely eradicated."

[26] Cf. Colenbrander, 1921, p. 469 concerning a Javanese plan (which "by God's grace came to nothing") to "go to each of these houses in succession, kill the people of the General Company and plunder everything."

with food, which could be accomplished by means a christian colony in the Indies. Then both trade and religion might be able to make some progress against the "Indians [who] manage to outwit the Company officers in matters of trade, state and policy as well as in the promotion of the Moorish religion in several places in the Indies".[27] As is the case with virtually all great colonial visions - from Coen's policy of colonization to the 'ethical policy', expressed in noble and often grandiloquent words at the beginning of the twentieth century - this was merely talk for the most part as well and the vision was only partially realized. The extremely negative attitude towards the Muslims, however, was to remain a constant factor for a long time.

The One Constant in Diplomacy: Accommodation

The *cantus firmus* of fear and disapproval with regard to the Muslims which set the tone for colonial politics for such a long time had a number of local and historical variations. These variations were mainly determined by developments in the balance of power between the Dutch and their trading partners. The collection of more than a thousand political contracts made by the Dutch with local rulers between 1600 and 1800 provides good documentation of these developments. Quite often these contracts include a paragraph on religion. During the time of the Company's influence this paragraph always expressed a negative attitude toward Catholics. In Sri Lanka and southern India, which the Company captured from the Portuguese, a special provision was quite often made for the safe retreat of the 'papists', even for respect to be shown to churches, liturgical articles and images. On the other hand, Jesuits and all other European priests were "exiled from here for all eternity".[28] If possible, attempts were made to spread the Christian religion in its Reformed variety and in accordance with the stipulations of Synod of Dort. The Company did make an exception, however, for the 'Thomas Christians' or Malabar Christians in southern India. In 1664 the Company drew up a contract with the Rajah of Teckencour, on the coast of Malabar, in which this ruler promised to refuse admittance to all "Roman Catholic papists or supporters of the same" to his territory and not even to grant them passage. The Christians, however, "who are under the authority of the Bishop of the Thomas Christians of the mountain" were explicitly exempted from this clause.[29]

The fact that some contracts safeguarded the privileges of pagans or Muslims reveals a lenient (and therefore possibly weak) position of the Com-

---

[27] Colenbrander, 1922, p. 599.

[28] This happened, for example, after Colombo was captured from the Portuguese in May, 1656; cf. *Corpus Diplomaticum*, II, pp. 85, 140, 194, 236, 245, 290, 492.

[29] *Corpus Diplomaticum*, II, pp. 290, 345.

pany in some cases. A contract made with Trimelapatnam in southern India in 1674, for example, specifies that "the pagan pagodas ... will continue to retain their former privileges and belong to their Brahmans who will not be deprived of any income from them."[30] In other cases the Company did attempt to gain advantages for its Christian subjects. When the Company's position was weak, the only significant advantage was that the Christians could retain their exemption from taxes, as happened in southern India when the Company was forced to leave in 1785.[31] In the Moluccas, however, the Company was strong enough to impose its will. The Christian parts of this mosaic of Islamic and Christian villages were subject to strict regulations in order to promote "the true Reformed Christian religion". Local rulers in these areas could only allow Christian marriages to be contracted and all Roman Catholics were to be refused admittance.[32]

Religion was not a politically neutral affair. Capital punishment was not only taken over from the orientals in instances of illicit sexual relations, but it was sometimes also applied in the case of apostasy.[33] This applied not only to individuals but also in cases of collective apostasy. As we noted above, Coen commended the Company director Speult of Ambon in 1622 for having razed the village of Way to the ground and deporting the inhabitants after more than half of the village population had become Muslim.[34] Changing religion was often treated on a par with desertion and included in the treaties with native rulers. A number of treaties stipulated that these deserters were not allowed to convert to Islam and that they had to be extradited.[35]

Muslims within the Dutch Fortress: A Group which "Could not be Tolerated"

The Company's influence on the local population was strongest in Sri Lanka, Malabar and the Moluccas.[36] A paragraph on religion is often contained in treaties with these areas especially. Relations with the rulers of Sumatra and

---

[30] *Corpus Diplomaticum*, II, p. 516.

[31] *Corpus Diplomaticum*, VI, p. 561.

[32] *Corpus Diplomaticum*, VI, pp. 14, 68, 130, 276, 312, 389, 410, 513, 671.

[33] See, for example, Valentijn on Ambon (1648), III, p. 54: "... a renegade Christian, who was captured on Ihamahoe ... was burned because he burst out in very blasphemous words against the Lord Jesus Christ ...."

[34] Colenbrander, 1921, p. 249.

[35] See, for example, *Corpus Diplomaticum*, I, pp. 68, 79, 93, 102, 111, 123, 164, 189 (on Persia), 227-8, 374; II, p. 157; V, pp. 479, 910; VI, pp. 13, 246, 447, 577.

[36] Cf. Van Goor, 1978, and 's Jacob, 1976, on Sri Lanka and Malabar.

central Java were still only superficial in the seventeenth and eighteenth centuries, which is probably why religion was not discussed. There is a general insistence on maintaining the status quo in the seventeenth-century treaties with the Moluccan rulers. The Company demanded that neither side make any attempt to promote conversion: "To each party its own religion", or in the words of Koran 109:6: "To you your religion, and to me my religion". In a treaty made in 1657 with the Sultan of Tidore the Company director promised "not to confuse [the Muslims] in regard to their religion and faith, nor treat them with mockery or scorn, and much less force the Christian religion on them."[37] The 1669 treaty with the ruler of Sumbawa formulated it even more strongly: "Christians who enter the service of the above-mentioned kings and show themselves favourably disposed to embrace the Mohammedan faith will not by any means be accepted ... nor shall the Company draw any of the kings' subjects to the Christian faith against the explicit will of Their Highnesses."[38] Diplomatic communications emphasized that both religious groups could practise their own rights and rituals. Indeed, the final clause of such contracts often includes not only an oath on the Bible but also one on the Koran also and the parties "by way of further confirmation drank water that had been poured over krisses [daggers], which from ancient times till now signifies a pact of the highest order."[39]

Prohibitions against mixed marriages and the sale of Christian slaves to Muslims were also among the means of maintaining the status quo.[40] Since these regulations had to be restated frequently, they do not seem to have been enforced consistently.

In general, the Chinese were subject the Company's direct authority. This was certainly the case in cities such as Batavia where the Company was in control. The Chinese were required to pay higher taxes than the native population. If the Chinese, however, became Muslim, they were looked upon and treated in the same way as natives. In Banten (western Java), on the other hand, such changes of religion did not immediately reflect on societal status: only the children of these Chinese converts would be legally treated as natives, while the converts themselves were still under the direct authority of the Company and especially subject to higher taxes.[41] Regulations were fre-

---

[37] *Corpus Diplomaticum*, II, p. 103.

[38] *Corpus Diplomaticum*, II, p. 423; Cf. II, p. 547 for a similar treaty with Tambora.

[39] Cf., for example, *Corpus Diplomaticum*, II, pp. 11, 426, 453.

[40] *Corpus Diplomaticum*, II, p. 17: "Neither shall we permit any young men of the Moorish persuasion to marry any Christian girls without the special consent of [the girls'] parents and friends." Cf. also VI, p. 203.

[41] *Corpus Diplomaticum*, VI, pp. 13, 415.

quently issued in Batavia as well to keep the Chinese from becoming Muslims. In 1755 the Company specified that Chinese Muslims would be required to continue paying the poll-tax and that they would not be given freedom to travel.[42]

In 1635 the municipal authorities of Batavia stipulated that every one who was baptized would receive 2 crowns of 40 pennies from the Company in order to "stimulate others to adopt the Reformed faith as well, and to show how we appreciate that our pagan and Moorish community attempt to seek their salvation through the only Saviour, the Lord Christ".[43] This measure, however, was only temporary. A few years later the municipal government (or the Company directors, since there was no real distinction between civil authorities and that of the Company) prescribed a number of "means for promoting the conversion of the pagans". These regulations laid particular emphasis on the refutation of Islam and defense of Christianity "on the basis of natural reason" in the form of a catechism which was to be printed in both the Dutch and native languages.[44] The financial relief the church gave a number of people monthly also benefited some non-Christians. A proposal was made in 1676 by which the unbelievers could be aided by a general collection or otherwise, without affecting the resources for the Christian poor. This proved to be impractical, however, and the church fund for the poor continued to be used for the benefit of believers and unbelievers alike.[45] The exhortation to Muslims sentenced to death to convert was a curious affair: a few times such exhortation led to conversion but did not involve any mitigation of the sentence.[46]

The Company was by no means lenient toward those Dutchmen who crossed the line of division and became Muslim. The theology of baptism of the Company's employees greatly emphasized one's birth "in the covenant". A special baptism formula, therefore, was used for a pagan child who was "still outside your covenant in the blindness of paganism ...."[47] In 1651 Rijklof van Goens returned from a journey to Mataram and brought along a boy who had born within the marriage of a Javanese woman and a Dutchman. This Dutchman had been imprisoned and was said "to have been circumcised by the Javanese and to have renounced Christ". After Van Goens promised

---

[42] *Plakaatboek*, (Collection of Edicts) VII, p. 153.

[43] *Plakaatboek*, I, p. 371.

[44] *Plakaatboek*, II, p. 45.

[45] Mooij, III, p. 282.

[46] Mooij, II, pp. 88, 102-104.

[47] Mooij, I, pp. 186-187.

that he would give the boy a proper education, the child was allowed to be baptised "not primarily on account of the child's father, who was supposed to have renounced his faith, but on account of his believing forefathers, in whom also this boy is sanctified and accepted."[48]

Time and again the Batavia church council turned its attention to the Chinese temples and Islamic places of worship in the city.[49] Requests made to the municipal authorities to forbid such places only resulted in a number of unkept promises to close the buildings and in advice to the church council to try to spread the faith in other and more effective ways. In 1651 the government in Batavia banned any "public or secret meetings for practising their evil and Mahometan religion ...." Mosque services were apparently regarded as "an act which should not be tolerated by a praiseworthy government where the pure and unadulterated teaching of the only and true Saviour Jesus Christ was taught and served." Besides, the government added, the majority of native Christians had only just "emerged from the Moorish religion" and were still weak in the new faith.[50] Nonetheless the church council kept complaining and in 1654 the council decided that each minister was to carry out an inquiry in his own district as to the "Moorish, Chinese and Javanese schools" by which the "younger generation is attracted and educated, not in any civilized morality, but in the principles and rudiments of idolatry, in their despicable service, in fact, to the Devil".[51] "As [had] often been done before but in vain," the church council again requested in 1662 that the Chinese temples be closed down, but this attempt was unsuccessful as well.[52] Another investigation by the ministers in 1674 revealed no less than six Islamic places of worship and schools. In spite of their renewed attempt, however, no effective measure to have them closed was taken.[53]

There was certainly a difference in accent between the church's attitude, generally represented by the ministers, and that of the Company directors who were also members of the church council. The ministers strongly disap-

---

[48] Mooij, II, p. 203. See also II, pp. 157-163, for the discussion in the church council involving Hendrik de Rijke, who was held prisoner for 17 years and fathered five children by two Javanese wives and was then again accepted into the church in 1650.

[49] For the seventeenth century cf. the minutes of the church council in Batavia, published in three volumes by Mooij. The church council's attempts to impose a ban on non-Christian places of worship are to be found, for example, in I, p. 699; II, pp. 42-43, 62, 66, 77-78, 127, 188-89, 202, 210, 256, 264, 389, 633; III, pp. 207, 380-81, 568, 600, 686, 695, 697.

[50] *Plakaatboek*, II, p. 169.

[51] Mooij, II, p. 389.

[52] Mooij, II, p. 633.

[53] Mooij, III, p. 200.

proved of non-Christian religious practices, but they were in fact so dependent on the Company that this disapproval did not affect Company policy in any way. There was hardly any political and strategic difference between the church council and the municipal authorities on essential points, however: both continued to argue for the maintenance of the status quo and the segregation of the religions groups. The occasional minister who was in favour of a tough policy was quite soon faced with so many problems that it was impossible for him to accomplish anything, since sufficient supporters in the church council could not be found. The case of Rev. Ruterus, who had protested in Sri Lanka against the presence of Company employees at "pagan dances", is notorious. This case was also brought before the Batavia church council, who viewed this matter of temple women as an innocent diversion. The council's view was only that

> the pagans as well as the Moors allow these women into their houses or other suitable places in order to have them sing at weddings, banquets or other festive occasions, to dance and perform skilful and amazing jumps as a means of civilized entertainment for the guests who are being treated, where the host's praises, rather than the devil's, are sounded.

Thus Ruterus also failed to find support among his colleagues.[54]

Many lines of division ran through colonial Batavia. Racial differences were important, but religious differences were certainly not unimportant. The question of a 'politics of apartheid', based only or mainly on race never arose in that society. White and coloured people alike were allowed to partake of the Lord's Supper. The church council minutes even mention one case in which an unbaptized slave, Anthoni of Bengal, shared in the Lord's Supper "out of ignorance ... because he saw other slaves of the noble Company stepping forward." When the council examined Anthoni, he said that he wished to be taught the Christian faith and they warned him to "refrain from such disorderly behaviour from that time on."[55]

As we have already seen above, the municipal authorities in Batavia more than once banned non-Christian religious services within the city limits, if only with the further specification that this was to be enforced "without there being a substantial change" in the situation.[56] Nevertheless, the administration was finally forced to recognize and regulate Islamic affairs to some degree. Provision was made in 1681 for a salary to be paid to the "Mahomedan priest who had to administer the oath to Mahomedan witnesses on behalf of the

---

[54] Mooij, III, p. 659; see also Van Goor, 1982, pp. 116-119.

[55] Mooij, III, p. 74.

[56] *Plakaatboek*, II, pp. 572, 169, 172.

college of aldermen"[57] and a Muslim priest was appointed as "principal
supervisor of the mosque of the Coromandel Moors outside the Utrecht gate
at Batavia" in 1748.[58] In 1754 a *Compendium of the Most Important Mahomedan Laws and Customs Concerning Inheritance, Marriage and Divorce* was
composed after consultations between the 'Delegate for Native Affairs' and
'some Machomethan priests and Kampong officers'. This agreement stated
that Islamic law was to apply to Muslims in cases where civil law would apply
for Europeans.[59] These regulations did not imply that Europeans were
beginning to accept Muslims. Within the actual city limits of Batavia non-
Christian places of worship continued to be banned, as was once again stated
in the *New Statutes of Batavia* (1776). Although these statutes were never
officially endorsed, they were certainly enforced.[60] This same 'civil code' took
up the status quo policy as a means of reinforcing itself: "all marriages
outside one's own nationality are forbidden and declared to be invalid." As
we already saw to be the case with the Chinese, religion also played a role in
deciding one's nationality: native Christians were dealt with in the same way
as Europeans.[61]

The Company had no consistent policy with regard to those who partook
in the pilgrimages to Mecca. They did arrange transport (in part) to Mecca
for rulers with whom it was desirable to remain friends, but more often than
not the captains of the ships were absolutely forbidden to take pilgrims along
as passengers.[62] Arabs who travelled around as traders and preachers and
pilgrims who passed through on their return often wanted to visit their fellow
believers in Batavia, but prohibitions against their coming ashore were often
issued "since such tramps are only harmful here because of their following
among the Mohammedans."[63] In respect to its laws, the Company city of
Batavia sometimes resembled a strict Christian enclave in an Islamic country.
It certainly was not a community that took an active missionary interest in its
surroundings. Above all else, the lines of division between Christians and non-
Christians had to be maintained. There were nonetheless, quite a number of
cracks in that wall since trade, after all, was the centre around which everything, including religion, turned.

---

[57] *Plakaatboek*, III, p. 68.

[58] *Plakaatboek*, V, p. 548.

[59] *Plakaatboek*, VIII, pp. 392-407.

[60] *Plakaatboek*, IX, pp. 29-30.

[61] *Plakaatboek*, IV, pp. 410-431, especially p. 424.

[62] Vredenbregt, 1962, pp. 94-96.

[63] *Plakaatboek*, IV, pp. 76, 80.

Sir Thomas Stanford Raffles and the Biased Re-evaluation of Oriental Cultures

The British exercised full control over the East Indies from 1811-16. In general, their highest ranking officials had a low opinion of the economic and cultural policy of the Dutch. In his great work *History of Java* Sir Thomas Stanford Raffles scornfully observes: "The Dutch must always have contemplated the prosperity of the eastern tribes with the invidious regret of a rival shopkeeper, and regarded their progress in civilisation with the jealousy of a timid despot."[64] The British held the view that the Dutch East India Company was a corrupt business enterprise which could only continue to exercise authority through despotic means. The British vision was different: "In the first place, the British would conciliate Asian potentates who would of their own accord seek close relations with them on a basis of mutual trust and advantage".[65] In his *History of Java*, Raffles, the highest ranking British administrator in the East Indies, provides an eloquent defence of this British policy. Raffles employed a few prominent Javanese rulers as personal advisers, particularly in regard to cultural affairs, one of which, Kiai Adipati Sura Adimanggala, was the regent or *Bupati* of Semarang. Two of his sons were sent to India to receive a British education[66] and he himself translated some classical Javanese historical works into English. Another cultural advisor, Natakusuma, the regent of Sumenep, was a great authority on Javanese and Arabic. On the basis of these sources Raffles incorporated a great deal of historical and cultural information in his *History of Java*, with the result that it is much less focused on colonial history than Valentijn's major work one hundred years earlier. A closer look at the work reveals that Raffles was also selective in his material. In the eighth chapter, which concerns Javanese language and literature, he centres his discussion on pre-Islamic literature. In a discussion which covers more than seventy pages he quotes an Islamic poem only once and that briefly[67] but devotes forty-seven pages to summarizing the Javanese version of the Mahabharata epic.[68] In his discussion of religion he

---

[64] Raffles, 1978, I, p. 232. Compare the observation made by his contemporary Robert Percival concerning the Dutch in Sri Lanka, quoted in Marshall, 1988, p. 2: "As they were usually men of no education and entirely of mercantile habits, they could not extend their views to distant advantages."

[65] Marshall, 1988, p. 7.

[66] See De Graaf, 1978, on this regent; Cf. Bastin's introduction in Raffles (1978), pp. I, IX, concerning the education of the two sons. The Raden Saleh mentioned there is not the well-known painter but his cousin. See also Harsja Bachtiar, 1978.

[67] Raffles, 1978, I, p. 406, where a stanza about the Kaabah is quoted in order to illustrate a certain metre.

[68] Raffles, 1978, pp. 415-468.

manages to discuss Islam in four pages[69] but takes sixty pages to discuss the remnants of Hinduism and Buddhism. In addition, Raffles provides a number of beautiful prints of remnants of pre-Islamic architecture.

Raffles did not pursue a pro-islamic policy in the field of politics either. He considered the Muslim leaders, especially the *hajis* who had completed the pilgrimage to Mecca, as the greatest enemies of every colonial regime:

> Every Arab from Mecca, as well as every Javanese, who had returned from a pilgrimage thither, assumed on Java the character of a saint, and the credulity of the common people was such that they too often attributed to such persons supernatural powers. Thus respected it was not difficult for them to rouse the country to rebellion .... The Mohammedan priests have almost invariably been found most active in every case of insurrection. Numbers of them, generally a mixed breed between the Arabs and the inlanders go about from state to state in the Eastern Islands and it is generally by their intrigues and exhortations that the native chiefs are stirred up to attack or massacre the Europeans, as infidels and intruders.[70]

Raffles lent his approval to a policy that held regents' sons to be unsuitable for an administrative post if they had made the pilgrimage unfit to Mecca.[71] After his term in Java, when he was appointed to West Sumatra he took the part of the aristocratic *adat* party in the conflict between them and the Islamic leaders [whom he called *Padri*, employing the term used in India for Catholic priests and islamic leaders, because of their long white garments].[72]

Dutch Officials Pro and Contra the Padris

Beginning in the early part of the nineteenth century, a religious revival occurred in the highlands of Minangkaban in West Sumatra that was known as the *Padri* movement. This religious revival also took the form of a social struggle on the part of the small traders against the feudal nobility and in some places resulted in a savage civil war.[73] The nobility appealed to the colonial authorities for assistance and thus they also became involved in the conflict. The reports of the colonial officials, however, reveal great differences of opinion with regard to this conflict and therefore reveals that there was no consensus of opinion within the colonial administrations. These differences in

---

[69] Raffles, 1978, II, pp. 1-4.

[70] Raffles, 1978, II, p. 3.

[71] Vredenbregt, 1962, p. 97.

[72] Raffles' journey to the uplands of West Sumatra is described in full detail in Raffles, 1830, where his position is clearly evident.

[73] Dobbin, 1983, *passim*; Wertheim, 1978, pp. 56-58; Roff, 1987, pp. 37-39.

the reports seem to arise especially from the desire to defend Dutch policy and not so much from a desire to be accurate and objective.

One who played an important role in the assessment of the *Padri* movement was H.J.J.L. Ridder De Stuers, the Resident of West Sumatra from 1824 to 1829. The East Indian army was occupied during this period with the Java war (1825-1830), so De Stuers had to send most of the few troops at his disposal to Java. His hands were therefore completely tied and he was only able to control the port of Padang and the immediately surrounding area. The region beyond he had to abandon to the parties concerned, and to the *Padri* in particular. His successors from 1830 onwards had more troops at their disposal for military and political purposes and began to pursue an policy of aggression against the *Padri* until the main leader, Imam Bonjol, gave up the struggle in 1834.

There are considerable differences between De Stuers and one of his successors, General Michiels, in their assessment of the *Padri*. De Stuers portrays the *Padri* in a way which shows understanding and appreciation: they prohibited excessive drinking and gambling and in the areas under their control they protected trade from robbers and arbitrary tolls. Michiels, on the other hand, defended his aggressive policy by particularly emphasizing that in their attacks the *Padri* burnt down the villages of the 'unbelievers', killed the men and carried off the women to their harems. The difference in assessment, which can also be described as that between doves and hawks, is connected with the difference in political and military background.[74]

Similar observations can be made with respect to the other three great wars of expansion which occurred in the nineteenth century: the Java War (1825-1830), the Banjarmasin War (1859-1862) and the Achinese War (1873-1904). Because a discussion of these and 'lesser wars' would offer generally more of the same, we will not deal with them here. We have dealt with these developments in connection with the *Padri* here in order to underline the fact that the pattern of 'natural hostility' continued well into the nineteenth century. This was the case even when, as a result of control over extensive areas, a entirely different pattern, completely under the supervision and control of the Dutch, began to unfold.

---

[74] H.J.J.L. Ridder de Stuers, *De vestiging en uitbreiding der Nederlanders ter Westkust van Sumatra* (The Settlement and Expansion of the Dutch on the West Coast of Sumatra), Vol. I-II, (Amsterdam: Van Kampen, 1849-1850). For more polemics on the struggle of the *Padri* cf. Boland, 1983, pp. 7-9 and the literature mentioned there.

CHAPTER 5

Holle, Hurgronje and Hazeu:
Tutors to "Members of a Backward Religion"

Colonial history consisted of a process in which one phase was replaced by another. The early phase of exploration, represented by the 'guesthouse', was followed by a period which can best be represented by the fortress. Using the fortress as a base, the Company official became acquainted with the neighbouring rulers, played nations and kingdoms off against one another, but in the main managed his commercial interests. Although the country house replaced the fortress during the course of the eighteenth century - at least in some areas such as in the neighbourhood of Batavia, a few places on the Moluccas and on the northern coast of Java - it was not until the nineteenth century that the empire as such, represented by the palace and the plantation, came into its own. Colonial expansion reached its zenith only after 1850 when the acquisition of territory rather than commercial interests became the primary concern. The gradual abolition of the system of forced farming more or less ended the monopoly on trade in which the Dutch dealt mainly with the upper classes. By establishing lines of production and business which were intended to develop the export of tea, coffee, tobacco, sugar and other agricultural products, the contact between private Dutch individuals and the farming population increased.

The changes in social, economic and political position were accompanied by a shift in accent in respect to religious matters. Muslims were considered less as heretics or outright enemies and increasingly as backward and teachable inhabitants of a colony that was turning into a developing country. To attribute these changes only to economic and political developments would be too simple: changes in spiritual outlook that were independent of these developments occurred as well. Already in the eighteenth century the strict Calvinist public life began to give way to a cultural life that was inspired by the spirit of the Enlightenment and Romanticism. As we already observed in the third chapter, the Batavian Society of Arts and Sciences was founded in 1778 by the same man who had previously also set up the first Freemason lodge.[1] While the Society's influence was limited to a small group of academics and

---

[1] Lian The and Paul Van de Veur, 1973.

a few interested officials and planters, the influence of Freemasonry spread widely.

The nineteenth century in particular displayed a remarkably broad tolerance with respect to alternative worldviews. In 1883 the journalist and novelist P.A. Daum was able to publish a series of articles in a small newspaper which displayed a militant anti-clerical and anti-religious attitude. These articles did not lead to the cancellations of any subscriptions but rather marked the beginning of a new period of growth.[2] Daum directed his remarks chiefly against Christianity, but that did not mean that he was a fervent admirer of Islam. In his opinion, Islam was "an inferior religion, a religion that was by nature averse to development and progress ...."[3] On the other hand, Daum was the only Dutch novelist to devote an entire novel to a typical Islamic character. In *Aboe Bakar* the contrasts between Muslim and Christian, subject and colonial government are dramatically portrayed in the career of a man of Indo-Arabic descent who is brought up as a Dutchman but then finds himself in 'his' environment of Arabic traders. Daum draws the portrait with understanding and compassion, but shows quite clearly the inevitable result of Islam: hypocrisy, lack of productivity, unsettled relations and eventually ruin.[4] Daum was no exception to the general trend of the time but rather a good representative of it. Due to the development of the imperialist colonial system, the Dutch gained the upper hand over the Muslims in Indonesia and felt this to be true religiously as well. Islam was no longer viewed as a powerful heretical religion in competition with Christianity but as weak and backward. The advocates of the Enlightenment wanted to tutor Muslims using the methods of modern education.

As special representatives of the period 1850-1940 we will discuss three prominent civil officials here in more detail: Karel Frederik Holle, Christiaan Snouck Hurgronje and Godard Arend Hazeu. Not only were they representative of their age, but, in the position, which they all held, of *Adviseur voor Inlandsche Zaken* (Advisor for Native Affairs) to the colonial government, they also exercised great influence on the government's policy towards Islam. Their activities and writings reflect the basic aspects of the changing attitudes towards the Muslims.

---

[2] Termorshuizen, 1988, pp. 123-127; 1990, pp. 30-36.

[3] Termorshuizen, 1988, pp. 447-448.

[4] P.A. Daum, *Aboe Bakar* (The Hague: Thomas and Eras, 1980), 2nd impression. The book appeared as a serial in 1893 and as a book in 1894. Cf. Termorshuizen, 1988, pp. 442-454.

K.F. Holle (1829-1896): Education as a Neutralisation of Islam

Karel Frederik Holle came to the East Indies as a fourteen year old boy with his parents and became a clerk in a government office in 1846. Despite the fact that he managed to climb a few steps up the administrative ladder, he left this position in 1856 to manage a tea plantation and in 1862 obtained a licence to develop 'waste land' in the mountainous country of Java and start a plantation there himself. Without any formal education Holle built up an astonishing knowledge in many fields. He was considered to be a expert in linguistics in the East Indies at the time because of his knowledge of Malay, Sundanese and its related language of Javanese. He set up his plantation as a kind of experimental farm, researching into various facets of agriculture, such as dry terrace-culture for growing vegetables at high altitudes and fish-breeding in small ponds. He also proved to be an able advocate for his innovations. In order to acknowledge his merits and also to give him a more permanent position as a government official, Holle was appointed Honourary Advisor for Native Affairs in 1871. In order to circulate his ideas he cooperated for a long time with his loyal friend Raden Muhammad Musa, Chief-*Penghulu*[5] of Garut. Born into a family of which several members had chosen to enter the service of the colonial government, Muhammad Musa began his Civil Service career in 1852 as an accountant at the salt depot at Garut. In 1855, however, he had obtained the important position of Chief-*Penghulu* and in 1860 began to work closely with Holle, forming an association which was to last more than twenty-five years.

Musa assisted Holle in compiling a popular monthly and various brochures on agriculture. In the early 1860's Musa and Holle toured several places on Java, promoting the idea of fishponds that could easily be set up near private dwellings. Holle appreciated the religious charisma which Musa displayed as a religious official and later as a *haji*. They were also actively involved in founding the *Kweekschool voor Onderwijzers op Inlandsche Scholen* (Teachers' Training College for Native Schools) in Bandung in 1865. Together they tried to gather sufficient reading material by means of translation and particularly by publishing folktales at government cost. The booklets were distributed among the population by government services and there were even some proposals to set up simple lending libraries with these books. Holle published booklets in the Sundanese script, a more or less artificial variety of the Javanese script, which caused some violent reactions from various government officials. The Assistant Resident of Rankasbitung, for example, wrote that he did not understand why "this script should be forced upon the native popula-

---

[5] A Chief-*Penghulu* was the highest Islamic official in a regency. The colonial government had taken over the responsibility from the pre-colonial sultanates of appointing a person to such a position and providing him with a stipend.

tion." In his region the Sundanese already had to know two scripts: "The Arabic script in order to be able to read the Koran and the Dutch script in order to be appointed to a government position. Over against the few people familiar with the Javanese script are hundreds who are familiar with the Arabic script." Holle admitted that in much of West Java the Arabic script was used far more widely. All the same, he wanted to adhere to his policy of the promotion of the Sundanese script because further spread of the Arabic script would only reinforce the influence of religious fanatics. In his view colonial education, "without encroaching on the domain of religion," should be concerned with "eradicat[ing] superstition and at the same time moderat[ing] or stem[ming] the harmful influence of malicious or hostile priests and such, as well as fanaticism."[6] Fear of a Muslim reaction was also the reason for Holle's negative advice with regard to attempts to establish a mission in the Sundanese region. The same reason also figured in Holle's refusal to permit Christian religious instruction in 'his' school.[7]

Holle's attempt to drive back Islam's increasing social and political role characterized much of his activity. In 1873 he went to Singapore with Musa on a secret mission in order to ascertain the extent of international Islamic support of anti-Dutch resistance in Achin. In the same connection the government had him investigate the social influence of the *haji*'s who made the pilgrimage to Mecca. According to Holle, the *haji*'s were the instigators of fanaticism and zealotry and he advised that under no circumstances whatsoever were they to be appointed to higher governmental posts.[8] While he did not request that the special "*haji* clothing" be banned, he did suggest that the government alter the military uniform according to that of the French army in Algeria, which would give it a more or less Arabic look. On the one hand, the resemblance to the *haji*'s clothing would make enlistment more attractive, whereas on the other hand it cause "confusion with the holy dress": hatred towards the army might also arouse hatred toward the *haji*'s. As was the case with several similar proposals, however, this advice was never followed.[9]

---

[6] Bt. 5 March, 1860 nos 10f. "Holle-papieren" (Holle Papers) in the ANRI which have not yet been catalogued. The Assistant Resident's letter is dated 26 September, 1869. Similar advice was given by the Resident of Bantan, 1 October, 1869.

[7] In documentation dated August, 1871, from the Holle papers not yet catalogued at the ANRI. A regent in the Preanger is supposed to have remarked to Holle "first a school, then a mission."

[8] Holle's advice to the Governor-General on 20 August, 1873. His advice was not formally accepted, but the Governor-General makes a marginal note to the advice given the Council for the Dutch East Indies: "Without making this principle a government order, I will nevertheless apply it." Cf. Bt. 29 November, 1873, no. C7.

[9] *Ibid.*

Several times Holle tried to deny or minimize the religious function and influence of the regent or *bupati*, which was the highest position a native Indonesian could attain within the colonial administration. In the Government Regulations for the Dutch East Indies regents were named "Commissioners of Religion". When Holle was requested to make a Sundanese translation of the regulations in 1871, he did not translate the term literally. His translation emphasized that the regents should control religion through "police surveillance". In the extensive correspondence which followed this translation he protested violently against regents "who play at priest or pope". He gave examples of regents who promoted the quality of Islamic education in their regions and had the teachers examined before they were allowed to start a new *pesantren*. There were also regents who, in order to avoid difficult conflicts, themselves calculated the beginning and end of Ramadan, the ninth month that was dedicated to fasting. In some regions the regent himself wished to be mentioned in the Friday prayer as the "Guide of the Believers". Holle, who suggested a strict separation of political power and religion, felt all this should be opposed. J.H. Zoetelief, the Chief Inspector of Agricultural Crops and Holle's chief opponent in the matter of the translation, more or less agreed with Holle that a watchful eye should be kept on fanaticism. At the same time, he considered the policy already in effect at the time to be sufficient for that purpose. Zoetelief did not believe that there were any "fanatic" regents at all. He commended a regent from Cilacap for seeing to it that practically nobody in his region made the pilgrimage to Mecca. The regent summoned anyone who intended to make the pilgrimage to Mecca to appear before him and managed to keep the candidates from carrying out their journey. Holle similarly commended the regent of Purwokerto, who would no longer allow a certain teacher to give religious instruction, "not because his teaching was dangerous for the authorities, but because the number of his pupils was growing too fast and the regent thought it undesirable that so many were trained to be *santri*'s in that way."[10]

Although Holle warned of religious fanaticism among the regents and the officially appointed religious functionaries, the *penghulu*'s, he considered the *haji*'s and teachers to constitute the greatest danger that Islam posed. Among these, in Holle's opinion, the most dangerous were the preachers of the Islamic brotherhood known as the *tarekat*. In most cases a *tarekat* very much resembled a medieval Marian confraternity in Europe. The members, both men and women, promise first of all to observe all the customary obligations of their religion faithfully and, in addition, to say a number of extra prayers at least once a week. From 1850 on the Naqshbandi brotherhood on Java partic-

---

[10] Zoetelief was Holle's main opponent and their discussion is to be found in ANRI, Bt. 4 May, 1872, no. 23.

ularly attracted a large number of new supporters among the social and political upper class. In 1885 Holle wrote a general article on this brotherhood in a scientific journal,[11] but in his official advice he also warned against certain persons. In West Java especially, a larger number of regents and *penghulu*'s were supposed to have become members of this new group. The *penghulu* of Cianjur was described as "quite fanatic and anti-European": he refused wine at receptions held in the Assistant Resident's home and as a consequence a number of Dutchmen forced his mouth open on one occasion and poured wine into it. Since then he tried to avoid Europeans as much as possible. This *penghulu* was reported to be involved with some teachers of religion in a conspiracy to kill all the Europeans of the Preanger at one time. Holle's warnings to the Residents of Batavia and Bandung did not achieve anything and he eventually appealed directly to the Governor-General.[12]

In order to gain even wider support for and attention to his warnings he also enlisted the services of a journalist on *De Javabode* (The Java Messenger). On 29 September, 1885 subscribers to the *De Javabode* in Batavia and elsewhere were treated to a piece of sensationalist journalism. The editor-in-chief, Brunner, entitled his main contribution of that day "*Prang Sabil*", ('Holy War') and reported on preparations for a "raid, murder and robbery, in which the Europeans would be the victims ... a *ketju*-party on an gigantic scale." The article followed earlier reports of a milder nature, but which also mentioned growing fanaticism and "living on a volcano". On the 29th Brunner specified the danger by naming the leaders involved. The religious leaders in the regions of Cianjur and Sukabumi, about 80 kilometres south of Batavia, were reported to be preparing for a great revolt through the foundation of a secret society. Brunner received much of his information from a retired *penghulu* in Achin, Muhammad Al Segaf, who estimated that the "outburst would occur in two or three months' time." Since the local authorities were too lax, Al Segaf had taken the initiative upon himself to inform the press and later the police in Batavia as well. *De Javabode* published the reports in large print and a few other papers followed suit. One of these, *De Locomotief*, added some information of its own. These articles always concluded with an appeal for a more stringent government policy, proper control of rebellious movements and stronger action in Achin. The risings were connected with the *Mutiny*, the great rebellion in India that claimed 40,000 lives. It was suggested that "It had been the same in British India before the rising in 1857, when murder plots and other atrocities were planned and designed under the very

---

[11] Holle, 1886.

[12] Holle to the Governor-General, 5 September, 1885, in MGS 23 May, 1886, no. 91/C, ANRI.

noses of the unsuspecting English. There were warnings at that time as well, but they were mockingly brushed aside."[13]

The government's reaction to the articles was not as Brunner had hoped. Some of the natives who were supposed to be involved in the murder conspiracy against the Europeans were in fact interrogated, but the authorities did not take any strong action. On the other hand, however, *De Javabode* was closed down on 6 October, 1885, which prevented the newspaper from appearing for a few months and thus losing its readership. This remained a notorious case in the history of the Indonesian press. P.A. Daum, the most prominent journalist in Indonesia, was faced with censorship as well. His newspaper, *Het Indisch Vaderland* (The Indian Fatherland) was also affected by a ban on printing.[14] In subsequent discussion journalists and politicians connected this case to internal changes within the colonial administration: the Governor-General at the time, O. van Rees (1884-1886), was a liberal but nonetheless was far from lenient where the freedom of the press was concerned.[15] It was also suggested that the whole incident had been influenced by budget debates: if one could show that the situation in the Dutch East Indies was unstable, there was a possibility that more funds could be released for the army.

The Governor-General also dealt with the expected uprising through official channels. He asked the Resident of Bandung for information and inquired as to why the latter had not reported any possible uprisings earlier. The Resident answered in the usual way: for some time he had been aware of increased activity on the part of the 'Sect of Naksa Bandrija', as well as of the fact that many native civil servants were members of this sect. The regent of Cianjur had been a member for more than twenty years. The movement, however, still did not give any real cause for alarm. He therefore regretted the fact that a few Europeans, in good faith or otherwise, driven by fear or the need to create fear, had spread such exaggerated rumours. The story that all the Europeans would be killed during the horseraces and the later one that they would all be murdered in a fire belonged to such exaggerations.[16]

---

[13] *De Javabode*, 29 September, 1885; for more Indonesian reactions to the Mutiny see Jaquet, 1980, pp. 283-312.

[14] See, among others, Gerard Termorshuizen, *P.A. Daum, Journalist en romancier van tempo doeloe* (Amsterdam: Nijgh and Van Ditmar, 1988), pp. 276-285.

[15] F.J.G. van Emden, "P.A. Daum, De Stichter van het Bataviaasch Nieuwsblad," *Vijftig jaren Bataviaasch Nieuwsblad* (Batavia, 1935), pp. 39-41.

[16] Resident of Bandung, A.G.G. Pletzer to the Governor-General, 29 September, 1885 in MGS 23 May, 1886, no. 91/C, ANRI.

The Governor-General was not satisfied by this reply and asked for the names of the Europeans who had spread the rumours. In his first reply[17] the Resident related information about a plot centring on the position of the *patih* of Sukabumi, the highest local native official. The son of the late *patih* had been passed over in a recent appointment and was now trying to regain his father's position. His method here was to cast doubt on the new official's integrity by describing his pious conduct as fanatic. With the assistance of an Indo-Arab intermediary, Sayid Muhammad al Segaf, who had been involved in conspiracies between Europeans and natives for a long time, this son began a slander campaign against the *patih* and his friends, all of whom were members of the religious brotherhood.[18] In respect to Holle, the Resident at first tried to smooth things over:

> Although his mind is clear, his physical condition prevents him from going much further than his own home and its immediate surroundings. This can only make Holle despondent and it seems to me that Waspada, [Holle's plantation] with the dark mountain of Guntur on its horizon is bound to have influenced his judgement of affairs and persons somewhat. One must also add that the Chief-*Penghulu* of Garut, his loyal adviser and friend, has become an old, listless man following a prolonged disease and is no longer able to travel as he used to do.

In a letter dated somewhat later,[19] the Resident of Bandung made more serious and concrete accusations against Holle. Musa, Holle's friend and adviser, had three sons, of whom two of them had already climbed high up the administrative ladder. The prospects for the third, however, were less favourable because he had been physically and mentally disabled after a fall from a horse when he was twelve. All the same, he had managed to acquire a position as a minor religious official in the small town of Wanaraja through his father's help. If the post of Chief-*Penghulu* at Sukabumi or Cianjur were now to become vacant as a result of the religious conspiracy, this son could still be placed in a comfortable and high position before his father's death.

---

[17] Resident Bandung to the Governor-General, 18 October, 1855 in MGS 23 May, 1886, no. 91/C, ANRI.

[18] An account of Sayid al Segaf's busy and adventuresome career can be found in ANRI, Bt 16 February, 1880, no. 2. He was dismissed from his position as *penghulu* of Kotaradja because he ran a brothel at home and the believers left the mosque the moment he (as leader of the mosque) entered (Malay text in Steenbrink, 1988b, pp. 73-78). He had been appointed at the behest of the army in an attempt to neutralize the religious sentiments in Achin in connection with the war that began in 1873. For his appointment see ANRI, Bt. 2 April, 1877, no. 2.

[19] Resident of Bandung to the Governor-General, 26 January, 1886, also in ANRI, MGS 23 May, 1886, no. 91/C.

Musa had indeed made such a formal request to Van Rees in December, 1885.[20]

Holle also involved the quite scholarly and respected Sayid Uthman bin Yahya al Alawi of Batavia in this affair. Sayid Uthman (1822-1913) was of Arab descent and had settled in Batavia in 1862. He ran a printing shop where his numerous brochures and booklets on religious subjects in particular were printed.[21] Sayid Uthman had already written a pamphlet prior to 1885 opposing the *tarekat*. At Holle's instigation a large number of free copies of this pamphlet were distributed in the Preanger. Thus Holle also tried to gain the theological support of Islam in his struggle against these religious societies. But the Resident of Bandung took the part of other devout Muslims who were advocates of this new form of piety and he proposed banning the distribution of Sayid Uthman's booklet on the grounds that it was too inflammatory. This case was taken to the highest level: the Council of the Dutch East Indies, who acted on the advice of the *Adviseur voor Arabische Zaken en islamitisch Recht* (Counsellor for Arabic Affairs and Islamic Law) when it decided that Sayid Uthman's booklet by no means was to be viewed as

stirring up hatred against the adherents of that form of piety.... On the contrary, according to its [the council's] judgment, it should be regarded as being of a useful and desirable nature in that it combats a devotion which many have often considered to be dangerous, since it deviates from the usual religious forms and customs ordained in the Koran.

This was more a matter of politics than of theology: a small group of liberal Dutchmen declared itself in favour of Islamic orthodoxy.[22]

We have dealt here so extensively with the entire affair concerning the 'plot' in the middle of 1885 in order to indicate how complex the relations were between 'the' Dutch and 'the' Muslims. A man such as Holle would certainly have seen the Muslims as a great danger to the stability and development of 'his Dutch Indies' and he pointed to the danger in many different ways. Although Holle attempted to make use of important and influential Islamic leaders like the liberal Muslim Raden Muhammad Musa and the certainly orthodox Sayid Uthman in order to achieve his ends, he was also expected to pay in kind for this cooperation. Thus one person displayed quite different interests and his attitude alternated between principle and pragmatic concerns. It is impossible, therefore, to draw any simple conclusions regarding

---

[20] In ANRI, Bt. 29 April, no. 4. This request was not pursued any further after this information about the son had been received.

[21] On Sayid Uthman cf. Van den Berg, 1886, and Snouck Hurgronje, 1923, IV, 1, pp. 69-83 ('An Arab Ally of the Dutch East Indian Government'), (1957), I, pp. 840-930.

[22] ARA, Mr (1886) p. 362f., Advice dated 29 April, 1886, nr. 326.

the attitude of 'the' Dutch towards 'the' Indonesian Muslims. That the air still hung heavy with the fear of hostility does, nonetheless, appear from the above account. In Holle's time educational activity was still at a rudimentary level and had not yet produced any significant results.

The Colonial Government and their Subsidizing of Islamic Education

Already before colonization the Islamic areas in Indonesia had an educational system which emphasized reading the Koran, practising prayers and learning the main religious duties. The most basic form of this education was for the most part called *Pengajian al-Qur'an*: instruction in the recitation of the Koran. This education took place (and still often does) in the homes of mosque leaders or other devout members of the islamic community. For advanced education, the island of Java had the *pesantren* system. A *pesantren* was a monastic school of sorts where students were taught from the age of about ten until they were past thirty by a teacher or *kiyahi*. At larger *pesantren*'s the *kiyahi* taught only the advanced pupils or *santri*'s, who in turn taught the beginners. In this way a *pesantren* under the leadership of a single *kiyahi* was still able to develop into a large school with thousands of pupils.[23]

In 1819 Governor-General Van der Capellen ordered an inquiry into the state of education among the Javanese "with the particular aim of setting up ways in which the existing laws and regulations can be more effective through a broader extension of reading and writing among the Javanese." He requested that special attention be paid to the possibility of "whether it would be useful in this case to stimulate the present teachers by appropriate measures or whether it would be necessary to employ entirely different objects for that purpose." In his *Geschiedenis van het onderwijs in Nederlands-Indië* (History of Education in The Dutch East Indies) of 1938 Brugmans assumed that Van der Capellen wanted to set up education "on a purely indigenous basis organised in relation to the village economy and in accordance with the already existing Mohammedan religious education."[24] If Van der Capellen ever had any concrete plans, he never carried them into effect. Yet Brugmans phrases his conclusion in rather extravagant language: "However weak at times and often interrupted, the policy of the Dutch colonial government has always remained the same: to do justice to the native elements in society while avoiding the subjection of native culture to foreign Western civilization."[25] Although beautifully worded in the style of ethical politics, combined with the need for

---

[23] For the previous history of the *pesantren* cf. Steenbrink, 1974, pp. 1-23.

[24] Brugmans, 1938, p. 74; HIOC, 1930, I, p. 9; Van der Wal, 1963, p. xii.

[25] Brugmans, (1938), p. 74.

economy in the thirties, this conclusion will not stand. There were a number of proposals over the years which dealt with the possibility of merging the education of the colonial government with the existing Islamic education, but apart from one or two exceptions all were rejected.

We have already met the first such rejection in connection with Holle's educational program. Holle explicitly refused to admit Islamic religious instruction in his school and in the face of strong opposition he even proposed a script entirely different from the Arabic one. The conservation of the Arabic script, if necessary, might safely be left to *pesantren*'s and *langgar*'s.[26]

J.A. van Chijs, who as Inspector of Native Education was the first government official to be able to devote his time to education for non-Europeans, seems to have taken a decisive step. In his report in 1865 on native education he points out that he "wish[es] to see the native school grafted onto native customs," but Islamic instruction is unsuited to such a project. He points especially to the mechanical memorization of Arabic texts, which are read without any comprehension.[27] This conclusion seems a little farfetched, considering his description of Christian education in the Minahassa and the Moluccas in 1867. He comments in respect to the latter:

> At present their social character is still so amphibious that it would be impossible to say what they really are: schoolteachers or religious instructors. They are usually called schoolteachers, but they might just as well be called catechists or visitors.

Like the Islamic educational institutions in Islamic areas, much of the instruction in these schools was religious instruction. Just as the Arabic version of the Koran was the principal text for the different forms of Islamic instruction book, the Malay translation of the Bible performed the same role at these mission schools. For most pupils, however, Malay - certainly in Leijendekker's translation - was more or less a foreign language. Reading and writing was almost exclusively connected to the Bible and the biblical stories and geography was limited to Palestine and the Apostle Paul's travels. History was practically identical with the biblical history. Singing, in preparation for the church service, certainly received as much attention as ritual instruction in prayer in the Islamic schools. Indeed, since the local teachers had been trained at mission schools themselves, their education was geared to produce suitable pastors for

---

[26] In ANRI, Bt. 5 March, 1860, no. 10. A *langgar* is a chapel for the practice of prayer and is also used for elementary instruction in the recitation of the Koran. More positive proposals for integrating Islamic education within government education, among other things, are to be found in Kerkerk Pistorins, 1871, pp. 203-204; Van der Wal, 1963, pp. 62, 145-151; HIOC, 1930, II, pp. 8-12; Van Nieuwenhuijze, 1949, p. 74.

[27] Van der Chijs, (1865), p. 12.

the local Christian community.[28] In contrast to what happened in respect to Islamic education, Van der Chijs did suggest improvements in the Christian schools: instruction in religious subjects gave way to instruction in secular subjects.

Although it is certainly possible to point to educational differences between Islamic and Christian education, they are of such a limited nature that the only explanation for the decision to keep Islamic education outside of the government system as much as possible must be one of political motivation. Keuchenius, the first minister in the colonies to be a member of a Christian political party, expressed it clearly enough in 1888 when he rejected the idea of subsidizing islamic schools and wrote that he feared

> that the involvement of the colonial government and the financial sacrifice required for the sake of those schools would eventually only lead to the promotion of a type of religious education that would surely be of little profit to our authority and our influence.[29]

Islamic education was thus forced to go its own way, without any connection to the colonial government through which it could retain its own traditions but at the same time be open to change. In the long run this meant that traditional Islamic education had to adapt to the Western, colonial system of education.[30]

C. Snouck Hurgronje and the Emancipation of the Muslims

Christiaan Snouck Hurgronje is one of the most controversial figures in Dutch colonial history.[31] The discussion focusing on him originated in, among other things, in the presence of a number of contradictions which co-existed in this great scholar. Pursuing his ideal of an emancipated and educated Indonesian people Snouck thought it best to advise a systematic and ruthless oppression of sections of the East Indies such as Achin and Jambi, which were still trying to maintain their independence. He favoured a separation between politics and religion, but his political advice led towards the increasing involvement of the colonial government in the daily affairs of the "islamic

---

[28] Van der Chijs, 1867, pp. 346-387.

[29] Dispatch of February 28, 1888, in HIOC (1930), II, p. 217.

[30] Cf. Geertz, 1960, and Steenbrink, 1974, pp. 33-78 on this topic.

[31] For the discussion that occurred in the 1970's see the articles in Van Koningsveld, 1988.

church."[32] This involvement developed to such an extent that the Office for Native Affairs, which he himself proposed and founded, may rightly be viewed as the predecessor and pioneer of the Indonesian Ministry of Religious Affairs.[33] Snouck tried to distinguish clearly between Islam's religious ideals and values on the one hand and its political involvement and aims on the other, yet when he arrived in the Dutch East Indies in 1889 he discovered an Islam that was largely apolitical. At his death in 1936, however, the situation had changed to such a degree that a modern political party and trade union formed on an Islamic basis had already come into existence.

After a thorough education in Arabic languages and literature at Leiden, which was - as was the case with so many others - the continuation of a study which had begun with theology, Snouck Hurgronje visited Arabia during the period from 1885-1886. By formally adopting Islam he was able to stay in Mecca for six months. He went to the Dutch East Indies in 1889 with the intention of studying Islam in that locale and with the special aim of putting colonial policy on a more scientific basis. In order to gain the confidence of the Muslims he acted like a Muslim. He was employed in the Dutch Indies as a counsellor for native affairs from 1889 till 1906. After his return to the Netherlands until his death he continued to exercise influence on colonial politics as an adviser to the minister for the colonies, especially in the field of education and religion.

Snouck himself made a theoretic summary of his "Islam policy" in four lectures addressed to the Dutch East Indian Academy for Administrative Studies in 1911.[34] These lectures constituted a strong plea for "association", by which Snouck means the "birth of a Dutch state, consisting of two geographically distant, but spiritually connected parts, one of which would be in northwestern Europe and the other in southeast Asia."[35] In his view the Islamic system had become so rigid that it was no longer capable of adapting

---

[32] Snouck Hurgronje, *Adviezen*, II, p. 1073. "When I was sent to the Indies in 1889 in order to study the practice of Islam there, Keuchenius in particular impressed on me that, if at all possible, I was to look for a way in which *the organisation of the Mohammedan community as a church* might be achieved. Thus that statesman, among other things, hoped to relieve the government of the responsibility of appointing *pengkulu's* etc. The idea proved to be impracticable."

[33] See Steenbrink, 1972. The Ministry of Religious Affairs, for that matter, is not the only religious institution which originated from colonial involvement in religion. The Office of the Missionary Consul, which eventually developed into the Indonesian Council of Churches, was also established at the initiative of the colonial government. Cf. Jongeling, 1966.

[34] See Snouck Hurgronje, 1911; Cf. also Benda, 1958, for a very extensive but uncritical summary. Benda does not sufficiently distinguish between theory and practice in Snouck's political ideals. Kernkamp, 1946, is more critical. Cf. also in this respect Suminto, 1985, and Algadri, 1984.

[35] Snouck Hurgronje, (1911), p. 85.

to a new age. Only through the large-scale organization of education on a universal and religiously neutral basis would the colonial government be able to "emancipate" or liberate the Muslims from their religion:

> Upbringing and education are the means for achieving that end. Even in countries of a much older Muslim culture than our archipelago we see them working effectively to relieve the Mohammedans of some of the medieval rubbish which Islam has been dragging along in its wake for too long.[36]

Snouck himself struggled during his years in India to begin the realization of that ideal. He took several sons of the West Javanese nobility and highly-placed civil servants into his home, became a member of the board of the Batavia Grammar School and exerted himself to find suitable posts for those who graduated.[37] This education had to begin with the nation's upper classes and to be strongly oriented to the Dutch system as well as to Dutch culture. For that reason he attached great importance to schools of high quality for his pupils and a thorough training in the Dutch language, if possible placing them as boarders with Dutch-speaking families. He could not foresee that his first Indonesian doctoral student at Leiden, Dr. Husein Djajadiningrat, would become the highest religious authority within the bureaucracy during the period of 1942-1945 and that from 1947 onwards student movements such as the Young Muslims' Association and the *Himpunan Mahasiswa Islam* would quite successfully support the continuation of Islamic ideals within the modern academic world. Nor could he foresee that from 1965 onwards the mosques of the modern universities would become the centres of an Islamic revival.[38]

The achievement of the final aim of this policy required the rejection of the Muslims' political ideals and the state would have to assume as neutral a position as possible in religion. However, this was not quite possible because of the historical obligations binding on the colonial government. These obligations consisted of the appointment of religious judges, the leaders and preachers of the main mosques, and several other matters which, according to Western law, could not be handled directly by religion, such as the regulation of marriages and inheritances. As an expert in Islamic law Snouck felt obliged to follow the Islamic rules in this respect quite strictly and advised others to do the same. At the beginning of his career in the Indies he tried to abolish the incorrect use of terms such as 'priest' for Islamic teachers and 'priests' coun-

---

[36] Snouck Hurgronje, 1911, p. 79.

[37] *Adviezen*, II, pp. 1110-1144.

[38] Cf. Victor Tanja, 1982, on the *Himpunan Mahasiswa Islam* and Rusli Karim, 1985, on the most important developments since 1965, especially in intellectual circles.

cil' for the Islamic court of law.[39] Snouck's elaborate account of Islam as a layperson's religion in which priests are not distinguished from the ordinary laity through ordination or other means caused another counsellor, L.W.C. van den Berg, to comment scathingly: "That gentleman indeed assumes the attitude of an orthodox Mussulman and as such assesses a matter of legislation as if the Government were concerned with the purity of the Mohammedan doctrine ...."[40]

During his research in the Dutch East Indies Snouck discovered several instances where customs deviated from the "orthodox teaching" of Islam. This was the case not only on Java, which was generally considered to be more syncretistic but also in areas such as Achin where Islam was dominant. In Snouck's view, these 'deviations' were not limited to Indonesia nor was there any reason to give Indonesia a distinct status within the islamic world. By way of comparison he used the example of a purely Arabic region like Hadramaut to show that next to "the doctrine and law that is generally regarded to be divine but nevertheless is very much neglected, a completely different standard of religion, law and morality is practised."[41] Thus, to take the position that Islamic law must either completely or not at all apply to Indonesia would be misguided. Traditional Islamic law was to be applied in accordance with the proper rules to Indonesian affairs for which it was considered relevant. Corrupt and unwitting judges had to deal frequently with Snouck, who, as the Advisor for Native Affairs, handled complaints of unjust treatment. Several times he reprimanded *penghulu*'s severely when they granted divorce on such insufficient grounds as apostasy. In his opinion, native women could make use of these particular grounds for divorce only if they had been prompted by those well acquainted with the law: "As a rule, the only motivation that leads the priests' council to such a decision is an unusual reward privately furnished by the woman who is eager to have another husband."[42] This practice would only discredit religious jurisprudence, the judges who had been appointed by the government and consequently the colonial government. Such practices, therefore, called for strong measures.

Snouck also criticized the appointment process with respect to Islamic jurisprudence. These appointments came under the jurisdiction of the native

---

[39] *Adviezen*, p. 658; VG, IV, 1, pp. 277-282.

[40] Van den Berg to Minister, ANRI Ag 24a, 1891. This is a reaction to a Snouck Hurgronje's report on the "Mohammedan legal system", also printed in *Verspreide Geschriften*, (Miscellaneous Writings), IV, I and Adatrechtbundel Vol. I.

[41] Snouck Hurgronje, (1893-94), II, p. 304.

[42] *Adviezen*, II, p. 968. According to Islamic law only the husband and not the wife can initiate divorce proceedings, with the result that wives are compelled to look for alternate means if they wish to divorce their husbands.

officials within the twofold administration and Snouck did not feel that the Dutch supervised the process closely enough. The consequence was that the religious administration was far too easily controlled by incompetent and corrupt people. During Snouck's tenure as counsellor, therefore, he introduced the regulation that candidates for the position of Chief-*Penghulu* would have to be examined by the Dutch Counsellor.[43] Snouck was also responsible for the marriage decree of 1906 which reinforced the position of the official Islamic holders of the office considerably.[44]

Snouck's activities in the Dutch East Indies coincided with the 'peak' of colonialism. Contacts between the ruling colonial government and the Indonesian population were intensified in every area and religion was no exception. The official theory of 'emancipation from Islam' was offset by the actual reinforcement and purification of islamic jurisprudence.

The Indonesian assessment of Snouck is as varied as his influence was contradictory. In Achin in particular, but elsewhere as well, in legal and orthodox religious circles he is despised as the personification of all the evils of colonialism, while at the same time he is respected as an expert on Islam, especially in Islamic law. He was prepared to make the required effort to become acquainted with Indonesian Muslims' own values. This does not entail by any means that his cooperation with the colonial administration is defended - on the contrary - but some reactions show that the Indonesian citizen of a later era is proud of having had such an interesting and formidable opponent.[45]

Godard Arend Hazeu: "The Only Real Ethicist"[46]

Snouck Hurgronje was not only of great significance because of his own numerous activities - he also founded a entire school of pupils.[47] These pupils were all trained in literary studies and read manuscripts in Arabic, Malay and Javanese. They were also well-informed in the field of literature and history. In addition, all of them spent some time doing fieldwork and in this way acquired direct experience of a variety of social and religious groups. A number

---

[43] *Adviezen*, I, pp. 762-798. For a number of similar inquiries by a later counsellor cf. Pijper, 1977, pp. 63-96.

[44] *Adviezen*, II, pp. 857-915, Cf. also Van Ophuijsen, 1907.

[45] Cf., for example, Suminto, 1985, and Algadri, 1984.

[46] L. de Hoop, *Ethicus in een Koloniaal conflict. Een studie naar Dr. G.A.J. Hazeu, in de onderwijs- en bestuursverhoudingen in Nederlands-Indië (1900-1920)*, Master's Thesis, (University of Groningen: 1984).

[47] Cf. especially Boland and Farjon, 1983, pp. 30-37, for an overview of 'Snouck's school'.

of them were employed by the *Kantoor van Inlandsche Zaken* (Office for Native Affairs), while others worked for the (academically) somewhat less highly esteemed *Bureau voor de Volkslectuur* (Office for Popular Literature), which was the most important publisher of Malay and Javanese texts between 1920 and 1940. All of them adhered to that complex ideology known as "ethical politics", a term stemming from Brooshooft's publication of a pamphlet in 1901 entitled *De ethische koers in de koloniale politiek* (The Ethical Direction in Colonial Politics).[48]

The period of ethical politics is often regarded as the third major period since the beginning of the 19th century. 1830-1870 was known as the period of the system of forced farming in which the export of agricultural products from Java was emphasized: the native chiefs were required to cultivate a number of agricultural products in fixed quantities. The colonial administrators had only indirect contact with the population, since the farming system was administered by the local native authorities who also had a financial interest in this system. The second period (1870-1900) was known as the liberal period. Plots were distributed among individual Dutchmen for the purpose of setting up plantations. The year 1900 saw the dawn of ethical politics. Such a description, however, serves only as a general outline and is certainly not a reflection of what occurred in all areas: Holle, for example, began work on his tea plantation far earlier than 1870.

The concept of ethical politics especially is a quite large umbrella which includes a variety of things. Locher-Scholten indicates that the term covered a policy of guardianship followed by a policy of emancipation, a welfare policy for the benefit of the Indonesian population, a policy of association, a policy of safeguarding the interests of Dutch exports - the Dutch variant of modern imperialism.[49] All these aspects were included in an ideology that was often formulated in a slightly sermonic way in which many aspects of the colonial system were depicted as a "moral vocation" which the Dutch people supposedly possessed with respect to the still underdeveloped Indonesian people.[50]

Probably Hazeu (1870-1929) can be called the "only real ethicist", because he was neither involved in the world of the planters, as Holle was,

---

[48] For the origin and definition of the concept of 'ethical politics' cf. Locher-Scholten, 1981, and pp. 11-54 on Brooshooft.

[49] Locher-Scholten, 1981, p. 176.

[50] Governor-General de Jonge's arrival in 1930 introduced a 'no-nonsense' policy, which was reinforced even more by the economic crisis, as a result of which 'ethical politics' lost much of its appeal. Official theorizing on colonial politics in the 'ethical direction' reached its culmination in the work of De Kat Angelino, 1930. De Kat Angelino had been the Advisor for Chinese Affairs. He did not award any place to the Islamic experts in the Office of Native Affairs in his lengthy work and hardly mentions Islam at all in his cultural history spanning 2100 pages.

nor in the military and continuation of colonial power, as Snouck Hurgronje was. In other respects as well he did not have any links with the economic powers. He "came out" to Indonesia as a teacher of Javanese in the William III Grammar School (1898-1904) and was subsequently assigned a post as an assistant in Snouck Hurgronje's office. In 1906 Hazeu succeeded Snouck as Advisor for Native Affairs and held this position until 1920. Unlike his predecessor, Hazeu was not an expert on Islam. Rather, as a scholar in the area of language and culture he applied his energies mainly to the Javanese theatre and then to the compilation of a dictionary of Gajo, the language spoken on the mountainous inland of Achin. His position, however, brought him into close contact with the Muslim population. In this section we will examine rather closely four of the different areas in which he became involved: 1) the conflicts between the Islamic and Christian missions in Northern Sumatra, 2) neutral or even Christian education for Muslim pupils, 3) the colonial government's attitude to the rise of the national movement that had an Islamic hue to it, especially Sarekat Islam, and finally 4) his attitude towards what were called "Islamic fanatic and extremist movements".

Colonial strategists sometimes took advantage of Christian missionary work in order to ward off the "danger of Islam." About the turn of the century, for instance, a controller in Eastern Java still cherished the hope that the Tengger region in Java, which had not yet become Muslim, could be maintained as a buffer zone between the largely Muslim eastern corner of Java and the rest of the island.[51] A similar notion was raised more than once concerning the Batak region on Sumatra, which could serve as a buffer between the largely Muslim regions of Achin and Minangkabau. This idea not only occurred to individual civil servants and missionaries[52] but was even supported by a secret decision by the Governor-General in 1891 not to appoint Muslims as village chiefs in areas that were not Muslim.[53] In 1903 a village chief in the Angkola area on the border of North and South Tapanuli was converted to Islam by his son and, despite the fact that he had been a chief for twenty-three years, the Dutch controller relieved him of his post. The son, Shaikh Ibrahim, who had already made the pilgrimage to Mecca although he was only a first-generation Muslim, did not let the matter rest but registered a protest with Hazeu. At first Hazeu thought that he was simply faced with a single act on the part of a pro-Christian civil servant but discovered that this anti-Islamic action was based on an official government injunction. Hazeu felt that

---

[51] La Chappelle, 1899; Freijburg, 1901.

[52] Van Limburg Stirum, 1891, p. 112.

[53] Geh. Bt. (Secret Order) 3 June, 1889 no. 1, in Suminto, 1985, p. 185. Cf. also my discussion of G.K. Simon in chapter VI.

this systematic favouring of Christians would not only embitter Muslims but might even give some of them the aura of martyrdom. He appealed within government circles that they pay attention to the fact that the Islamic press was increasingly gaining influence and that such discriminating measures would be difficult to defend. For the time being Hazeu's advocacy was unsuccessful. Shaikh Ibrahim barely escaped exile in 1910 and in 1916 he was sentenced to two month's hard labour for attempting to gain for himself the position of village chief from which his father had been expelled. Hazeu then resumed his attack. In an official criticism of Lulofs, the Advisor for the Outlying Provinces, Hazeu pleaded for the abolition of the obstruction of Islamisation. A committee of inquiry was appointed which exposed additional cases in which people had been imprisoned simply for the promotion of Islam. Lulofs was relieved of his post and Shaikh Ibrahim was elected chief by a population of which the majority were Christian.[54]

This case contradicts the complaint often voiced in missionary circles that the colonial government hampered missionary work. Because missionary activity was forbidden in a number of areas and during certain periods, this complaint is not entirely unfounded. On the other hand, however, there are also many cases in which the colonial government favoured Protestant and Catholic missions. We will return to this in the next chapter. In this incident Hazeu made himself clearly known as a consistent advocate of Muslim rights, but this was an attitude which was not greatly appreciated by certain members of the colonial civil service.

In addition to serving as Advisor for Native Affairs, Hazeu also served for some time as Director of Education, Public Worship and Industry (1912-1914) and continued to be very much involved in education policy later as well. He is one of the architects of HIS, the *Hollands-Indische School* (Dutch-Native School), a high quality Dutch-speaking primary school. It is true that he did not explicitly express himself negatively in regard to the qualities of Islamic instruction, but he never accepted it as a basis for universal and good public education in the Indies. He continued the course set by Snouck Hurgronje by his direct involvement in favour of high quality education for children of the native nobility. The Islamic press attacked him vehemently when it discovered that, at his instigation, the daughter of an aristocrat, the future bride of Raden Wiranatakusuma, who was the son of the Regent of Cianjur, and who would later be the Regent of Bandung, attended the school of the Ursuline nuns at Batavia and boarded there. This did not reflect any deliberate policy on Hazeu's part, however, who, during the administration of the quite explicitly Christian Governor-General Idenburg (1909-1916), repeatedly and success

---

[54] Cf. Castles, 1972, pp. 91-105 for an account of the whole affair.

fully argued against Christian education being forced on the Muslims, since this would be tantamount to playing with fire.[55]

Hazeu was one of the most powerful champions of *Sarekat Islam*'s right to exist, the first extensive nationalist movement founded in 1912. Although Governor-General Idenburg's name in particular was connected with this national movement which was connected to Islam,[56] his opinion of his adviser was that "Dr. Hazeu's judgment counterbalances the fallacies of a great many other people."[57] Hazeu's extensive advice and that of his assistant, Dr. Rinkes, were of the utmost importance for the development of this movement in its early phase. In the opinion of supporters as well as opponents both advisors behaved as if they were "advisors to the movement".[58]

Hazeu's persistent attempts to serve the rights of the native subjects of the colonial empire culminated in his actions during the so-called Garut Incident of 1919. This incident began with the government's attempts to force people in western Java to sell their surplus rice to the colonial authorities for the benefit of areas with had suffered a shortage. Local regents were left with the task of implementing this measure. The regent of Garut wanted to buy the rice far in advance of the harvest so that he would not have to pay as high a price. One farmer, Haji Hasan, refused to sign a contract of sale so far before the harvest. As a result of negligence, misunderstanding and obstinacy a military unit was sent to the wealthy *haji*'s home. Hasan had retreated inside the house with a group of friends and relatives and, since they possessed only amulets and ordinary agricultural tools to defend themselves with, he began a prayer of lament. On 7 July, when the regent was occupied with betting on an important horserace, the military unit attacked and the house was riddled with bullets. Haji Hassan and three of his supporters were killed and nineteen people were wounded and taken to a hospital.

A government investigation approved the police action but Hazeu came to an entirely different conclusion. He not only consulted with the higher-ranking civil servants but also with a number of farmers and religious leaders. According to his sources, the whole affair was proof of the corruption and

---

[55] Cf., e.g., Governor-General Idenburg's letter to the Minister for the Colonies, 7 October, 1912, in Van der Wal, 1963, pp. 215-219, especially p. 216 and a different note from Idenburg to Kuiper, 19 September, 1912 in De Bruijn, 1985, pp. 310-312.

[56] This connection can be seen by, among other things, by the pun on the initials *SI* as *Salah Idenburg* ('Idenburg's Mistake').

[57] De Bruijn, 1985, p. 118.

[58] De Bruijn, 1985, pp. 369, 391.

abuse of power by both European and native officials. Hazeu did not gain any support because a secret and militant branch of the political movement *Sarekat Islam* had been discovered in the same area at the time. Neither the authorities nor Governor-General Van Liburg Stirum accepted the results of Hazeu's investigation. Hazeu resigned and left his post in the Indies as a broken man. The rightist European press was rejoicing:

> Thank God! Is that bungler going at last? It is almost too good to be true. Someone lacking completely in firmness, a weak, wavering, old-womanish, narrow-minded, sentimental little fellow, too spinelessly good-natured to exercise authority - if only over his own garden boy, was appointed advisor to the authorities, simply because he speaks the language of the subjects. But even his garden boy does that better![59]

These rightwing journalists expressed themselves in a way completely different from Coen in his letters where he conveys the insecurity he felt among the "untrustworthy Muslims" who dominated Indonesia in his day.

A number of adherents of ethical politics supported Hazeu and some Indonesians as well wrote in his defence. The two most important were the Muslim politician and journalist Abdul Muis in his newspaper *Neratja* and the scholarly Dr. Husein Djajadiningrat, a student of Snouck Hurgronje. Djajadiningrat, for that matter, wrote a rather calm reaction in which he already displayed his future qualities as administrator and politician. He wrote that Hazeu's departure as advisor was "to be regretted in the light of the development in the Indies" but his becoming a professor at Leiden would benefit the academic world. Of the effects of Hazeu's efforts Djajadiningrat especially commends his academic publications and the foundation of the *Hollands-Indische School*.

In one respect Hazeu's attitude resembles Coen's very much: both tried to avoid religious matters as much as possible. This eventually made Hazeu promote a type of education which would be equivalent to a sound introduction to the West while ignoring the traditional Islamic system of education. In spite of all his good intentions in this respect he was not able to discover the way that the later independent Indonesians would choose.

The advisors displayed a great deal of benevolence. In more than one respect they shared heartfelt cooperation and sometimes even common interests with the Indonesians. They worked in a situation in which there was no equal balance of power and they had to serve the interests of the oppressed while employed by the oppressor. They tried to transcend this opposition by dealing

---

[59] *Nieuws van de Dag* (Daily News), 23 September, 1919. For a long time this newspaper had been conducting a smear campaign against the 'gentle powers' of ethical politics, or Hazeuism, as it was called in an article that appeared on 8 April, 1919. An extensive collection of clippings on this subject can be found in the Hazeu archives which are stored in the KITLV in Leiden.

with both parties as partners in a process of development. For Holle Islam still counted as a threat, while Snouck Hurgronje felt that an Islam deprived of its political content would be tamed. Hazeu, meanwhile, made no effort to reflect on its importance. Certainly these three had successful and significant encounters with Indonesians, but these took place despite the fact that they were Muslims. The main issue in these encounters were intellectual and economic development rather than religious considerations.

CHAPTER 6

The Age of Mission (1850-1940): Between Anticipation and Accommodation

The 19th century is sometimes called the "Age of Mission"[1], but in 1850 Catholic and Protestant missions were still only in the initial stages of the great missionary movement. In reference to the Protestants, an organisational separation between the established churches and missions occurred, which would continue until the end of the colonial period. Since the most important denomination, the *Reformed Church*, was suffering from a significant shortage of ministers in the Indies, a number of missionaries were also required to serve among the Europeans for some time. The *Regeringsalmanak voor Neder-landsch-Indië* (Government Almanac for the Dutch Indies) of 1850 lists only seventeen Protestant ministers and twenty-seven missionaries, while there were only nine Roman Catholic priests. In 1900 the numbers had increased to seventy-seven, seventy-three, and forty-nine respectively and after 1900 these numbers continued to increase.

Like many others that left for the colonies, Protestant and Catholic missionaries were a mixed group. Frustration caused by failure at home, idealism, a sense of adventure and a longing to perform great and heroic deeds all contributed in different ways to the motivations and attitudes of many of the Dutch citizens who decided to go overseas. The missionaries also displayed different attitudes to the Muslims whom they encountered. In this chapter we will briefly sketch the portraits of ten missionaries in their encounters with the Muslims of the East Indies. As different as these portraits may be from one another, one significant element appears to emerge again and again: Islam was the intimidating opponent[2] that should not be attacked directly but whose power should be curtailed through any means available - from the promotion of ancient folk customs, adat and folk religions, regional dialects (in contrast to Malay, thought to be of Islamic origin) to the modernization of

---

[1] S. Coolsma, *De Zendingseeuw voor Nederlandsch Oost-Indië* (The Age of Mission for the Dutch East Indies) (Utrecht, 1901).

[2] Jongeling, (1966), p. 110, cites a question that was sighed at the 25th General Dutch Missionary Conference in 1911: "Why has God allowed such a intimidating opponent?"

health care and education in particular. The common aim of all representatives of the diverse and varied world of missions was the curtailment of Islam's power and influence, especially through economic, political and educational means. Next to 'heathendom', Islam was the obvious target of Protestant and Catholic missionary activity, but the missionaries avoided direct confrontation. The former missionary consul Van Randwijck characterized their strategy with the words: "It skirted Islam."[3]

Samuel Eliza Harthoorn (1831-1883):
From Civilization as a Means to Civilization as an End[4]

Harthoorn arrived with his wife in the East Indies in 1854. By the end of 1855 he was studying Javanese at Modjowarno and from 1856 until 1862 worked as a missionary in Malang. He was quite liberal in his theological views, as was the case with ministers in the Indies on average and more often with the missionaries at the time.[5] Already in his first year as a missionary Harthoorn proved to be a man adept at making contact with the various native groups. He was a prolific writer as well and submitted several articles to missionary periodicals. From the start he was critical of the missionary methods which had been employed up to that time. In his view, the practice of handing out free tracts devalued the Christian faith, whereas in the Javanese tradition the pupil was initiated only gradually and after adequate testing into their sacred doctrine. Harthoorn did not want to be too quick to forbid various pagan or Islamic customs. He felt that it was impossible to produce pure Christians within one generation and was prepared to allow both circumcision and the *slametan*, a religious meal to which the Javanese invited their neighbours and acquaintances. Nor did he see any harm in the innocent children's games disallowed by Christians in East Java on the grounds that "otherwise the righteousness of Christians would be inferior to that of the *santri*'s, since even they prohibit[ed] their children from the display of such impiety."[6]

---

[3] Van Randwijck, 1981, p. 397.

[4] W. Nortier, *Het leven van Samuel Eliza Harthoorn*, (Life of Samuel Eliza Harthoorn) an unpublished manuscript of 52 pp. written "during the winter of famine 1944-1945 in Leiden", available in the library of the Hendrik Kraemer Institute in Oegstgeest. See also Enklaar, 1981, pp. 101-105.

[5] De Bruijn, 1985, p. 17, mentions that when Idenburg arrived in the East Indies in 1882, he wrote that "At the time there was one, and only one, orthodox minister in that entire church, Rev. Klomp in Batavia." Cf. Kruijf, 1894, pp. 472-507 and Enklaar, 1981, pp. 67-88 concerning liberal views in the Nederlandsch Zendelingsgenootschap (Dutch Missionary Society).

[6] Nortier, 1944-45, p. 27.

Harthoorn did not want to treat all unbelievers on the same level and made an exception for "those among them who were devout - for even in that dark pagan world the shades of light and brown have not been forgotten by the great creator."[7] In a fierce attack on mission strategy and tactics he states that it was the missionaries' usual practice "to call Mohammed a false prophet - but *not* in the presence of his followers - [and] to label the Moham-medans as unbelievers - but not in their presence." He viewed this as hypoc-risy: "Indeed, if in Mohammedanism I did not perceive one of many forms of religious life but the work of an impostor and sheer unbelief, then I would certainly be ready to say frankly what I thought of it. Then, at least, one remains sincere and does not generate hypocrisy."[8]

The most important issues in the conflict between Harthoorn and the leadership of the Dutch Missionary Society, however, do not seem to have been of a theological nature. Harthoorn himself held the view that the actual religion in the inland areas of Java was not Islam but an older folk religion. It was impossible to eradicate this folk religion all at once and a lengthy process of education was required: before the native population could be con-verted, they needed to be civilized first. This strategy caused Harthoorn to come into conflict even more with the few missionaries in his own immediate area than with the mission directors in the Netherlands. He resigned his posi-tion in 1862 and went to the Netherlands to argue "his case" and then left for the island of Madura as a private missionary, and applied his method. In 1865 he published a more elaborate account of that method entitled *De Toestand en de behoeften van het Onderwijs bij de Volken van Neêrlands Oost-Indië* (The Situation and Needs of Education among the Peoples of the Dutch East In-dies). Here he showed himself to be an advocate of the colonial system:

> The interests of the Netherlands and of the Indies are one. No thoughtful person will deny this. Everyone knows what the Netherlands are without the Indies. What the In-dies are without the Netherlands is indicated by the interior of the Archipelago which lacks Dutch influence. There the fertile soil lies waste; there the inhabitants roam about the woods without any permanent dwellings; there the chiefs have persons and goods at their unlimited arbitrary disposal; there wars are fought incessantly over triv-ialities. Dutch capital, Dutch talent, and Dutch government make the Indies a rich and blessed country.[9]

---

[7] Harthoorn, 1864, p. 4.

[8] Harthoorn, 1864, p. 108.

[9] Harthoorn, 1865, p. 1.

Harthoorn repeatedly speaks of "Mohammedan ecclesiastical education" in this work and describes the famous Islamic school (*pesantren*) at Tegelsari.[10] At the end of his book he responds to the question "What are the available means by which education can be improved?" He discusses extensively the "connection of education with the internal and external world of the native," but never takes up the elaborate system of Islamic education here at all.[11] Harthoorn's conception of education was modelled on the Dutch model, adapted to some extent to the climate, condition of the country and other particulars, but not to the religious traditions of the majority of the Javanese. He never discussed these subjects again.

Harthoorn's life took a tragic turn when his wife was murdered at Pamekasan on Madura in 1868. The regent had been involved in this affair and was therefore sentenced to death. Harthoorn then abandoned missionary work, remarried and became a teacher of anthropology and history at the William III Grammar School, dept. B. in Batavia. In the East Indies at the time this school provided the highest level of training for those intending to enter the civil service. It seems that Harthoorn had come to view civilization or education no longer as simply a means to the goal of conversion but as the most important goal itself. In a speech delivered in 1875 he says:

> I consider it a privilege that I am no longer prevented by unavoidable professional duties from living with my thoughts among people that I have loved from my youth as my own people, making no distinction between the Dutch and the Javanese; above all I consider it a privilege to be able to assist in the development of Dutch-Indonesian civil servants, [teaching them to] link the Indies and the Netherlands together not, indeed, with chains of gold, but more firmly and permanently with moral ties.[12]

At the end of his book on colonial history he sketches a similar picture of the blessings of education:

> The kris [Javanese dagger], which used to be an indispensable weapon for self-defence on the street and in one's own yard, is now an ornament. The farmer, who used to be a slave in the hands of tight-fisted and narrow-minded masters, now enjoys the protection of the law. Civilization and learning are slowly dispersing the dense clouds of ignorance and prejudice.[13]

In missionary circles Harthoorn was often regarded as an apostate who had yielded completely to the liberal and progressive criticism of the Christian

---

[10] Harthoorn, 1865, pp. 22-44, 268-273; cf. also Fokkens, 1877, on Tegelsari.

[11] Harthoorn, 1865, pp. 203-206.

[12] Harthoorn, 1875, p. 24.

[13] Harthoorn, 1873, p. 241.

religion. He still received some recognition, however, even in missionary circles. Nortier remarked on a different kind of criticism of religion in Harthoorn - the Barthian aversion to 'religiosity' in general:

From Harthoorn's criticism it is clear that he feels that preaching the gospel is not preaching a 'doctrine' and that essentially Christianity is not a religion, just as there are also pagan, Mohammedan or Buddhist religions, but he forgets that it should not lead to the neglect of church life and dogmatics."[14]

Nortier's remark and his mild criticism echoes the respect that Harthoorn continued to receive from subsequent missionaries in spite of his 'apostasy'. The sources provide no justification for such a strong distinction between religion and faith in Harthoorn, as was the case with Kraemer and Barth. On the contrary, for him Western civilization and the Christian faith seem to be connected almost inseparably with each other. Education eventually completely replaced the preaching of the gospel in Harthoorn's activities and goals.

Neither Islam nor Christianity were of any importance to Harthoorn in that later phase. The developments in modern Indonesia, where the great world religions are acquiring an increasingly more distinct and stronger position in society, seem to be diametrically opposed to the process of secularization, which not only the progressive champions of "the ethical policy" but also this (former) member of the missionary movement initiated.

Carel Poensen (1836-1919):
Building up a Christian Congregation Among Muslims[15]

Poensen's life seems to have been as smooth as Harthoorn's life was eventful. Born in 1836, he left for Java in 1860 in the service of the Dutch Missionary Society. From December, 1862 until March, 1889 he worked at Kediri as a missionary, after which he went back to the Netherlands on furlough. He returned to the East Indies in 1890 but only for a short period since he had been appointed a professor at the training college for East Indian civil servants in Delft sometime in the middle of 1991. For 28 years he worked in the same place. He followed the discussion of Harthoorn's 'apostasy' and was quite balanced in his opinion and to a certain extent he sympathized with Harthoorn's ideas. His assessment of Islam was also balanced and moderately positive: because of Mohammed "there was more unity among the Arabs ... the social situation of women and slaves was improved and infanticide re-

---

[14] Nortier, 1944-45, p. 47.

[15] An obituary on Poensen can be found in MNZG (1919): 97-99 and 193-207 (the latter written by N. Adriani); for an account of his activities with Kediri as his base cf. especially Kruijf, 1894, pp. 569-578.

pressed; the poor were looked after, idolatry was kept in check and some forms of immorality were counteracted."[16] Poensen saw the positive aspects of Islam not only in relation to the past and the Arab world but he also considered it to be a positive force in nineteenth-century Java because of its opposition to headhunting, the burning of widows and the Hindu caste system. He could also testify to a great many more victims of alcohol, opium and gambling among Europeans and Chinese in the Indies than among the Javanese.[17] Poensen, however, was not another Relandus, who attempted to be an apologist for Islam. According to Poensen, Islam was unable to satisfy the ultimate "needs of the human soul". For this purpose this religion settled too easily for the external appearances and superficiality.[18]

Poensen also viewed the Islamic regulations regarding marriage and sexual morality as especially weak elements. One could note these weaknesses not only in the practise of polygamy and frequent divorce but particularly in the lack of a "domestic life as that ... which obtains as a standard of life among Christians".[19]

Because of his profound knowledge of Javanese language and culture, Poensen saw quite clearly that it was impossible to form a Christian community from the individual believers who were dispersed among an Islamic majority; folk customs and religion were too closely interwoven. Village feasts and religious feasts were practically identical for the Javanese and a Christian was therefore more or less forced to live in isolation from his surroundings. The result was the existence of a few small Christian villages surrounded by Islamic ones. Poensen made a virtue of necessity and argued repeatedly for the foundation of a large Christian plantation as a mission centre, but this idea was never put into practice.[20]

In line with Holle, Poensen also argued for a separation between those in charge of administration and those in charge of religious concerns, an attempt at secularization that was ahead of its time - in the *Regeringsreglement* (Government Regulations), after all, the native chiefs had also been formally

---

[16] Poensen, (1886), p. 113.

[17] Poensen, 1886, pp. 113-115.

[18] Poensen, 1886, pp. 113-115.

[19] Poensen, 1886, p. 27.

[20] Poensen wrote at least one article, sometimes more, every year between 1862 and 1895 for MNZG and repeatedly brings up the topic of these Christian villages. In MNZG (1879): 198 he relates that he had had the opportunity to buy some excellent property for such a Christian village, but a Chinese had bought it before he had the chance to do so. In all probability, Poensen was no businessman and the mission was not prepared to spend a great deal of money on his plans.

declared to be chiefs of religion as well. But whereas Holle protested this reg-ulation [21] because he suspected it of possibly providing a support for Islamic fanaticism, Poensen protested it on the grounds that this regulation seriously diminished the possibility of converting native leaders.[22]

Poensen was a missionary who was also rightly regarded and respected as a scholar[23] and who because of his great gifts was able to maintain close contact with many circles of native society. On a number of points he also criticized the government as a repressive administrator who left the poor peasant with hardly any opportunities for development. It struck him as "rather peculiar for a Dutchman" to speak to the Javanese about the Phar-aoh's oppression of the Israelites.[24] He saw no great objection to making Christianity more attractive by creating employment or providing material prosperity: "Christian truth need not always hesitate to ride a horse as humble as material interest."[25] This view, however, led him to a politics that resembled apartheid: a Christian community that lived within but was socially and culturally separated from the Islamic community. The Javanese Muslim could be converted but should then become a member of a new and separate social community that consisted of Christians only.

Lion Cachet (1835-1899): The Outsider's Easy Assurance[26]

Frans Lion Cachet entered the service of what was later called the Reformed (*gereformeerd*) mission about 1850. He worked in South Africa until 1880, briefly as a "missionary to the Mohammedans" but mostly as a minister in an established congregation. In 1880 he became the minister of the Nieuwe West-erkerk in Rotterdam, which he served till 1891, when he went to the East In-

---

[21] Cf. chapter 5.

[22] In MNZG (1890): 391-415.

[23] Cf., for example, Snouck Hurgronje's assessment, (1923-24), IV, 1, pp. 55-67, of Poensen's *Brieven van een desaman* (Letters from a Villager), a collection of some seventeen articles on Islam on Java, first published in the *Soerebajasche Handelsblad* (Surabaja Business Paper) and later collected and published as *Brieven over den Islam, uit den binnenlanden van Java* (Letters on Islam from the Interior of Java). Snouck Hurgronje surely modelled his own series, *Brieven van een Wedono Pensioen* (Letters from a Wedono Pension), published in *De Locomotief* in 1891-1892, on Poensen's collection. See Snouck Hurgronje (1923-1924), pp. 111-248.

[24] Kruijf, 1894, p. 571.

[25] Kruijf, 1894, p. 538.

[26] For a short biography see the *Biografisch Lexicon voor de Geschiedenis van het Neder-landse Protestantisme* (Biographical Lexicon for the History of Dutch Protestantism), Vol. I, pp. 128-129.

dies for a year-long trip to inspect the mission work.[27] In his travel account he recorded several impressions of the history of mission, as well as the places he visited, and used the description of the journey through the Red Sea to make a number of remarks on Islam:

Arabia, that land of poetry and blood; of ancient cities and a nomadic population ... especially the land of the false Prophet, of the Bible of lies and of anti-Jerusalem towards which 170 million people are turning in more or less fanatic ecstasy at this moment, calling upon their Allah. Arabia, steeped in blood before bending the knee to Mohammed, that has made the blood of nations flow in its struggle for Islam and for centuries has been one of the strongest bulwarks of Satan against the spread of the Gospel.[28]

Lion Cachet was not a man to make subtle distinctions: for him Islam was the absolute negation of Christian teaching. He spoke of Buitenzorg, "the Residency of the Dutch Indies, where the High Governor resides in a princely palace," in apocalyptic terms: "Will the men of Buitenzorg then not rise up in judgment on the Christian Netherlands and condemn it for having ruled here for three centuries already - in pomp and luxury even - without making any effort to plant the Banner of the Cross among the Pagans and the Mohammedans?"[29] Writers such as Poensen clearly displayed a different tone than this inspector of missions who gave a predominantly negative and bleak picture of the colonies and particularly of its spiritual life. In Lion Cachet's opinion, the low social position of the missionaries only entailed disadvantages. Already on the voyage *to* the East Indies he wrote several pages on the frugality of the missions treasurer who had the missionaries travel second class. Lion Cachet felt this to be detrimental to their prestige.[30] He also complained extensively about the bureaucracy and expenses needed for providing missionaries with the necessary permits.[31] "With an eye directed to the idol *prestige*" he very much regretted that in Purworejo "... the church's external appearance was so dilapidated".[32] His strongly developed sense of prestige and superiority was also behind a very painful decision that the mission in Central Java was forced to make because of his unconditional condemnation of the doctrine and practice of Sadrach, a Javanese Christian.

---

[27] His report on that trip, *Een jaar op reis in dienst der zending* (A Year's Journey in the Service of Mission) (Amsterdam: Wormser, 1896), totalled no less than 879 pages.

[28] Lion Cachet, 1896, p. 39.

[29] Lion Cachet, 1897, pp. 216-217.

[30] Lion Cachet, 1897, pp. 10-18.

[31] Lion Cachet, 1897, pp. 187-197.

[32] Lion Cachet, 1897, pp. 251-252.

Sadrach (born c. 1835) had been baptized in 1867 after he had been taught by Javanese Christians who assured him that he did not have to give up Javanese customs in order to become a Christian. Sadrach first worked as a distributor of tracts for the mission and afterwards established a religious centre of his own in the vicinity of Purworejo. It was Christian in character, but resembled the Islamic *pesantren* in architecture and organization and Sadrach acted independent of the missionaries, who themselves did not agree with respect to how they were to respond to him. Only one of them, Wilhelm, was inclined to treat Sadrach as an independent leader of the native community, and this was also expressed by the fact that when they met he and Sadrach were seated on chairs which were the same height, something that many other missionaries considered to be improper. Lion Cachet took a definite position in this affair and as a result of his visit all contacts with Sadrach were severed. In Lion Cachet's own words, "The mission *had* to break with the liar Sadrach, who poisoned our mission field completely and had brought a 'Javanese Christianity' into existence in which there is no place for Christ".[33] The Indonesian theologian Sutarman Partonadi, who earned his doctor's degree in 1988 with a dissertation on this affair, defined Sadrach's christology as "an adequate and meaningful image for use in the Javanese context" and his assessment of Lion Cachet's visit was that "the effort to place Sadrach's community under the control of the Dutch missionaries represents a direct attack on contextualization."[34] Because of Lion Cachet's great and overriding aversion to syncreticism, coupled with a strong leaning towards holding to the superiority of the white race - especially in its eminent representatives, ministers and missionaries - he saw only obstacles to Indonesia's conversion to Christianity. Islam was only one of the many negative factors in this respect.

G. Simon: The Missionary Attempt to Anticipate Islam

In missionary circles a great deal of attention was paid to the question whether their limited resources should be used primarily for the benefit of the pagans or for that of the Muslims. Most Indonesians were adherents of Islam and this religion was also the dominant one on Java and Sumatra, the most important islands. On the whole, the missionaries were convinced that regions which had become Muslim would no longer embrace Christianity[35] and missionary activity focussed therefore mostly on 'pagan' regions, especially those

---

[33] Lion Cachet, 1897, p. 842.

[34] Partonadi, 1988, Theses 2 and 3.

[35] Simon, 1912, p. 113: "For a variety of reasons the Mohammedan resists Christianity; he does not want to become a Christian."

in the "outlying provinces". An argument that was used in respect to those regions was that christians "ought to anticipate Islam."[36]

It was the German missionary G. Simon especially who wrote extensively on the challenge to missions constituted by the promotion of Islam. In a short piece written in 1909 he gives a fascinating picture of the competitive rivalry between Islam and Christianity for the pagan soul and speaks quite negatively of the role which colonialism played. As early as the fourteenth century Islam had penetrated practically the entire coastal area of Sumatra, but at the beginning of the nineteenth century the larger part of the interior had not yet been Islamised. When the Dutch conquered the southern part of the Batak region in 1837, they opened the way for Islam as well: "What the centuries-long pressure of the Mohammedans had been unable to achieve, now developed automatically, as it were, under the protection of the colonial government."[37] According to Simon, the same situation obtained at the beginning of the twentieth century: "Islam accompanies the colonial government."[38] In the previous chapter we noted how Hazeu tried to get the colonial officials to abandon their systematic obstruction of Islam's advance. Simon may well, therefore, be accused of a certain one-sidedness. Thus, it will be our primary task to clarify his aim regarding the progress of Islam in his attempt to exert pressure on the government to assist Catholic and Protestant missions (more substantially). In a later elaboration on this view, however, he does express himself more subtly. His only comment on the general suggestion that the colonial government had to all appearances supported the promotion of Islam was that this "had repeatedly been the case with the Dutch Government."[39] He points to the example, among others, that strong action was taken against paganism by prohibiting headhunting, human sacrifice and similar practices, whereas no action was taken against Islam. The colonial government used and promoted the use of Malay, which was regarded as an Islamic language because, among other things, it was written in Arabic script. Since there were several Muslims among the teachers in the government schools and hardly any "pagans", education also contributed to Islam's progress.[40]

---

[36] Adriani, "The Mohammedan Part of the Dutch Indies," originally published in 1907 and rpr. 1932, I, pp. 160-70; cf. Bigalke, 1984.

[37] Simon, 1909, p. 4.

[38] Simon, 1909, p. 5.

[39] Simon, 1910, p. 31.

[40] Simon, 1910, pp. 30-45; summarized in Simon, 1912, pp. 15-19.

Simon's approach and use of language, which often seems militaristic, is by no means representative of the world of mission.[41] Others have been more subtle in writing about and applying their resources to the complex relations between Christianity, Islam and government. The fact that many translations have been made of Simon's work, however, indicates that many in missionary circles shared his views.

Baron van Boetzelaer (1873-1956):
Tactician and Expert in Arranging Subsidies
in Negotiation with "the Government of a Christian Nation"

Beginning in 1906, the popular and governmental support for missions that Simon tried to achieve with his books and articles, written for the general public in a rather sensational and militaristic language, became the diplomatic task of Baron van Boetzelaer, the first *Zendingsconsul* (Consul for Missions). This consulate had been founded in order to function as a contact point between the spokesmen for missions and the government in Batavia. These contacts were often concerned with the colonial government's political and financial support for missionary activities. In his 1909 annual report Van Boetzelaer wrote in no uncertain terms that he would like to see the government admit every now and then admit "that it is the government of a Christian nation."[42] Van Boetzelaer's practical policy and that of his successors as consuls do not yield a clear picture of the actual policy of mission with regard to the Muslims and the government. It did not follow an even course by any means; rather, mission policy was guided by changing situations and the plans for the study of Islam and evangelization among the Muslims were adjusted accordingly.[43]

Missions received political, administrative and financial support in a number of areas where Islam threatened to advance quickly. We have already seen in the previous chapter how governmental support was given to the efforts to stem the progress of Islam in the Batak areas. In her study on the mission consulate, Jongeling characterizes these *Maatregelen met betrekking tot de mohammedaansche propaganda in the Bataklanden* (Measures regarding Mohammedan Propaganda in the Batak Areas) of 1889 as an "interesting gov-

---

[41] Cf., for example, Adriani, 1932, III, pp. 199-214.

[42] Quoted in Jongeling, 1966, p. 112.

[43] For a general picture of the policy of the consuls cf. Jongeling, 1966, pp. 110-119. She typifies the policy in this way (p. 111): "Insofar as it is possible to speak of a policy, it swung between 'anticipating' and 'accommodating' Islam".

ernment document, issued as a field order for the struggle against Islam."[44] A similar situation occurred in southern Celebes, now Sulawesi, which had been brought under Dutch rule in 1905. The governor gave moral support and later financial support as well to missions "because of the political concern that the Torajans, Murians and other tribes not become Muslim."[45] Financial support from Germany for the missionaries of the *Rheinische Mission Gesellschaft* came to a halt during World War I. During that period, as well as during the period 1920-1929, when German money was practically worthless because of inflation, the RMG received "advances" from the government.[46] In certain areas where Dutch authority had not yet been effectively established, the missionary post was an important factor in the establishment of a regular administration. From 1909 onwards, therefore, a "civilization subsidy" was granted to missions in connection with the island of Mentawei.[47] Missionaries on the Sangi islands had received a comparable subsidy already in 1904.[48]

Government support was not always accepted and a few missionary societies, such as the Mennonite Missionary Society, did not want any subsidy at all.[49] The former consul for missions, Van Randwijck, felt that the missionary organizations ought to hold to the "limit of what missions in a religiously divided nation could ask from the colonial government of a country predominantly inhabited by Muslims. Sometimes they exceeded that limit."[50] Baron van Boetzelaer was more restrained in this than Gunning, the director of missions in the Netherlands.[51]

There were also differences among the authorities themselves. Idenburg, the Governor-General from 1909 to 1916, has sometimes been called "the first Christian on the throne of Buitenzorg". He declared clearly himself in favour of support for missions in a letter to Abraham Kuyper in 1911, as well as elsewhere:

---

[44] Jongeling, 1966, p. 113.

[45] Van Randwijck, 1981, p. 192; Bigalke 1984.

[46] Van Randwijck, 1981, p. 245; Jongeling, 1966, pp. 189-198.

[47] Jongeling, 1966, p. 188.

[48] De Bruijn, 1985, p. 233.

[49] Jongeling, 1966, p. 43.

[50] Van Randwijck, 1981, p. 247.

[51] Cf., for example, Van Randwijck, 1981, p. 247 on the subsidy for supervision that Van Boetzelaer rejected.

I have sent word to the consul for missions [Van Boetzelaer] that I am prepared to consider applications for financial support to established native Christian communities (missionary communities) on the same terms as was done in the Sangi Islands. That is all I can do. The missions themselves must make the applications.

I am quite busy with the Christianization of the outlying areas, but I am quite pessimistic. We lack the strength to stand against Islam - that is repeatedly my impression: dozens stand for Christ while thousands for Mahomed. We must not falter and must work on in faith, but when one sees here the crippled condition of Christianity and the spiritual power of Islam, then one's heart becomes anxious ....[52]

Van Limburg Stirum, who succeeded Idenburg as Governor-General from 1916 to 1921, still supported mission work, but from 1918 on this support was substantially curtailed as a result of the influence of Indonesian Muslims through the People's Council, founded in 1918.[53] Until the end of the 1920's missionary efforts were still very much needed in order to be able to maintain the level of education in respect to both quality and quantity. After 1930 the government itself was able to support a sufficient number of teachers with the result that missions found itself in a weaker position. In 1915 it was still possible for Governor-General Idenburg to urge the consul for missions Van Boetzelaer to a more energetic policy with respect to the government. Van Boetzelaer was able to threaten missions with the following declaration, "If you do not take our wishes into account, the day will come when we will close all our schools and then it will be left up to you," but after 1930 such a threat would not have been very effective.[54]

A number of problems between missions and the government also arose. The main controversy concerned the interpretation of art. 123 of the *Regeringsreglement* which stipulated that "Christian teachers, priests and missionaries must be given special permission issued by or on behalf of the Governor-General in order to be allowed to perform their services in any specified area of the Dutch Indies." This article was used more than once to declare certain strongly Islamicized areas from Achin to western Java closed to Protestant and Catholic missions for a long time. The mission societies often protested - and most strongly about 1930, when this measure still applied also to the island of Bali.[55]

As consul for missions, Van Boetzelaer was a mediating figure: it was up to him to coordinate the policies of mission and the colonial government. As

---

[52] De Bruijn, 1985, p. 228.

[53] Van Randwijck, (1981), p. 247.

[54] Van Randwijck, 1981, p. 254.

[55] Eykman, 1934.

'Baron Subsidy'[56] he managed to capitalize on the common interests of missions and the government so as to anticipate Islam in a number of areas, even though at the same time he was responsible for the idea that this weapon was to be handled with care.

Hendrik Kraemer (1888-1965): The Continuing Unsolved Riddle of Islam

Just as Christiaan Snouck Hurgronje is a central figure in the view which secularized religious studies and governmental policy took of Islam, Hendrik Kraemer has become as important and, at the same time, as controversial for the world of church and missions - not only in reference to Indonesia, but on an international scale. Kraemer studied Indology at Leiden and received his doctorate in 1921 on the basis of a thorough study on a Javanese Islamic text.[57] In that same year he was sent to the East Indies by the Dutch Bible Society (*Nederlands Bijbelgenootschap*), another organization that worked in missions. He was not only assigned the task of assisting with the revision of the Javanese translation of the Bible because of his linguistic background, but he was also required to study more recent trends in Indonesian society (in particular those among the younger Javanese intellectuals) and developments within Islam.

Kraemer accomplished the task of establishing contacts with young intellectuals by, among other things, becoming an adviser to the student society *Jong Java* (Young Java). He gave a series of lectures on Christianity for this society, as well as on theosophy and Catholicism. The more orthodox Muslim students therefore requested that the society sponsor a series of lectures on Islam as well. The chairman, Raden Samsurijal, put forward a proposal to this effect at the society's seventh annual meeting, held in Yogyakarta towards the end of 1924. When the proposal was rejected, Samsurijal and a number of sympathizers left to found a new society, *Jong Islamieten Bond* (JIB - Young Muslim Society). In the fierce discussion that surrounded this split in the youth movement, the Muslim leader Haji Agus Salim was said to have promoted the lectures on Islam and the split. Kraemer, on the other hand, was said to have infiltrated the *Jong Java* society with the purpose of excluding the Islamic element at any price. That price was high indeed: during the period from 1925 to 1942 the JIB developed into a self-confident organization of young Muslim intellectuals which, among other things, agitated strongly against Catholic and Protestant missions both inside and outside the People's Council and published a number of anti-Christian articles in the periodical

---

[56] Jongeling, 1966, p. 211.

[57] *Een Javaansche primbon uit de zestiende eeuw. Inleiding, vertaling en aantekeningen* (Leiden: Trap, 1921).

Het Licht (The Light) and other publications. The JIB was also an important training ground for the leaders of the *Masyumi*, the political party of progressive Muslims.[58] Kraemer put himself and large missionary circles outside of and even in opposition to that group.

Within Javanese culture an orthodox Islamic movement exists alongside a movement called 'Javanism' which maintains a number of traditional customs and values. The 'Islamic' group is sometimes also called *santri*, the name for students in the *pesantren*, and also 'whites' (*putihan*), in accordance with the white clothing of the *haji*'s. The 'Javanist' group, on the other hand, is sometimes referred to as *abangan* after the chthonic, earthly element of red clay. Both movements may be compared to the more biblical tendency on the one hand and the philosophical tendency, oriented towards Aristotle, Plato and Homer, on the other, in Christianity. Just as depictions of Pallas Athene, Zeus and Apollo stand alongside those of David, Jesus and Mary in the palaces of the Vatican, so the gods and goddesses, dwarfs and giants of the Hindu stories from the Mahabharata and Ramayana function alongside the traditions about Mohammed and his successors in 'Javanism'. Indonesian Islam has indeed sometimes rightly been called "the only Muslim group in the world today who have a strong and ancient indigenous liberalism."[59]

Within the dynamics of these two movements Kraemer deliberately chose for 'Javanism' and against the more orthodox Islam through his contacts and his resistance to holding lectures on Islam in the JIB. It was not sympathy for 'Javanism' as such that led him to this choice; it was prompted by the more orthodox Muslims' inaccessibility to mission work. Kraemer later described this inaccessibility as follows: "Islam as a missions problem: there is no religion for which missions has worked itself to the bone with less result and on which it has scratched its fingers till they were bloody and torn than Islam."[60] On the one hand, Kraemer gives a detailed description of Islamic teaching, especially its mystical aspects, in an intelligent, learned and refined way. On the other hand, however, particularly in some of his later writings he often displays the attitude of a lay theologian with a quite pronounced negative view of Islam. In the latter, general statements that which seem pathetic and sometimes slightly bombastic occur frequently. The following serves as an example: "The riddle of Islam is that, though as a religion it is shallow and

---

[58] See especially Abdurrachman, 1986, and also Petrus Blumberger, 1931, and Kwantes, 1978.

[59] Smith, 1959, p. 296. Wilfred Cantwell Smith never made any thorough and extensive research of Indonesia, but he certainly had a number of prominent Indonesians as students at McGill University in Montreal. They acquired so many important positions in the ministry of religious affairs and at the islamic universities that there was sometimes mention of a 'McGill Mafia'.

[60] Kraemer, 1938, p. 7.

poor in regard to content, it surpasses all religions of the world in the power by which it holds those who profess it."[61]

Although not all of Kraemer's later statements regarding Islam were as negative as the one just quoted,[62] this does appear to be his general tendency. For those unfamiliar with theological jargon, Kraemer, imitating Karl Barth, complicated matters by pronouncing a harsh judgement on religion in general. In Karl Barth, this judgement on religion was prompted by criticism of the cultural and political abuse of religion, previous to but also particularly during the time that Hitler was in power. In a quite sympathetic interpretation of Kraemer's harsh statements about the World Mission Conference at Tambaram in 1938 J. van Butselaar writes:

> Western society was designated as 'Christian culture'. For many people, transmitting Western society as much a goal of mission as communicating the gospel. At Tambaram Hendrik Kraemer brought up the question of whether Western society or Jesus should take the central position in mission, whether it was Christianity or the gospel that was unique. Today we find the answer of the conference to be self-evident; for that time, however, it was new: the gospel ought to be liberated from captivity to Western society and Western theology ....[63]

Although Van Butselaar may be correct in his interpretation of Kraemer, many others, particularly Third World theologians, have understood Kraemer differently. For many, he has "become a symbol of missionary arrogance and intolerance."[64] The very man who, because of his studies and perceptive qualities, seemed preeminently suited for preparing and initiating the encounter with Islam, eventually became an obstacle to this encounter, not only for himself but also for the generation after him. It does not seem to be very easy to combine detailed and balanced religious studies with rigidly implemented theological dogmatics. At any rate, such a combination will by no means contribute to a solution of the riddle of Islam so long as it is formulated in such a black-and-white way as in Kraemer.

Barend Schuurman (1889-1945):
The Exclusion of Mysticism as a Link

Barend Schuurman arrived on Java in 1922, the same year as Kraemer. After working separately for some years, both of them worked for missions and the

---

[61] Kraemer, 1938, p. 5; cf. also Van Koningsveld (1978).

[62] A balanced survey can be found in Slomp, 1988.

[63] Van Butselaar, 1988, pp. 208-209.

[64] Spindler, 1988, p. 4.

newly founded theological college in Malang from 1926-1928. Kraemer wrote later:

> That we directed our activities towards the town was not based on the idea that the existing village communities were considered to be of less importance nor on the assumption that we might win the town easily and from there penetrate into the surrounding countryside with the message of the Gospel. Far from that! This would have been a very superficial, not to say stupid, approach. It would have been more so the case since a Mohammedan country soon teaches missionaries not to think in terms of conquest. Two other things were of importance: to establish significant contact as a mission with the full reality of Javanese life and to remove east Javanese Christianity from its involuntary isolation and to place it in the midst of Javanese life.[65]

The transition from Mohammedan to Javanese in this quote is typical: the remarks on Islam are negative while those on Javanese life are positive. Barend Schuurman, who founded the theological college in Malang, is without a doubt the Dutch theologian to achieve the most fruitful results in the encounter between Christianity and Javanese culture. Whereas the intellectual elite of future Indonesia mainly spoke Dutch (such as the students in *Jong Java* and the *Jong Islamieten Bond*) or after 1928 began to use the modern version of Malay, Schuurman deliberately chose the complex, rich, but also thoroughly feudal, Javanese. Is this choice simply a desire to adapt, when in the past this choice so often meant a choice for the already antiquated past? From the perspective of the present, one could easily regard it in such a light, now that Javanese books are no longer available. At any rate, whereas orthodox Islam was and is identified with the coastal regions, with the harbours where the first Islamic traders arrived centuries ago, 'Javanism' is more readily identified with the mountains, the place of the gods and traditions. Malang, situated close to the mountainous areas of eastern Java, seemed to be the proper place for the theological college of the mountaineer Schuurman.

He used his time during the twenty years that he was allowed to work on Java to initiate "Javanese theological thought". Islamic-Javanese mysticism, which Kraemer had already thoroughly studied, could be of only limited assistance here. Schuurman's way of thinking was too much dominated by dialectical theology for this purpose. In his view there was a gulf between mysticism and faith that could not be bridged. Thus, while he was developing the notion of humanity as God's image, it was only with the greatest reservation that he was willing to employ the use of the concept of the human soul as God's image in the Islamic-Javanese mysticism. In order to prevent a final pantheistic merging of God and humans it was "necessary in this country of

---

[65] Cited in Schuurman, 1951, p. 22.

mysticism and Islam to establish as clearly as possible the human condition *over against God*, the real human condition."[66]

From 1930 to 1933 Schuurman interrupted his work on Java to write a doctoral dissertation. For that purpose he studied under Emil Brunner in Zurich, because as a graduate from the Free University of Amsterdam he could not obtain his doctorate from a Dutch State University. The title of his dissertation was *Mystik und Glaube im Zusammenhang mit der Mission auf Java* (Mysticism and Faith in the Context of the Mission on Java). He describes this work in the preface as a kind of contextual theology: "The present work has sprung from a missionary praxis to which, after having pursued its theoretical detours, it may return again."[67] Schuurman goes into far less detail in his religious studies and is less original than Kraemer. The subject clearly sprang from his Javanese environment which, far more than Dutch Calvinism, prefers to emphasize and enjoy the mystical aspects of religion. This more or less pantheistic mysticism is simply designated as "unorthodox" in the tradition of religious studies.[68] Schuurman avoided reaching any firm conclusion on the matter and interpreted this mysticism as favourably as possible. In the end, nevertheless, he emphasized the absolute separation of faith and mysticism in line with dialectical theology.[69]

Father F. Van Lith S.J. (1863-1926): A Flexible Educator on Java

The Catholic mission in Indonesia was considerably slower in getting started than the various Protestant missions. Until 1850 hardly anything was done apart from the pastoral care of Europeans in the Indies. In the decade of the 1850's Flores definitely came under Dutch rule (cf. the 1859 treaty with Portugal) and missionary work among non-Europeans began, as well as elsewhere in the Indies. On Java mission work started only with the Jesuit F. van Lith. In 1896 Van Lith arrived in Muntilan, in the heart of Central Java, where he thoroughly prepared himself by studying the language and became acquainted with several aspects of Javanese culture. In 1904 he opened a

---

[66] Schuurman, 1951, p. 153.

[67] Schuurman, (1933), p. vii.

[68] Schuurman, 1933, p. 2. In this connection it is interesting to consider the judgement of the Jesuit Father Dr. P. Zoetmulder on the Muslim mystic al-Hallaj, sentenced to death for adhering to the doctrine of the incarnation and pantheism. Of his doctrine of incarnation ("I have become Him whom I love and He whom I love has become me") Zoetmulder writes: "This union may after all be best compared to God living in humans through His *gratia sanctificans* as taught by the Catholic doctrine, in which divine transcendence is fully preserved." Zoetmulder, (1935), pp. 38-39, also defends al-Hallaj against the charge of pantheism and monism.

[69] Cf. also Hoekstra, 1989.

teachers' training college which became the centre of Catholic mission work on Java. The boys who attended this boarding school eventually formed a Catholic elite which became the basis for the further expansion of the Catholic community on Java.[70]

There are a number of parallels between Schuurman and Van Lith: both were culturally aware and were appreciative of the Javanese language and society; both of them were also very much aware of their limitations as Westerners and made only provisional efforts to translate the message of the gospel into Javanese, realizing that the actual work should be left to 'real' Javanese. Schuurman wrote works of a more theological nature and worked for a small group, whereas most of Van Lith's writings were of a more popular nature and he worked on a much wider scale among larger groups of pupils.

As a comparison between the Catholic and Protestant missionary traditions we intend to discuss here one of Van Lith's works in which he took up the matter concerning Sadrach, whom we have already encountered in connection with Lion Cachet. While on leave in the Netherlands from 1921 till 1924, Van Lith wrote a study, using seventeen workbooks, entitled: *Kjahi Sadrach. Eene les voor ons uit de Protestantsche Zending van Midden-Java* (Kjahi Sadrach: A Lesson for Us from the Protestant Mission on Central Java). This work has never been published. Someone other than Van Lith wrote in the margin: "On the whole your sympathy for the Protestant mission has made a good impression on me and I think it is useful that you express it, particularly since you do not hesitate to criticise certain practices and ministers ...."[71] Van Lith commended the missionary Wilhelm highly, who had acted as Sadrach's servant and assistant. Van Lith's positive attitude towards a Protestant may well have been the reason why this work was never published.

In a very original and at the same time very Catholic way, Van Lith tried to avoid the problems encountered by Poensen, Sadrach, Wilhelm and a number of others who wanted to develop a purely Javanese form of Christianity, but at the same time, for reasons of purity of doctrine, objected to baptized Christians joining in that mixture of social society and religion that is always part of village life. When solemnizing marriages Van Lith chose to be radically lenient, making particular efforts to respect as much as possible those in the village and mosque who were authorized to solemnize marriages:

We Catholics have thought it best to adopt a different position. We have taken great pains to ensure that the marriage register is filled out in precisely the same way for the Catholic Javanese and brought to us by *kahoem* (the officials of the mosque on the village level), so that the benefits for the village would remain intact for all of

---

[70] L. van Rijckevorsel, 1952.

[71] I have used the typewritten copy of this manuscript, prepared by Dr. J. Weitjes SJ, in the Jesuit College Kolsani at Yogyakarta. The quote is found on p. 77 of this copy.

them. In our view this whole arrangement was not primarily established for the sake of religion. The Koran does not require that marriages be solemnized in the mosque or by the *pangulu*. It is required by the Dutch government so as to have a civil register of sorts and to supervise marriages in view of the civil consequences, primarily involving questions about inheritances. Besides, the officials in the desa do not have a very large income for the most part, but they are needed and do have to live. Therefore we have followed a different strategy and have left those revenues undisturbed. Both the Protestants and the *Sadrachians* consider it their Christian duty to remove these village ties because they were simultaneously religious ties. Is it not, however, the best policy to break such religious ties by employing the entire village staff in exactly the same way in the services of the church and the *missigit* (mosque) alike?[72]

The Koran does not give specific instructions for the solemnization of marriage any more than the Bible. These directions are found in the "second source" for the Islamic code of behaviour - the traditions of the prophet. But these traditions do not specify any persons in particular as those whose responsibility it is to solemnize marriages. Local Islamic customs everywhere, however, acknowledge regulations for the solemnization of marriage. In 1906, in order to deal with a number of abuses in the Indies, the Dutch government drew up a marriage act which gave certain people the authority to solemnize marriages.[73] Many people held that this act strengthened the position of the (more orthodox) Islamic officials. Van Lith was of a different opinion and proposed a radical distinction between local customs and their religious significance. The person appointed by the village chief as an official of the mosque and, at the same time, to perform marriages would also have to work for the Christian Catholics. He would not lose any income and he would be employed both by the mosque and the church. In this way Van Lith applied a radical 'secularization' of social customs which had been connected to (Islamic) religion. He applied the same argumentation to the calculation of lucky and unlucky days: "We would certainly be guilty of superstition if we attached any value to that. Should one, however, also say the same of the simple Javanese? Most certainly not."[74] Using a similar argument, Van Lith did not consider it absolutely objectionable that Catholics were passively present during the *slametan* when the Javanese prayer for the traditional local village god or the Arabic, Islamic prayer was pronounced. The same reasoning was applied to the circumcision of children.[75] He did require in the latter case that the strictly Islamic prayers be omitted, so that circumcision would be seen as a purely Javanese, rather than Islamic, affair:

---

[72] Van Lith, *Kjahi Sadrach*, pp. 78-79.

[73] Van Ophuysen, 1907.

[74] Van Lith, *Kjahi Sadrach*, p. 147.

[75] Van Lith, *Kjahi Sadrach*, pp. 152-53, 159.

Which gives expression to a more vigorous protest against Islam: keeping silent and not letting oneself be circumcised or submitting to the circumcision as a Javanese custom in order to become a Javanese youth, with the explicit demand that anything that reeks of Islam be omitted?[76]

In all respects Van Lith's position lies in the tradition of the Protestant missionaries who, faced with the choice between Javanism and the more orthodox Islam unconditionally chose the former and left the latter out of consideration. Van Lith's choice in this respect was made even easier by the fact that, like De Nobili in India and Ricci in China, as a Catholic theologian it was somewhat easier to differentiate between religion and social customs. In his view Javanism was purely cultural, not religious, and one could therefore follow it. Islam, on the other hand, is regarded purely as a religion which must be avoided.

The Ten Berge Affair (1931-1941): The Muslims Respond

In 1931 the Jesuit priest J.J. ten Berge published two articles on the Koran in the journal *Studiën*, edited by the Dutch Jesuits. Ten Berge worked at the missionary post in Muntilan founded by Van Lith. The articles are largely based on studies by the Jesuit Islamologist H. Lammens, a specialist in Mid-Eastern archeology. In a few places Ten Berge gives the Malay or Javanese form of a technical Islamic term next to the Arabic form. He drew his material for the articles from studies rather than from direct encounters with Muslims. The articles are written in a steady 'objective' style, but in the conclusion of the second article Ten Berge offers a few sarcastic and vitriolic remarks. Ten Berge first quotes the Koran (5:79): "Christ, the son of Mary, is no more than an apostle; other apostles have preceded him and his mother was in truth a woman. Both of them needed nourishment."[77] He comments on this text in the following way: "One can see that according to Mohammed Christians conceive of a father and a mother and a son in a sexual sense. How would it have been possible for him, the anthropomorphist, the ignorant Arab, the gross sensualist, who was in the habit of sleeping with women, to conceive of a different and more elevated conception of Fatherhood!"[78] Ten Berge continues in this style for some time. On the next page he mentions that the "Koran teaches that Christ was not crucified. This is not a discovery of Mo-

---

[76] Van Lith, *Kjahi Sadrach*, p. 166.

[77] Ten Berge uses the so-called oriental method of verse division. This verse is 5:75 in the Muslim division. 'Christ' is a rendering of the Arabic *masih* which probably has the same roots as *Messiah*.

[78] Ten Berge, 1931, p. 302.

hammed's hardly original mind, but can be traced to the ancient docetic sects ...."[79] His final conclusion is that the Koran can only be considered as a "confirmation and interpretation of the historic gospels - a very poor result!" If one discounts that result, "what is left is a mere collection of fables, concoctions and misunderstood stories."[80]

In contrast to many similar products of Dutch anti-Islamic apologetics, this article did not go unnoticed in Islamic circles and the *Persatuan Islam* society established at Bandung began a protest campaign.[81] The society published a pamphlet in which the anti-Islamic attitude of the Western colonial powers in general was criticized, of which the Italian invasion of Libya and Ten Berge's article were mentioned as examples. The Resident of Bandung and the Attorney-General took great pains to hush up the matter and promised to bring the case to court. The leaders of the *Persatuan Islam* society acquiesced and reclaimed a number of copies of the pamphlet from the post office. By the end of July, 1931, however, an extensive report of the case appeared in the Malay press of Batavia.[82] Most likely the leader of this counteraction was the twenty-three year old Muhammad Natsir, a graduate of the *Hollands-Inlandsche Kweekschool* (Dutch-Native Teachers' Training College) in Bandung. From 1930 onwards he proved himself to be a sharp and critical observer of colonial policy towards Islam in a number of articles in the periodical *Pembela Islam*.[83] He criticized the policy for exercising a double standard because the Indonesian Muslims were quickly punished for "articles which sowed hatred," whereas it was impossible to bring Ten Berge formally to trial. The "offence" had not been committed in the Indies, since the journal was printed and circulated in the Netherlands. Natsir made also mention of the discussion in the *Nederlands Juristenblad* (May, 1931) on the "Penalization of Blasphemy."[84] His article showed that he had reviewed the parliamentary reports of the Upper House regarding the policy of the colonial government towards Islam.

The Governor-General's account of this affair in the People's Council did not satisfy the Muslims and a series of protest meetings all over the country

---

[79] Ten Berge, 1931, p. 303.

[80] Ten Berge, 1931, p. 307.

[81] See Federspiel, 1970, on this society.

[82] ARA Mr (1931): 797x.

[83] In 1969 these articles were collected in M. Natsir, *Islam dan Kristen di Indonesia*.

[84] *Nederlands Juristenblad* 6 (1931): 313-316. This discussion did not arise because of the incident in the Indies but in connection with a bill which was particularly directed against the Dutch Communist paper *De Tribune*.

was convened 11 October, 1931. These meetings were held in a number of large towns and especially attended by educated Muslims, who were often members or sympathizers of organizations such as the *Muhammadiyah*, *Persatuan Islam* or the *Partai Sarekat Islam* which favoured modernization. These meetings, under strict police surveillance and restrictions (the Italian invasion of Tripoly in particular was not to be mentioned), proceeded in good order and a few weeks later the matter disappeared from the Indonesian press for the time being.[85] The content of Ten Berge's article was only indirectly discussed: a few incidents, such as those mentioned above, were described as being offensive to the Muslims, after which an appeal was made to the government to exercise neutrality in a fair way and prohibit such statements.

The case still had some consequences within the Catholic community of the Indies. Mgr. Willekens, Apostolic Vicar of Batavia, disagreed entirely with the government's criticism of Ten Berge's statements and rejected it as a "completely unjustified and imprudent statement", which could be detrimental to the relations between Muslims and Catholics. The chairman of the *Indische Katholieke Partij*, however, shared the government's criticism and because of this affair (once again) collided with Mgr. Willekens, whereupon he resigned as chairman in 1932. Together with other discordant views this affair led to a split in the Catholic party in the Indies.[86]

The affair continued to hold people's interest, because, as in the Rushdie case in Europe in 1989, various other matters were involved as well. Natsir stirred up the issue again in 1939, just after a complaint from the Islamic community had met with a quite formal reaction. He therefore reported again in full detail the police's lenient treatment of the Catholic priest in 1931. After the government, represented by the Director of Education and Public Worship, had "seriously" pointed out "the reprehensibility of his words" to Ten Berge, the Ministry of Justice sent a telegram to seize all the copies of the periodical. The seizure was not successful because the telegram had been incompletely and inaccurately addressed to the parsonage in Muntillan with the result that it was not legally valid. No further action was taken. At the end of his article Natsir asked, "May our people expect such mild treatment as well?"[87] Natsir brought the case up once more in 1941, including even more details regarding different treatment in this and similar cases of slander.[88]

[85] For the final result see ARA Mr, 1931: 963x, 1066x, 1025x, 1095x. For the PID report, cf. Poeze, 1988, pp. XXXVIII, 90, 100, 116, 211-12.

[86] Bank, 1983, pp. 49-50.

[87] Natsir, 1969, 87-94.

[88] Natsir, 1969, pp. 158-161.

I have been unable to locate any sign of any response by Ten Berge himself. They are indeed of little consequence.[89] The affair that bears his name is indicative of a change in relations, which was certainly connected with a hardening of general policy in the very tight administration of Governor-General de Jonge, the collapse of the global economy, and the slow decline of the ethical policy in the 1930's. Others, such as Kraemer and Van Boetzelaer, were also attacked by Natsir and his sympathizers, even if considerably less fiercely and for a shorter period.[90] In the emancipation movement, which was also a nationalist movement, Islam played an important part. Snouck Hurgronje's hopes and expectations regarding the non-political character of Islam did not materialize. On the contrary, the Muslim reaction, which was possible only through improvements in education, caused a worsening of relations rather than a "spiritual association".

1945-1949: The Catholic Preparation for a Muslim Indonesian Republic

From 1600-1950 there were only a very few leadership positions in the Indies held by Catholics. After the Belgian Count Du Bus de Gisignies, who was Governor-General on behalf of the United Netherlands from 1826-1830, the next Catholic to hold such a high position in the Indies was Beel in 1948. In 1938 only three of forty-two residents and governors were Catholic. Of the assistant residents only nine of the 169 were Catholic and only 0.3% of the Indonesian population were registered as Catholics in the 1930 census.[91] The Catholic church could hardly be said to occupy a strong position at the beginning of Indonesian independence. This small minority watched the political developments with mixed feelings. Nevertheless, it is also possible to point to clear differences. The attitude of the Catholics in the Netherlands was at first

---

[89] After this affair Ten Berge no longer wrote any substantial articles in *Studien*, but only a few book reviews of a popular kind such as in (1932) I: 186-187 on *De grote Zwartrok, Pater de Smet SJ* in his missionary letters, followed by (1932) I: 357: *Apostel der Roodhuiden*. Afterwards his job as reviewer as well was taken over by a far more learned writer with the pseudonym R. Artati, but probably to be understood as the younger Jesuit brother of Ten Berge, P. Zoetmulder SJ, at the time still a student of Indology at Leiden. In (1933) II, 316 this scholar furnished a review of Schuurman's book in which he criticised Schuurman's view of pantheism on the basis of his own Catholic tradition: "Here [in Schuurman] mysticism is largely regarded as a psychological phenomenon in which religion is completely overrun by 'anthropology' .... It is indeed characteristic of the writer not to incorporate into his study the genuinely Christian mysticism which manages to retain the proper distance between God and humanity, the mysticism, for example, of St. Theresa and St. John of the Cross." In this and other reviews 'R. Artati' shows himself to be a great expert not only on Western but also on oriental mysticism.

[90] For Van Boetzelaer cf. Natsir, 1969, pp. 23-29 and for Kraemer, pp. 28-34, 49, 83, 90-97, 234.

[91] Cf. Bank, 1983, pp. 506-508 on this data.

considerably more negative towards Indonesian independence than that of the missionaries: Mgr. Willekens of Batavia had far more fear and misgivings than his Indonesian colleague Soegiojopramata of Semarang. Frans Seda, who was still a young man at the time but was later to become a politician and minister in the Cabinet, supported the cause of the United Republic, whereas a considerable number of Catholics on the eastern islands were apprehensive of the danger of "neo-colonialism" on the part of the Javanese. In spite of all this the Catholics managed to maintain unity without much difficulty. Catholic activities were centred on the promotion of the faith, health care and education and outside of these concerns politics was regarded as a neutral question. Thus they continued the tradition of Catholic missions which, even in colonial times, had refrained from becoming too easily identified with the government in the East Indies and certainly with the objectives of the plantation owners and businessmen.[92]

Insofar as the church authorities were called upon to take a political stand, everything was determined by "the spectre of a quiet transition from the Dutch-Indian restriction to an Indonesian one, from the policy of a liberal colonial administration to limitation by an Islamic government."[93] Under colonial rule a number of priests received their salary from the government. Mgr. Willekens argued strongly that the church renounce this privilege entirely, as well as any final financial settlement by the Dutch government, since this could be interpreted as giving preferential status to Christianity at the expense of other religions.[94]

Typical of the debates that occurred during these years is the *Minimum Program inzake godsdienst, onderwijs, sociale zaken en volksgezondheid in 1948 uitgegeven door het Centraal Missie Bureau* (Minimum Program for Religion, Education, Social Affairs and Public Health issued in 1948 by the Central Missionary Office).[95] In this political document the state and private institutions are juxtaposed, with the state's chief obligation being to safeguard the rights of the private institutions. Freedom of religion has to be achieved through equal (including financial) government support of all religions: "If the ministers of one religion, for example Islam, continue to be vested with the

---

[92] Bank, 1983, p. 250.

[93] Bank, 1983, p. 245.

[94] Bank, 1983, p. 249.

[95] This organization was located at 10 Van Heutzplein in Batavia. Through one of history's little ironies, the Van Heutzplein has now been renamed Taman Cut. Mutiah, after a female Achinese guerilla fighter who was Van Heutz's enemy. The central office of the Catholic church is still located at No. 10. The *Minimum Program* was published in the *Indisch Missietijdschrift* (East Indian Missionary Review) 31 (1948): 137-146. Cf. Bank, 1983, pp. 248-49 for the history of its origin.

authority to perform marriages, the same authority, if necessary, should be granted to ministers of other religions, such as Christianity."[96] The following argument is given with regard to education: "What Catholic and Protestant missions have achieved so far in the field of education is of such importance for the Indonesian community that these activities can hardly be considered as something that has only been tolerated or allowed to happen."[97] The proposals regarding health care reflected not only their confessional aversion to an all-powerful state but also the fear of ecclesiastical institutions being taken over by the Islamic government: health care: "The task of the government in this respect is directed towards leadership and planning, as well as towards the supplementation of what has been achieved in this respect by private initiative ...."[98]

In 1949 Mgr. Willekens wrote rather pessimistically of Catholicism finding itself "face to face with the rivalry of Protestantism, with the strength of Islam and with that of Freemasonry, now quite active again ...."[99] It was hardly surprising that the Franciscan fathers in West Irian carried on a campaign of their own in order to continue the special status this area enjoyed. Its transfer to Indonesia would mean the further progress of Islam, an "infiltration of the Protestant Ambonnese in all administrative posts" and an end to the "substantial subsidy spent on education by the Dutch government."[100]

In the outlying provinces efforts were made to anticipate Islam, if it was still possible. On Java and in other Islamic areas Islam would have to be respected and private Christian organizations expanded. This was the policy that the leaders of Protestant and Catholic missions had in mind. Fortunately, this strategy has by no means proved to be representative of the Indonesian Christians. Lay people especially have self-consciously assumed the political initiative and have achieved the natural and integrated role of the Indonesian Catholic community, as well as the Protestant community, in the national East Indian society.[101]

---

[96] *Minimum Program*, p. 140.

[97] *Minimum Program*, pp. 144-145.

[98] *Minimum Program*, p. 145.

[99] Bank, 1983, p. 461.

[100] Cf. Bank, 1983, p. 462.

[101] Although one can dispute the particulars and sometimes biased approach to the Catholic cause, the general picture as outlined in the work of Muskens, 1969, is certainly acceptable for the period in which that research took place.

CHAPTER 7

Indonesian Reactions
to the Christians' Arrival

In the previous chapters we were primarily concerned with describing the Dutch colonial image of Muslims and the policies they adopted towards Islam. Discussion of the Indonesian response arose only occasionally. In this chapter we will take up this question. As in the preceding chapters, our approach here will be to describe a number of concrete examples rather than engage in survey that would prove to be far too general.

Closely associated with this subject is the question of the Indonesian Muslims' general approach to other religions. How did the Muslims view Hinduism, Buddhism and what is often referred to now as 'animism'? We will answer this question by discussing some conversion accounts found in a number of Malay and Javanese historical and literary texts. Conversion here refers to conversion from a pre-Islamic religion to Islam. These conversion accounts provide an excellent access to the characteristic features of the Islamic understanding of other religious traditions.

Islam's Arrival in the East Indies
in the Malay and Javanese Literary Traditions

The *Sejarah Malayu*, (History of Malaysia), which was probably composed in the approximate area of what is known today as Singapore between 1612-1615,[1] certainly ranks as one of the classics of early Malay literature. This work also includes an account of Islam's arrival in this area and the kingdom of Samutra on Achin's north coast is cited as one of the first areas in the East Indies to adopt Islam. According to the *Sejarah Malayu*, the prophet Mohammed had told his companions that a kingdom called Samudra would embrace Islam and many holy people would live there. The king of Malabar was to be taken there and some time later the king of Mecca sent a ship to Malabar, amply provided with provisions and gifts. It arrived in the kingdom of Sultan Muhammad and when he heard the story about Sumadra, he appointed his son to be king in his place and joined the mission. They called at various

---

[1] Cf. the introduction in Situmorang and Teeuw, 1952. This edition of the *Sejarah Melayu* has been used throughout this chapter.

places in northern Sumatra but, while the inhabitants in these places adopted Islam, none fit the prophet's description of Samudra. When they arrived in Merah Silu's kingdom in Samudra, he immediately embraced Islam as well. The following night Merah Silu had a dream in which the prophet Moham-med appeared to him and ordered him to open his mouth, into which the prophet spit, after Merah Silu had done so. Merah Silu then awoke and smelled the lovely fragrance of balm enveloping his body. The next day the former king Muhammad of Malabar entered his palace and handed him the Koran with the request that he read it. Since Merah appeared to be able to recite the entire Koran, Muhammad of Malabar decided that Merah Silu was the ruler of the kingdom of holy ones that the prophet Muhammad had fore-told. They then presented all their gifts to Merah Silu and changed his name and title to Sultan Malikul Adil.[2]

The 'historical nucleus' of this account can be traced to the commercial relations that existed between northern Sumatra and Malabar. In adopting Is-lam, Sumatra was admitted into the international Islamic trade network which dominated the entire Indian Ocean from the east African coast to the Philip-pines from the twelfth to the eighteenth century. Since Malabar is located on India's south coast, it was an important link in this network. The 'historical nucleus' of this story also includes the fact that the conversion to Islam was a clear conversion. Islam is not an disinterested religion which gradually, piece by piece, presses its way into another culture; it involves a whole 'package' of religious truths, duties and rituals which are either accepted or rejected in principle. Conversion to Islam therefore always implies a clear break with the past in both human lives and cultures, as this account clearly demonstrates.[3]

Sumatra's role as the principal Islamic centre was taken over by the neighbouring kingdom of Pasai in 1350. Both Malacca on Java's north coast and Patani in southern Thailand were converted to Islam by scholarly Mus-lims from Pasai. According to the *History of Patani*,[4] conversion began as a result of a skin disease the king, then still a Buddhist, had contracted. After all the physicians's attempts to cure him had failed, the king promised his daughter to the person who could cure him. A certain Shaikh Said from the Kampong of Pasai, where the Pasai tradesmen lived, came and offered to cure him, but declared: "It is not your daughter I wish as a reward but that you

---

[2] Situmorang and Teeuw, 1952, pp. 58-61.

[3] The fact that conversion to Islam is regarded as a clear break does not imply that the en-tire population would immediately live according to all the doctrines and fulfil all the duties. Certainly in the feudal areas of Java, where conversion was also very much determined by the rulers, the further introduction of Islam to this culture was done more gradually. Cf. especially M.C. Ricklefs, 1979.

[4] Cf. Teeuw and Wyatt, 1970-71.

embrace Islam." The king accepted this condition and recovered but then refused to become a Muslim. Shortly thereafter he fell ill again, however, and the Shaikh was once more summoned. He cured the king on the same condition as before but the king again reneged on his promise. When he fell ill for the third time, he vowed solemnly: "By all the idols I worship, I will become a Muslim when I recover." The king again recovered after twenty days and summoned all the chiefs of the kingdom and his people, at which time he professed the creed and ordered his subjects to do the same. At Shaikh Said's suggestion, it was then also decided that the king would assume an Islamic name and that pork would no longer be eaten in his kingdom. The *History of Patani* then adds: "But that was all that he was prepared to change of his pagan customs. The people of the port city became Muslims, but those living in the uncultivated, wilderness areas did not."[5] This story also depicts conversion to Islam as an abrupt break, even though the author does note that people continued with a number of practices in their daily lives which Islamic teaching did not condone.

The main source for the history of Java is the *Babad Tanah Jawi*.[6] Entirely in agreement with traditional Javanese practice, this work glosses over and de-emphasizes conflicts as much as possible. Islam gained its first adherents in cities on the north coast, which became the centres of several independent Islamic kingdoms that eventually destroyed the pre-Islamic inland kingdom of Majapihit. The struggle between Majapihit and Giri, an Islamic kingdom on the north coast, is told vividly. For example, it relates how the saintly priest-king of Giri was busy writing at the precise moment when the Majapahit army went into battle against the Muslims:

> He threw down the pen which he was using and prayed to God. When the pen was thrown down, it changed into a kris and began to attack on its own. It killed several Majapahit men and after the enemy's retreat, it returned and, stained with blood, lay in front of the ruler. When he saw the blood-stained kris, he prayed that his wrong deeds be forgiven.[7]

According to this history Raden Patah, the ruler of the Islamic port city of Demak, led the army that caused Majapahit's final ruin. Raden Patah was also a son of the last king of Majapahit, Brawijaya, and, when Raden Pateh arrived at the capital with his army, his father was waiting for him, wishing to see his son one last time: "Having seen his son, king Brawijaya ascended to

---

[5] Teeuw and Wyatt, 1970-71, I, pp. 71-75; Cf. Jones, 1979, as well.

[6] For a survey of recent research into this complex document and further literature cf. Ras, 1986, 1987. I have used the prose edition here, the so-called *Babad-Meinsma*, in Olthof, 1987.

[7] Olthof, 1987, p. 29.

heaven with the troops who had remained loyal to him."[8] The Javanese text uses the same Arabic term (*mi'raj*) to describe the king's ascension as is used to describe Mohammed's ascension to heaven. Thus this work indeed softens the conflict and clear separation between the religions, although it does not remove it entirely.[9]

As a final example of conversion accounts we will refer to a great work that is sometimes referred to as the 'Bible of Javanism', the encyclopedic poem *Serat Centini*, composed in the court of Surakarta in the early nineteenth century.[10] In this poem some *clerici vagi*, students of an Islamic school, are searching for their brother, Sajati ('the essential') and consequently make a trip across the whole of Java. During their search they encounter a hermit who was still an adherent of the "buddha-religion". The hermit is prepared to become a Muslim only if they can defeat him in a contest involving the secret arts and magic. He stacks a number of eggs on top of one another, but when the Muslims remove the bottom one the others remain in the air. The hermit then throws his head-covering into the air which flies away like a bird. The leader of the Muslims throws his cap into the air and when it falls back to the ground, the hermit's head-covering is inside. This contest of tricks continues for some time, after which the hermit hides in his temple bell, which one of the Muslims changes into powder. At that the hermit acquiesces, although on the remaining condition that a dead person be resuscitated. Only after this condition has been fulfilled does the hermit recite the creed and then immediately ascends to heaven (*mi'raj*).[11]

The four examples given here all indicate how conversion to Islam was regarded as a conversion to a different and distinct religion. This does not appear to be the case only in the slightly 'more orthodox' Malay texts but also in literary works such as the *Babad Tanah Jawi* and the *Serat Centini*. Frequently the religion that preceded Islam is not clearly indicated by name. The Malay texts mention only idol worship, while some Javanese texts only refer to the "Javanese religion" or "unbelief".[12]

---

[8] Olthof, 1987, p. 31.

[9] Cf. as well, in connection with this, Drewes' analysis, 1978, of one of the oldest sources for the history of Islam on Java. A clear distinction between Islam and Javanism is apparent in this fifteenth-century text. Cf. also Drewes, 1954, p. 3 on a sixteenth-century text that does not reflect anything specifically Javanese but "would apply to any Muslim country".

[10] Surveys of this work can be found in Pigeand, 1933, Soebardi, 1971, and especially in Berend, 1987. In reference to the first part of this poem I have used the Yayasan Centhini edition, published in Yogyakarta (1985).

[11] *Serat Centhini Latin*, I, pp. 138-141.

[12] Cf., for example, the text in Drewes, 1978, p. 37.

Christians in Malay and Javanese Texts before the 20th Century

As of 1511 Christians won a place for themselves in the East Indian world via the Portuguese fortress of Malacca. Remarkably, however, Malay and Javanese texts before the nineteenth century seldom mention Europeans and Christians. A slightly more extended treatment of Christianity can only be found in some writings of the Indian scholar Nuruddin ar-Raniri, who held a high post at the court of Achin from 1637-1644. Raniri was born in the trading colonies of Gujarat in northwest India, which contained a mixed population of Arabs and Indians. After a period of training which took him to Hadramant and Mecca, as well as other places, he began his career in the Malayan world, following in the footsteps of at least one other member of his family. During his time in Achin he led a fierce campaign against the mystic tradition represented by the writings of the poet Hamzah Fansuri and the theologian Shamsuddin as-Samatrani. Raniri, who had been appointed to the highest religious office in the sultanate, ordered their works burned and some of their adherents executed. In 1643 the mystics again gained influence and Raniri was forced to leave Achin in 1644.[13] This militant theologian was the author of a large number of works, among which was a king's manual, the *Bustanus-Salatin*, probably the longest work in Malay literature. Volume six contains an extensive discourse (no less than 260 handwritten pages) on 'holy war'. Raniri describes the warlike exploits of Muhammad and takes lessons from the accounts of Roman, Greek and Persian wars. Although the Portuguese had conquered the neighbouring kingdom of Malacca in 1511 and the Dutch captured Achin in 1641 (thus during Raniri's stay in Achin), Raniri makes no mention of any wars conducted by or against Christians.[14]

Elsewhere Raniri discusses ritual cleansing and indicates what may be used for such a purpose. Generally speaking, he states, one should use water, but if water is unavailable, paper may be used. In Raniri's opinion, paper on which the Rama narrative is printed can be so used since the story is pointless, anyway. As far as paper on which the Torah or the Gospel is printed is concerned, Raniri believes the Christian and Jewish scriptures to be forgeries and thus one may also calmly use it for cleansing after a visit to the toilet, "unless the name of God is written on it".[15]

Raniri writes more extensively concerning Christians in a work on the religions in the whole world, *Tibyan fi ma'rifati'l 'adyan*.[16] This work is com-

---

[13] Cf. Takeshi Ito, 1978, and al-Attas, 1986, among others.

[14] Abdul Salam Arief, 1988.

[15] Steenbrink, 1988.

[16] Voorhoeve, 1955.

posed in the tradition of religious studies and heresiology as developed in the Islamic world by Ash-Shahrastani as well as others. Raniri puts his own accent on these studies. His treatment of Hinduism betrays his own origins in the predominantly Hindu region of Gujarat: by tracing the word Brahman to Abraham, Hinduism becomes a "religion of the book" against which "holy war" is no longer required. In his discussion on Christianity Raniri relates a peculiar legend. After Jesus' death Christians began a terrible oppression of the Jews, with the result that many Jews were killed. A Jewish scholar (obviously Paul, although Raniri does not name him) pretended to want to become a Christian. He was accepted and managed to obtain an important position in the Christian community, until he eventually became their main teacher. He then summoned before him individually three of his best pupils, Malik, Masthur (Nestorius) and Ya'qub. He asked each of them, "Who is Jesus?" When they answered, "God's prophet, His messenger and Spirit," 'Paul' gave each a different interpretation of Jesus, all of which were heretical, with the message that this interpretation was indeed the real truth, but they were not to divulge this secret truth. After his death, a fierce conflict broke out among the three pupils so that the Christians became divided among themselves. The Jews were then able to fight back and forty thousand Christians were killed. As a result, Christians lost their dominant position.[17]

Raniri's accounts are not based on his own experience but reflect general Islamic traditions about Christians. We find a different Islamic tradition on Christians in works on the Islamic teaching concerning duties, which always contain a chapter on 'holy war' and in commentaries on the Koran, in which many passages that concern Christians are discussed. Our brief indication of such works is warranted here because these writings include the religious presuppositions that the Indonesians Muslims had already accepted before their first contact with Western Christianity.

At the end of the seventeenth century a certain Enci' Amin wrote a poem on the war between the Dutch and the Macassars (1666-1669). In this poem Amin praises the Sultan of Macassar as a holy and perfect human being, whereas he often describes the Dutch in theological and religious terminology as "infidels" or "devils".[18] Religious themes play a role in many other writings on the struggle between the Dutch and the Indonesians as well. Whoever died in the fight against the infidels would hardly notice the wounds: their effect would be the same "as if you are stung by a mosquito", in the words of the *Syair Perang Sabi*, a summons for holy war that originated in Achin in the late

---

[17] Cf. the text in Steenbrink, 1988, pp. 43-48.

[18] Cf. Skinner's edition, 1963, pp. 68-76 on the sultan and *passim* for the description of the Dutch.

nineteenth century.[19] These writings also describe how the heavenly nymphs, dressed only in thin veils, are waiting, ready to cover the martyrs' wounds with kisses. Indeed, they argue among themselves for the bodies of those who have been killed.[20]

More balanced accounts of Christians can be found in some works written by the interpreters whom the British employed. One Ahmad Rijaluddin travelled to Bengal in 1810 on behalf of the British government. In his report on Calcutta he hardly mentions any Muslims or mosques but does pay a great deal of attention to Hindu bathing places. He also describes a few Christian churches "where the christians honour the priest and "where they make a great deal of noise while saying their prayers."[21] One of Ahmad Rijaluddin's colleagues was the talented and versatile Munsyi Abdullah who served for some time as Sir Thomas Stanford Raffles' private secretary. In his autobiography, the first to appear in Malay literature, Abdullah offers an interesting description of the Singapore cathedral.[22]

The *Babad Suropati* contains a peculiar passage about the ethics of the Dutch. This work is the biography of the political adventurer Suropati, a man of Balinese descent who took part in the insurrections against the Dutch in western Java and eventually founded a kingdom in the far east of Java. One of the poems dealing with the story of his life emphasizes his noble birth and position by making him the Governor-General's adopted child, with whom the Governor-General's daughter falls in love. Islamic law prohibited such a relationship, but the girl argues: "The Dutch religion permits this kind of relationship even though you are my stepbrother, as long as we feel the same way. Let's go into this beautiful bedroom then and enjoy the pleasures of love."[23]

This literary account of Suropati's life includes a number of fictitious events which were the result of a rather fertile imagination. But if Malay literature displays imaginative excess in general, it is even more so the case in Javanese literature. A few experts in the field do assert that the power of

---

[19] Cf. Hasjmy, 1971, 1978.

[20] Cf. Woelders, 1975, p. 194 for a realistic and optimistic description of the holy war during the Palembang war of 1822.

[21] Skinner, 1982, pp. 127-129 and 135. In the description of Calcutta by another Malay interpreter employed by the British, Munsyi Abdullah, we do not find anything on churches but mainly descriptions of mosques; cf. Klinkert, 1889.

[22] Cf. *Hikajat Abdullah* (Jakarta, Djambatan: R.A. Datoek Besar and R. Roolvink, 1953), esp. pp. 379-403.

[23] Kumar, 1976, p. 300.

imagination in the creative process is generally uncontrolled.[24] An example of such unbridled imagination can be found in the *Serat Baron Sakender*, a Javanese poem that deals with the arrival of the Dutch in the Indies.[25] In a story replete with giants, hermits and deceptive magic spells, the author evokes the atmosphere of *The Arabian Nights* with its Bluebeards and abracadabras. The king of Spain and the twelve provinces of the Netherlands are placed within the dynastic line of Alexander the Great or Iskander Zulkarnain - as he is called in the Koran (Koran 18:83-98) - in the Islamic tradition. The author then ascribes the much deplored arrival of Java's new rulers, the Dutch, only partly to the Indonesians' failings and mainly to God's unvarying decree. The *Serat Baron Sakender* is undoubtedly a mythological story, but neither Islam nor Christianity figure in the final negative judgement on the Dutch: this story is too deeply rooted in the humanistic tradition of Javanism for that.

The image of the Dutch that emerges from most Indonesian writings of this period, varying as it did from neutral to quite negative, is often related to religious differences. This was not the only attitude, however, that was displayed: many Indonesians cooperated with the Dutch, were employed by them or dealt with them financially. Aside from periods of armed resistance and insurrection, the majority as well found ways in which they could live with the presence of the Dutch. We shall discuss in detail one nineteenth-century example, Sayid Uthman bin Yahya, a prominent theologian at Batavia and a member of the Arab community but nonetheless quite influential in the East Indian islamic community because of his Malay writings. We already met him briefly in chapter V as an adviser to K.F. Holle and L.W.C. van den Berg. They were not the only Dutchmen who readily worked together with him. Already in 1886, and thus even before his stay in the Indies, Snouck Hurgronje wrote quite positively about him:

> Those Muhammedans who are well versed in holy studies are never among the worst enemies of an unbelieving administration. On the contrary, the Islamic doctrine itself teaches them the precept that one should allow for the circumstances: if human reason cannot see any favourable results for Islam from a struggle against the infidels, then they consider the commencement of that struggle as a crime.[26]

---

[24] Amin Soedoro M.A., retired instructor in Javanese at the Universitas Gadjah Mada in Yogyakarta made this statement orally in 1987.

[25] Text and translation in Cohen Stuart, 1850; cf. also Pigeaud, 1927.

[26] Snouck Hurgronje, (1924), IV, I, p. 71.

More than two years later this scholarly Arab once more proved Hurgronje's assessment to be true by again attacking the Islamic brotherhoods as centres of irrational fanaticism. Sayid Uthman wrote a brief work, *Manhaj al-'isti-qamah fi'l din bi'l salamah*, shortly after the great insurrection at Cilegon in Western Java in which a number of adherents of such a brotherhood had killed some Europeans and Indonesians who had been cooperating with them. The counterattack by the Indian army cost the lives of nearly one hundred Muslims, but Sayid Uthman refused to see them as martyrs for a good cause: in his eyes, they were only victims of foolishness.[27]

In 1891 some pilgrims returned from Mecca with a curious letter which had already been circulated in the Islamic world. This letter had come, it was said, from the guard of Mohammed's grave in Medina. He had had a dream in which the prophet appeared to him and told him that the Almighty had complained that very few people, about seven per year (other versions mention either seventeen or seventy) were entering heaven. Allah had therefore decided that the Judgement Day would occur in the very near future and Mohammed had begged to be allowed to send a final exhortation to his followers to repent. This letter was that final exhortation. The circulation of such a *wasiat* ('final exhortation') by the prophet had given rise to an intensified religiosity several times before in the past and the colonial government regarded it with concern. The circulation of such a letter was therefore continually forbidden. The government also heavily subsidized the circulation of a booklet that Holle, on their behalf, had requested Sayid Uthman to write against this fraud (copies of the "final exhortation" were sold at a stiff price).[28]

The devout Sayid Uthman had once refused to pray in the house of a rich Arab who had a portrait of Queen Wilhelmina hanging on his wall, but this had more to do with his uncompromising aversion to portraits in general than an aversion to the colonial government as has occasionally been suggested. In a manual for religious courts his criticism of the government was mixed with quite liberal praise:

> We place our hopes therefore on the justice of the government of this country that does a great service to the Mohammedans by paying salaries to the chairmen of the priests' councils, so that they may return this service by choosing and members respectable people well versed in religious matters as chairmen.[29]

---

[27] Sayid Uthman Bin Yahya, *Manhaj al-'istiqamah fi'l din bi'l salamah*, pp. 16-22; Snouck Hurgronje, *Adviezen*, II, pp. 1511-1514; cf. also Sartono Kartodirdjo, 1966, pp. 160-161.

[28] Cf. ANRI, Geh. Bt. Dec. 7, 1891, no. 1.

[29] Quoted in Snouck Hurgronje, (1924), IV, I, p. 71.

In 1912 and 1913 the Governor-General and his principal advisers were positive and even enthusiastic about the growth and development of the nationalist movement, particularly about the rise of the *Sarekat Islam*. The government tried to stimulate and at the same time supervise the development of this movement. Idenburg and his main advisers in this matter, Hazeu and Rinkes, strongly supported the *Sarekat Islam* against criticism from Home Government circles as well as from conservative forces in the native Indonesian population. Sayid Uthman, then aged 91, went to the great inaugural meeting of the *Sarekat Islam* at Surakarta on March 23, 1913, probably on the suggestion of either Hazeu or Rinkes, in order to promote the new movement. He made a short speech which concluded with generous praise for the Dutch administration:

> Once again we consider it our duty to say thanks to the just Dutch colonial government which justly and dutifully enables us to perform our religious duties freely without any interference. Even more, they graciously help us to perform our religious duties by providing salaries to the religious judges, by cancelling regular court sessions in the month of fasting and by supporting the building of mosques, as well as by other kind deeds which we have mentioned in our writings and in our prayers.[30]

In Sayid Uthman, therefore, we see an orthodox Muslim who was able to feel a great respect for the freedom of religion, as he experienced it, and who also expressed this respect, even if stimulated to do so by a monthly allowance.

The 20th century: The Improvement of Education:
Rapprochement and Alienation

In the field of education, through the growth of the Dutch-Native School, the rise of so-called "ethical politics" at the beginning of the twentieth century brought primarily a better knowledge of Dutch. This better acquaintance with the Dutch language was also the cause of a certain softening of the Indonesian upper class' attitude toward Dutch culture. An effective example of such can be found in the letters of a Javanese princess, Kartini, to her Dutch penpal and a few other people.[31] Within those circles which advocated the study of Javanese culture some very warm relationships between Indonesians and Dutchmen occasionally developed, based on mutual admiration for the

---

[30] Two copies of this speech are available in the Hazeu archives, kept in the KITLV in Leiden.

[31] These letters have been published under the title, *Door duisternis tot licht; Gedachten over en voor het Javaansche volk van Raden Adjeng Kartini* (Through Darkness to Light: Reflections on and for the Javanese People by Raden Adjeng Kartini), (Semarang: Van Dorp, 1911 and later editions). See also Jacquet, 1987.

Javanese culture. A similar feeling of solidarity, going beyond the boundaries of nationality, is found among the activists for socialism. In religious matters, however, it was precisely this familiarity with the Dutch language that became the cause of additional tension. We have already seen examples of this previously in the conflict between Haji Agus Salim and Hendrik Kraemer and later in Muhammad Natsir's criticism of Father J.J. ten Berge (cf. chapter 6). It was not so much the traditional Muslims in the rural areas, only partly united in the *Nahdlatul Ulama*, who developed a new abhorrence of Christianity but especially the modernist Muslims who had been educated at modern schools in the cities and were often members of organizations such as the *Muhammadiyah*, the *Young Muslim Association* or the *Persatuan Islam*. This is not in itself so surprising because these Muslims were the ones who became aware of negative Christian opinions on Islam and also had the most intensive contact with Western culture.

Towards the end of the nineteenth century the entire Islamic world experienced the rise of a "renaissance" or reform movement. One of the principal figures of this movement was the Egyptian Muhammad 'Abduh (1849-1905),[32] who pleaded for a return to the original teachings of the Koran and the prophet and the removal of all the later additions of history. Aside from being a reformist, 'Abduh was also a modernist. He devoted a great deal of attention to the modernization of education as a reformer, among other things, of the mosque university of Al Azhar in Cairo. There he initiated a pro-Western policy by stimulating the knowledge of western languages and making room for the modern sciences, even in this bulwark of Islamic orthodoxy. In addition, he also founded a new type of apologetics by writing a critical work on the Christian Catholic and Protestant missionary activities.[33]

It is difficult to determine the precise extent of 'Abduh's influence within modern Indonesian Islam. Quite often the Indonesians themselves see his influence as more extensive than non-Indonesians do.[34] In any event, the combination of reformism and modernism with some lively apologetics against Christianity is clearly present in Indonesia as well. Ahmad Khatib Minangkabau (c. 1855-1916) is probably one of its first representatives. Khatib came of a wealthy family in western Sumatra and attended the so-called "*princesschool*" of Fort de Cock. He went to the holy city of Mecca afterwards for further study which he completed and lived there for the rest of his life. Kha-

---

[32] Hourani, 1962.

[33] Cf. Tibawi, 1972, pp. 8-72 on his work in education. His principal apologetic work is *Al-Islam wa'l Nasraniyyah ma'a'l'ilm madaniyyah* (Cairo: 1902).

[34] Cf. Hamka's oration on the occasion of his honourary degree at Al Azhar, January 21, 1958, published under the title *Pengaruh Muhammad 'Abduh di Indonesia*, (The Influence of Muh. 'Abduh in Indonesia), (Jakarta: Tintamas, 1958).

tib wrote a peculiar book on the calculation of inheritances according to Islamic law in which he introduced a Western form of long division into this holy science. He vehemently attacked the traditional law of succession (*adat*) in Minangkabau in western Sumatra,[35] which the Dutch authorities also supported. Snouck Hurgronje described this violent attack as "a polemical pamphlet prompted by unhealthy fanaticism, ambition and self-conceit."[36] In another work Ahmad Khatib discussed the belief in Mohammed's journey to heaven and in his introduction painted a depressing picture of

> the situation of our Malaysian brothers, who bear the name of Mohammedans, but who, even before they knew more of their own religion than the credal formula, associated with the white *kafirs*. The *kafirs* raised all sorts of doubts in them with regard to the Islamic religion, including doubt about our prophet's journey to heaven .... Know that my heart was moved with compassion for them when I learned about their situation, because they have thus become renegades who are excluded from the Islamic religion and it is not proper to hold the ritual service for them after their death; in this world they achieve nothing else but to become slaves to the white people, and in the next world they will end up in hell forever ....[37]

Although there is some question as to whether Ahmad Khatib was directly influenced by 'Abduh, the atmosphere of some of his writings do reflect the latter's. After a basic education at a school oriented to the West, Khatib, more so than 'Abduh, reacted to (aspects of) his education. This may also have been due to the conservative atmosphere of Mecca, where he spent the greater part of his life.

The *Muhammadiyah* society, founded at Yogyakarta in 1912, stood more definitely in the line of Islamic reform begun by 'Abduh. Through steady growth, a substantial extension of its own network of hospitals, clinics and schools ranging from kindergartens to universities, this society would claim a membership of more than three million in 1985. Although it is by no means the most revolutionary, *Muhammadiyah* is certainly the largest and most successful Islamic society in the twentieth century, even on an international scale.[38] Un-

---

[35] Ahmad Khatib Miningkabau, *Al-Manhaj al-masyru'* (Mekkah: al-Misriyyah, 1311H).

[36] Snouck Hurgronje, *Adviezen*, III, (1929). In considering Snouck's vehement reaction to Ahmad Khatib, one must also take into account the fact that Ahmad Khatib was involved in a 'battle of pamphlets' with Snouck's loyal associate, Sayid Uthman, concerning another issue - that of the legitimacy of a second Friday mosque in Palembang. Cf. *Adviezen*, I, pp. 823-845.

[37] The English translation here is a translation of Snouck Hurgronje's Dutch translation in *Adviezen*, III, pp. 1915-1916, which the author used in the Dutch version of this book. Translator's note.

[38] Alfian, 1969, Noer, 1978, Nakamura, 1976, Peacock, 1978a, 1978b.

der its founder and first leader, Ahmad Dahlan (1912-1923), the society maintained good relations with some Christians and any animosity that did exist was hardly worth comment. The society worked quietly, chiefly among its own members, and did not readily enter into politics. Under their second leader, K.H. Ibrahim (1923-1932) the external policy of the *Muhammadiyah*, especially towards political organizations, was influenced more by the youthful secretary, H. Fachruddin, who was at the same time a member of the executive of the political party *Sarekat Islam*. Socialist ideals, pan-Islamism and opposition to the growing influence of Christianity were important issues in guiding his actions. Fachruddin displayed this attitude clearly for the first time in 1925 when he protested the preferential treatment of the Protestant mission by the sultan of Yogyakarta and Resident L.F. Dingemans. Dingemans, a fervent supporter of Protestant missions[39], managed to persuade the sultan to cut back the subsidy for the *Muhammadiyah*'s orphanage in favour of a new subsidy for the sultanate's orphanage. At the same time the Christian Petronella Foundation was entrusted with its supervision. When the *Muhammadiyah* lodged a complaint with the sultan, the Resident charged the society with treason.[40] In a subsequent action that favoured Christianity the Resident backed down: he tried to postpone the celebration of Mohammed's birth, the most popular holiday in Yogyakarta, because it coincided with a Christian holiday. The sultan did not want to allow this and even complained directly to Governor-General Fock, who then ended Dingeman's colonial career by withdrawing his promise to nominate him as a member of the Council for the Indies.[41]

In the previous chapter we discussed the foundation of the *Young Muslim Association*, (JIB: *Jong Islamieten Bond*) in 1925 in connection with Hendrik Kraemer. Without any claim to a complete treatment of the society here, we do wish to bring a few important discussions and events from this association's history to the reader's attention. The *Young Muslim Association* recruited its members from students of secondary schools and advanced vocational schools. Later on members were also recruited from institutions of higher education such as the College of Law in Batavia and the technical college in Bandung. Here contacts between the Indonesians and the Dutch were on the highest level of education and training.

---

[39] Cf. the opinion of him entertained by his nephew, H.H. Dingemans, 1973, p. 15: "Of Mennonite background, and thus liberal enough, his religious impulses hardened during his years in Java into a Calvinism which showed elements of both intolerance and a missionary spirit."

[40] Alfian, 1969, pp. 340-341.

[41] Dingemans, 1973, p. 16.

The JIB was certainly not absolutely anti-Dutch or anti-Christian. The first volume of the association's magazine, *Het Licht*, contained a short article by Snouck Hurgronje which they included with approval.[42] During a later meeting their adviser, Agus Salim, at one time literally pulled away the curtain separating the boys' seats from the girls' and made a impassioned speech against the segregation of men and women at Islamic meetings as well as against the wearing of veils with an explicit reference to Snouck Hurgronje.[43] Members of the JIB generally did not know any Arabic, frequently showed contempt for the traditional Islamic education of the *pesantren* and read orientalist literature, while also often referring often to English publications circulated by the *Ahmadiyah* association. Their writings therefore sometimes contain quotations and excerpts from Western sources in which Mohammed is indiscriminately mentioned as the "author" of the Koran. The Jewish and Christian 'sources' of Islam are greatly emphasized, in which miracles are explained in a very rationalistic, liberal way.[44] At the JIB's first congress in the latter part of 1925 one of the people invited to address the congress was Rev. Pos on the subject of "The Vocation of Protestant Mission in the Indies". The consequent discussion included criticism of Protestant missions on the part of the JIB, but the response was not wholly negative.[45]

The JIB youth often endorsed their Dutch teachers but were sometimes critical as well, occasionally ending up defending Islam. In *Het Licht* examples of the negative view of Islam held by the Dutch are often given, particularly as they appear in history and geography texts used in the schools. They also took up national discussions such as the one related to the "Ten Berge Affair". This occurred more and more frequently when a former member of the JIB, Wiwoho, became a member of the People's Council in 1930 and there often voiced a typically Islamic opinion.

Discussions regarding love, marriage and sexuality were very popular among the members of the JIB. Free choice of partners, rejection of child marriages, romantic love, monogamy and a less convenient procedure of di-

---

[42] Snouck Hurgronje, "Het een en ander over de mystiek en den wijsgeer Ghazali," (A Few Ideas on Mysticism and the Philosopher Ghazali), *Het Licht* I (July, 1925): pp. 217-228. Snouck Hurgronje probably wrote this for the JIB - in any case, I have not been able to trace another reference for this short article.

[43] Agus Salim referred to Snouck Hurgronje's article, "Twee populaire dwalingen verbeterd" (Two Popular Errors Corrected) in *Verspreide Geschriften*, I, pp. 297-317. Cf. also Kasman Singodimedjo, "De positie van de vrouw in den Islam" (The Position of Women in Islam), *Het Licht* 3 (April, 1927): 32-35; (May, 1927): 50-53.

[44] Drs. Abrachman, lecturer at the IAIN, National Institute for Islamic Studies in Yogyakarta, is preparing a dissertation on this selective reading by the members of the JIB.

[45] Cf. *Het Licht* 2 (January-February, 1926) for a report on this congress.

138 DUTCH COLONIALISM AND INDONESIAN ISLAM

vorce were issues which they took up often. One may regard this as an acceptance of "Western" values. At the same time it was common for them to react to free social association between the sexes and all "its excesses" in which Westerners took part. We read, for example, in an comment made in 1931:

> The Western way of life, especially as regards intercourse between males and females, signifies in almost every respect a moral degeneration for our nation. At festive occasions and seaside resorts immorality is rampant. What goes on behind the scenes sometimes is beyond description. The *nikah* (Islamic marriage) abhors such an unchecked and extravagant life outside the home, since this may have disastrous consequences for the lives of married people.[46]

This comment is contained in the middle of an article on the "Evil of Divorce: The Divorce Epidemic," by which the author wanted to indicate his concern with the great number of divorces in western Java, which was quite large indeed. The author did not seek the underlying cause in his own cultural tradition where marriages were mostly arranged by parents, often at an early age, but blamed it on the contact with an unwholesome Western civilization.

In 1937, at the instigation of a few liberal Muslims, the colonial government was prepared to issue marriage regulations that also included the possibility of monogamous Islamic marriage. The JIB then protested vehemently but not because they favoured polygamy. To the contrary, they considered polygamy to be antiquated and old-fashioned. They protested because they viewed the bill as a Christian attack on the perfect doctrine of Islam which does permit polygamy in certain cases. The JIB member Jusuf Wibisono was one of those who wrote a book protesting the bill.[47] Apart from the English writings of the *Ahmadiyah* leader, Muhammad Ali, this work refers only to Western authors. Juynboll is his principal authority on Islamic law and Wibisono refers to a piece by Hendrik Kraemer for a description of the modernist Muslim Ameer Ali. Wibisono takes full advantage of European studies on prostitution to indicate the decline of Western morality and to prove the need for the traditional and legal outlet of polygamy. Nonetheless, one should view this defence of polygamy more as a defence of Islam than of polygamy.

The large variety of reactions that we have seen in this short chapter range from citation and adoption to resolute disregard, from approval to vigorous rejection and protest. In all these variations there is one constant theme: the

---

[46] An anonymous article entitled "Het echtscheidingskwaad, de hoedjan thalaq," (The Evil of Divorce: The Divorce Epidemic), *Het Licht* 6 (August 1931): 31.

[47] In 1980, after the Indonesian Parliament had finally accepted a similar arrangement in 1974, this book was reprinted. Jusuf Wibisono, *Monogamy atau Poligami, masalah sepanjang masa*, (Monogomy or Polygamy: A Neverending Problem) (Jakarta: Bulan Bintang, 1980). The first publication occurred in 1937.

constant division between two parties. In the case of rejection, everything of 'the Christians' or 'the West' is rejected, while in the case of acceptance, it virtually always involves only part of what "the other party' had to offer. A really successful encounter has never really occurred - certainly not between Christians and Muslims. The starting-point of each side made this impossible.

CHAPTER 8

Muslims and Christians
in Independent Indonesia 1945-2005

When this book was first published in a Dutch edition in 1991, post-colonial Indonesia was seen as an example of a harmonious and peaceful cohabitation of a minority of some 9% Christians amidst the world's largest Muslim majority country (in 2005 Muslims counted 87%, or some 205 million, out of 220 million citizens. At that time I had just finished seven years of teaching at the State Academy of Islamic Studies in Jakarta and Yogyakarta. In Jakarta I had lived with my family on the campus, amidst some 4000 Muslim students and 200 staff. Because of the green areas in the compound, it was one of the few places where children could safely ride their bicycles and many of the international schoolmates of my children came in the afternoon for a relaxed time in the campus. In Yogyakarta, a town dominated by tourism and universities, we lived in an upper middle class region with nearly all Muslims in our street, but also one Balinese Hindu family, an artist who trained small children for Hindu temple dances. A Jesuit monastery and church and a Javanese Protestant church were also close to our house. Until the early 1990s Indonesia looked like a wonderful example of religious harmony. Since then this has changed drastically and dramatically, culminating in numerous ethno-religious conflicts in the period 1996-2001. Therefore the second edition of this book requires a new concluding chapter. This chapter aims to give the general outline of this turbulent history in post-colonial Indonesia, as well as some more general interpretations.

1945-1955: Merdeka, Harmony of Religions as a Result
of the Struggle for Independence

Indonesian leaders declared independence on 17 August 1945, only two days after the capitulation of the Japanese army.[1] Under the leadership of the first president, Sukarno (no second name, he was president between 1945-1966), the constitution included a compromise between the promoters of a secular and those of an Islamic state. On 1 June 1945 Sukarno, as chairman of the preparatory committee for independence, proposed a Five-Pillar or *Pancasila* ideology as the basis for the future state. This ideology or state philosophy consisted of

---

[1] The following pages resume and elaborate ideas that have been described also in Karel Steenbrink, "Indonesian Politics and a Muslim Theology of Religions: 1965-1990," in: *Islam and Christian-Muslim Relations* 4 (1993): 223-46.

140

1) the belief in One Supreme Divinity; 2) humanism; 3) nationalism, seen as the national unity of Indonesia; 4) democracy; 5) social justice. On 22 June 1945 a nine-person committee proposed a text for the constitution of the new state, including in its preamble the "seven words" after the first pillar of Pancasila. These were (translated): "with the obligation for adherents of Islam to practise Islamic Law (*shariah*)." On 18 August 1945, one day after the declaration of independence, these seven words were deleted from the provisional constitution, as was the case also with the condition that the president of the state had to be a Muslim. This was done after protests from the Christian side. Christians had threatened that they would try to erect a state of their own in the eastern islands of the vast archipelago. Initially, the Christians also objected to the setting up of a ministry of religion, but on 3 January 1946 it was erected on the condition that it would also take care of some affairs of religions other than Islam alone.

During the first decade of the Indonesian Republic the Pancasila formula served as a binding factor between the many races that constitute the Indonesian nation. *Merdeka*, or freedom, was a more important idea. In the colonial bureaucracy as in the colonial army the Christians were over-represented. Some of them were afraid that after independence they would lose the privileges granted to them by the Dutch administration. In the Moluccas a rather large group of former native colonial soldiers rejected integration into the national republic and these soldiers were, by order of the former colonial power, deported to the Netherlands in 1950. More than 90% of these soldiers were Protestants, with a small number of Catholics and an even smaller number of Muslim soldiers who had promoted the Independent Moluccan Republic (*Republik Maluku Selatan* or RMS). In West Java and South Sulawesi more serious assaults against the new national state of Indonesia were carried out by Muslim separatists under the label of *Darul Islam*.

The majority of Christians and Muslims supported national unity under Sukarno's leadership. Because of their over-representation in the colonial army, many Protestant soldiers and officers were leaders in the fight against the Dutch during the period August 1945 until December 1949, when the Dutch finally recognised Indonesian independence. From 1949-1954 the outspoken Protestant Tahi Bonar Simatupang (1920-1990) was chief of staff of the armed forces in defence of the Republic of Indonesia. After being dismissed by Sukarno, he became the promoter of ecumenical cooperation in his country. On the Catholic side the bishop of Semarang, Albertus Soegijopranoto opted firmly in 1945 for the new independent state against the Dutch bishop of Jakarta, who was afraid for his small minority under an overwhelmingly Muslim rule.

1955-1965: Conflict and Disintegration;
Pancasila as a Symbol of Secularism and Tolerance towards Communism

In September 1955 the first general elections were held in Indonesia. During the preparation for these elections the conflict between the religious and ethnic groups intensified. The Nationalist Party of President Sukarno, PNI, became the largest, with 22.3% of the votes, followed by two Muslim parties: Masjumi 20.9% and Nahdlatul Ulama 18.4%. The Indonesian Communist Party gathered 16.4%. During the election campaign the idea of Pancasila did not play an important role.

The first elected parliament came together from 1956-1959 to discuss the final text of the constitution. The Muslim parties rejected Pancasila and asked that the state be established on an Islamic foundation. As a two-thirds majority was required for a constitution to be adopted, the debate in the assembly remained without final result and ended in a deadlock. In 1959 President Sukarno decided that the country (which had accepted a more decentralising constitution in 1950) would return to the original 1945 Constitution, with much power for the President and with Pancasila as the ideological basis of the state.

Between 1959 and 1965 Sukarno introduced a number of new ideological elements into political life, like the NASAKOM ideology, binding together Nationalism, *Agama* (religion), and Communism. Atheism had never been a strong element in the Indonesian Communist Party and therefore this party could also accept the rather vague first principle of Pancasila, confessing the common belief in the One, Supreme Divinity. The official ideology, not only of Pancasila but also *Nasakom* and more inventions by President Sukarno, was a compulsory subject in schools and offices under the name of Civics. The books on this subject are full of acronyms. Pancasila was only one of the major expressions of a permanently changing ideology. The religious character and the first principle of the Belief in the One Supreme Divinity were only seldom stressed in this period.

The Sukarno period was characterized by many separatist movements that nearly all had some religious connotation. Quite a few, however, were also of a mixed Muslim-Christian nature. This was the case with the PRRI-Permesta revolt, where local separatists of Sumatra and Sulawesi, both Christian and Muslim, conspired against the central government. Both religious groups were afraid of the ongoing influence of communism in Southeast Asia. With the examples of Vietnam, Laos and Cambodia so near and the civil war against communist guerrillas in Malaysia and the Philippines even closer, the threat of communism was not a phantasm. This made Muslim-Christian relations for the period rather good. Or, to say it in a less jubilant way, there were no major conflicts and incidents in this Sukarno period, other than the destructive strategy of the Darul Islam movement in West Java and South Sulawesi that destroyed a number of Christian villages. But these actions were not immediately seen as Christian-Muslim conflicts, but rather as local separatist protests against the central state.

1966-1978: Pancasila as the Condemnation of Communism;
The Islamic Interpretation and Acceptance of Pancasila

On 11 March 1966 General Suharto took over power from President Sukarno. This change of power was one of the consequences of the failure of a communist coup in September 1965. In a speech to Parliament on 16 August 1967 Suharto developed his new ideological language: this period should be called the New Order, with Pancasila and the 1945 Constitution as its most important foundations.

The Muslim and Christian communities welcomed this new emphasis on Pancasila as an important weapon against communism, atheism and secularism, a frequently mentioned and easily connected triad. Youth and student movements from both religions supported the new government of Suharto. From the beginning the New Order government also actively supported religious activities: religious lessons in government schools were intensified, the costs of new mosques were met by the government and a programme for the publication of holy books, not only the Koran and the Bible but also parts of Vedic scripture, was carried out. This was, however, not a complete break with the policy of the government of the Old Order: through the Ministry of Religion in the period before 1965 that government had also supported religion. The politics of the New Order therefore have to be considered as a shift in accent rather than as a complete change of policy.

Besides privileges, the religious and especially the Islamic communities, also experienced frustrations in this period. The Suharto government fully supported the religions in their doctrinal and liturgical functions but imposed heavy restrictions on their political role. In 1960 the greatest Islamic party, Masjumi, was banned by Sukarno for being too outspokenly anti-communist and for its support of the PRRI-Permesta revolt. In 1968 a new Islamic party was allowed, but not as a total revival of Masjumi and not under the old name. It was called Parmusi (*Partai Muslimin Indonesia*) and the most influential ex-Masjumi leaders were not permitted to take part in the Parmusi. In 1971 the chairmanship of the new party was taken over by two Muslim leaders, not very well grounded in party politics. These two men, Minister of Social Affairs H. Mintaredja and the lawyer Jaelani Naro, staged a coup within the party and received strong support from the government. Finally, in 1973, the four Islamic parties of Indonesia were obliged to unite into one new party, the United Party for Development (*Partai Persatuan Pembangunan*, PPP), with Mintaredja and Naro as the most influential leaders. It is within the framework of this government policy of strong interference in the religious communities and the manoeuvring of political life that the interreligious relations of this period should be understood.

An epoch-making event was the Makassar Riots of 1 October 1967. Muslim youth attacked several churches after rumours were spread that a Christian teacher had insulted Islam by stating that "Muhammad was only married to nine of his wives and lived in adultery with the others." Another issue that was at stake in this period was the construction of a grand church in front of the Great Mosque of Makassar, in the centre of the town, where, besides some Chinese traders, only a very few Christians lived. The national impact of what later was called the Makassar Affair of 1967 was great, although the immediate material damage of the attack on the churches was not too bad: only some furniture was damaged. On 30 November 1967 the government organised an interreligious consultation in Jakarta with the hope that the national leaders of Islam and Christianity should reach an agreement about this and some other affairs. At this meeting it proved that the communities had different goals. The primary goal of the Christians was freedom of religion with the right to carry out missionary work, and to establish visible signs of their presence through church buildings. Muslims proposed the mutual recognition of the communities with the firm promise not to engage in sheep-stealing. Missionary work should be restricted to those who "had not yet embraced one of the global religions." The 1967 interreligious consultation was a failure. The Minister of Religion, K.H.M. Dachlan, and President Suharto repeatedly blamed the Christians for not accepting the condition of not addressing Muslims for conversion to Christianity. The Muslim leader Anwar Haryono later commented that former army chief General T.B. Simatupang "fought like a lion in order to defend the missionary duty of the Christians."[2]

Like the colonial administration, the Suharto government developed an active policy of interreligious harmony, concentrating on preventing clashes by separating the communities. An important step in this direction was the decree by Minister of Religion Dachlan of 13 September 1969, on the construction of religious buildings. Paragraph 5 of this decree stated that the local government should act in cases of the "promotion of one's religion, spread of information, propaganda activities and religious speeches as well as religious buildings that would cause conflicts or discord." This was only the first in a long series that made it more and more difficult to build churches in Muslim regions or mosques in Christian areas. On 28 November 1975 this first regulation was followed by another instruction by the Ministry of Home Affairs stipulating that no private houses could be used as churches.[3]

In 1973 Parliament discussed a new marriage law. The first draft of the bill was quite liberal and invoked much protest from Muslims, who wanted to include regulations from Islamic law. Christians feared that the state would in this way promote the introduction of aspects of Islamic Law (*shariah*) for Muslim citizens. Finally, the result of the debate was a reinforcement for the Muslim religious courts and for the road towards a stricter implementation of Islamic rulings in the country. The law, accepted in Parliament on 22 December 1973 and signed by the president on 2 January 1974, did emphasize that

---

[2] For a description and more references, Karel Steenbrink, "Patterns of Muslim-Christian Dialogue in Indonesia, 1965-1998," in J. Waardenburg (ed.), *Muslim-Christian Perceptions of Dialogue Today* (Louvain: Peeters, 2000), p. 84; for this whole period see also Jan Aritonang, *Sejarah Perjumpaan Kristen dan Islam di Indonesia* (Jakarta: BPK Gunung Mulia, 2004), p. 391.

[3] This and many more regulations in Aritonang, *Sejarah Perjumpaan*, pp. 401-04.

marriages should always be based on the religion of the couple. It had no specific regulations for mixed marriages. After two decades of discussion, in the 1990s it was ruled nation-wide that no mixed marriages of Muslims and non-Muslims could be administered, not even at the civil administration. The Indonesian Council of Muslim Scholars (*Majelis Ulama Indonesia* MUI, erected in 1975) issued a *fatwa* or legal decision on 1 June 1980 that not only was a Muslim woman forbidden to marry a non-Muslim man, as was already a common opinion among Muslim scholars, but also that a Muslim man was forbidden to marry a non-Muslim woman. This last regulation is explicitly in contradiction to Koran 5:5: "Permitted to you are chaste women, be they either from among the believers or from those who have received the Book before you." This is a quite radical position, only to be explained by the growing fear in certain Muslim circles for Christian missionary activities or what was commonly called "Christianization."[4]

The first decade of the New Order government saw a tremendous increase in the influence of all of the major religions in Indonesia. As a result of the ban on communism, the massive killings of some 400,000 up to one million people suspected of communism or leftist sympathies in the period 1965-1966 and the internment for a shorter or very long period of another million, it was necessary to find an umbrella in Islam, Hinduism or Christianity.[5] This made the position of the 'big five' (Islam, Buddhism, Hinduism, Protestantism and Catholicism) much stronger in society. It became obligatory to accept formal membership in one of these religions. This caused a strong increase in the membership of Christian churches, especially on the island of Java, and caused reactions from the Muslim side, as already signalled above.

Former General Simatupang, who has been mentioned above already several times, occupied several ecumenical positions in the early 1970s. He was Secretary-General of the Indonesian Council of Churches and also a member of committees of the World Council of Churches (WCC). He proposed that the General Assembly of the WCC of 1975 should be held in Indonesia. Initially, he received permission from the Indonesian government. After protests by Muslims and the killing of an Anglican minister in Jakarta in July 1974, there was no longer support for this event, which was seen as a matter of Christian propaganda. The Assembly was thereupon relocated to Nairobi.

1978-1990: Further Depoliticization of Islam and the Birth of a Civil Religion

The late 1970s and the whole of the 1980s were the years of glory for Suharto's New Order. The economy was booming, prosperity seemed to reach a much

---

[4] Mohammad Atho Mudzhar, *Fatwa-Fatwa Majelis Ulama Indonesia* (Jakarta: INIS, 1993), pp. 84-93.

[5] Robert Cribb (ed.), *The Indonesian Killings: Studies from Java and Bali* (Layton Vic.: Monash University, Centre of Southeast Asian Studies, 1990).

broader middle class and there was a feeling of political stability under the tough leadership of the army. In this period the Suharto government promoted the Pancasila ideology more and more and even launched the idea of Pancasila as a civil religion. In 1978 the National Congress (a combination of the regular Parliament with members who came together only once in five years) accepted the so-called P4 Indoctrination Programme. P4 stands for *Pedoman Penghayatan dan Pengamalan Pancasila* or Guidelines for the Effectuation and Implementation of Pancasila, a course of 25-100 hours or one to four weeks, to be given to all government officials, students and many other groups within the country. Under the acronym BP7 in Jakarta a huge "laboratory for the development of the Pancasila doctrine" was started. Its leader, Ruslan Abdulgani, may perhaps be called the 'second founder' of Pancasila, of which we consider Sukarno the first founder. Pancasila should become the soul of the nation, creating religious harmony and preventing Muslims from establishing an Islamic state.

In 1985 Parliament accepted, after several years of hot debates, a new law that forced social and political organizations (including the Council of Churches, the Conference of Catholic Bishops, and also Muslim organizations like Muhammadiyah) to accept Pancasila as their "sole basis." In public life Pancasila became more and more important, through monthly or even weekly flag-celebrations, ceremonies on the 17th of every month in commemoration of Independence Day (17 August 1945) and similar rituals. Since 1975 all schools gave classes in PMP, *Pendidikan Moral Pancasila* or Pancasila Ethics. This development may be considered as the birth and growth of a new civil religion.

Some Christians, but many more Muslims, were not happy with this development, which was seen as a turn towards a state-guided pseudo-religion. In order to sooth Muslim parties, in 1978 the government issued two regulations, known as Decisions of the Minister of Religion no 70 and 77 of 1978. They forbade the public propaganda of any religion directed at adherents of another religion. This included the spread of pamphlets, leaflets, journals and books, visitation to houses, the sending of foreign religious personnel to Indonesia, except with special permits. For foreign subsidies to Indonesian religious institutions a special permit from the Ministry of Religion should be sought. The regulations caused many protests from Christians. In practise, however, not much was done with the regulations and especially the transfer of money was never effectively controlled.

In 1981 the Council of Muslim Scholars, MUI, issued a *fatwa* prohibiting Muslims from participating in Christmas celebrations. The reason for this decision was that the Council had received complaints about Muslim pupils in Christian schools who were urged to appear in pageants and to act as Joseph or Mary or as an angel in Christmas plays. Others complained that they had to sing Christmas carols at school or at Christmas meetings in private or government offices. To Muslims who protested this practice it was often answered that the harmony of religions would be endangered if they refused participation. Many

Muslim school pupils dared not refuse to join for fear of repercussions during their examinations.

The Minister of Religion, Haji Alamsyah, accused the chairman of the MUI of acting against the state ideology of Pancasila, while the latter accused the government of interference with religion and of attempts to introduce Pancasila as a new religion of the state. During most of the years to follow, the Muslim President and many of his ministers appeared at solemn celebrations of Christmas in the largest sports stadium in the country, in Senayan, Jakarta, broadcast nation-wide on television. The issue remained a point of debate between Muslims and Christians.[6]

In the New Order government there were three prominent persons who served as Minister of Religion. The first was Dr. Haji Abdul Mukti Ali (1923-2004), a scholar, graduate of the McGill Institute of Islamic Studies in Montreal. He hoped for interreligious cooperation for the sake of the development of the nation. He admired Max Weber and his theory of the relation between the spirit of Protestantism and the rise of capitalism. He hoped that Indonesian Islam would modernize and become the motor for a new, modern and dynamic country. In this sense the harmony of the religions would be fostered. He was Minister of Religion between 1971-1978. His successor was a retired army general, Alamsyah Ratu Perwiranegara (for the period 1978-1983) who used to talk about countries like Ireland and Lebanon, where religious pluralism was a very negative factor. He started a threefold programme of religious harmony: 1) internal harmony among various factions within the religions; 2) harmony between the various religions; 3) harmony between the religions and the government. In these three fields he started a series of encounters, where representatives of groups were invited to talk and work together. Interreligious dialogue was, in this period and later, very much a top-down affair, organized by the government and with the primary goal of preventing conflicts, supporting the political programme of economic development, under the firm and strict guidance of the national government.

For the period 1983-1993 it was the career diplomat Munawir Syadzali M.A. (who held a masters' degree in Political Science from Georgetown University) who led the Ministry. In his policy Munawir Syadzali paid less attention than his predecessors to interreligious relations. He also diminished the attention given to the relation between religion and development. His prime goal was the internal growth of the Muslim community through the improvement of the religious administration, especially the religious courts, and religious education. His policy was not reactionary, on the contrary. He sent several hundred men and women of the academic staff of his Ministry and of the theological Islamic academies abroad for study, mostly to Western countries like the Netherlands, USA and Canada (McGill University). He organized many continuing education courses for Islamic judges, but also increased the number

---

[6] Atho Mudzhar, *Fatwa-fatwa Majelis Ulama Indonesia*, pp. 101-06.

of women judges in religious *shariah* courts. Notwithstanding strong opposition from Christians, as well as the more secularized Muslims, in 1989 Parliament passed a new bill on religious courts, strengthening the basis of this institution. The process leading towards the law on the Islamic religious courts was accompanied by many discussions. Christians feared that the reinforcement of these *shariah* courts would lead to an introduction of more elements of Islamic law into public life in their country. They questioned the procedures that gave a special and privileged position to the religious rules of one religious community alone. Together with the compilation of Islamic Law in Indonesia, which started in the late 1980s, this was an indication that a firmer Islamic spirit was rising in broad circles in the country.

1991-2005: Indonesian Manifestations of Radical Islam

President Suharto, until 1990 a nominal Muslim who kept his distance from radical Muslims, decided to make the *haj* pilgrimage to Mecca in 1991. In that same year he consented to the establishment of ICMI, the *Ikatan Cendekiawan Muslim Indonesia* as the Indonesian Organization of Muslim Intellectuals. It provided him with a more solid basis of power than the Pancasila ideology that had become more and more identified with corruption and hypocrisy.

A sign of growing tensions between Muslims and Christians was the so-called Monitor affair. *Monitor* was a popular tabloid published in Jakarta, with the Protestant Arswendo Atmowiloto as its editor. On 15 October 1990 the tabloid published the result of an inquiry about "the 50 most respected persons among our readers." President Suharto was given the top position, while on this list other politicians, movie stars and singers held the positions 1-9 (with Saddam Hussein ranking as no. 7, the only non-Indonesian in the first section of this list). Position no 10 was for *Monitor* editor Atmowiloto himself and no. 11 was for the Prophet Muhammad. Muslim leaders questioned the validity of the process that had produced this list and issued strong statements in the press and in several mosques. The moderate Muslim leader and politician Abdurrahman Wahid (later president from 1999-2001), always good for a controversial opinion, remarked that Muslim leaders too easily sought political gain in this affair. In short time, however, the affair escalated. The Minister of Information, Harmoko (himself ranking no 9 on the list), banned the tabloid on 23 October 1990, Arswendo went to jail on 25 October and had to serve 5 years in prison before he could resume his previous activities. In the whole affair an important issue was that the tabloid was owned by the Catholic publishing company Gramedia, which also published the country's most prestigious newspaper *Kompas*. Although Jesus was never included in the list of the most admired persons of the tabloid's readership, the low ranking for Muhammad was already enough for the upheaval.

In May 1992, amidst the campaigns for the national elections, seven churches in the solidly Muslim province of East Java were burned, five of them in strongly Muslim Pasuruan. This was later seen as the beginning of a longer series of burnings and the (often partial) destruction of churches and other religious buildings that led, on 9 June 1996, with a series of attacks on ten churches in Surabaya. a strange series of events led to the destruction by fire of twenty-one churches and schools in Situbondo on 10 October 1996 , while an orphanage was also burned down and several more churches in the neighbourhood of this East Javanese town were damaged. The start of this affair was the court case of a certain Saleh, a young Muslim student at one of the huge Islamic boarding schools in the region but apparently somewhat insane. Saleh had declared that Muhammad was not a prophet. Therefore, he was tried and condemned to five years of internment, instead of the death penalty as requested by a number of hard-line Muslims. Thereupon a mob started a devastating tour of Christian buildings in the town, allegedly instigated by army personnel who were angry about East Timorese 'Catholic' attacks on mosques in Dili in mid-1995. The mosques in Dili had been seen as the symbol of Indonesian or 'Javanese rule' over the new 27th province of Indonesia that would be separated from the country in 1999 (only 24 years after being incorporated (1975)).

On Christmas 1996 several churches in West Java were subject to arson, especially in the Garut region. Some interpretations of these latter clashes accuse the army intelligence for these attacks: they were seen as masterminded by special forces in order to denounce the Muslim opposition leader Abdurrahman Wahid (who was to be elected President in October 1999) for these acts of violence. As in Situbondo, angry mobs attacked police offices and buildings of the court of justice but were most efficient in damaging churches. By blaming common Muslims for these attacks, their leader could also become suspect and more power could be given to the police and army to control religion.

Amidst growing political unrest and economic chaos President Suharto had to step down on 22 May 1998. He was succeeded by the former vice-president, Baharuddin Yusuf Habibie, who announced free elections for mid-1999.

From mid-November 1998 onwards many pamphlets were spread in Ambon, containing mutual slander of Christianity and Islam by the other parties with the threat that the time for a final battle and cleansing would come soon. On 14 November 1998 serious conflicts broke out between Christians of Hative Besar and their Muslim neighbours of Wailete, just across the town of Ambon in the bay, dividing Ambon more or less into Christian southern and Muslim northern halves.

On 22 November 1998 a Jakarta-based gang that controlled parking, shops as well as some gambling houses in Ketapang, North Jakarta, led by the 'Christians' Milton Matuanakota and Ongky Pieters, lost a battle against a Muslim gang, also from the Moluccan community in Jakarta, led by Ongen Sangaji: members of the *Pemuda Pancasila* and of the *Mahasiswa Muslim Maluku* (Moluccan Muslim Students), who were often hired by General Wiranto to fight anti-Habibie students in November 1998. Several hundred of the 'Christian group' returned to Ambon. Their opponents feared that they would take revenge in that region.

On Sunday 29 November 1998 a demonstration in Kupang, West Timor, by Christian youths ended in attacks on several mosques in that city and scores of houses in a district inhabited by Muslim fishermen were burned (in Oesapa). On 4

December, after the Friday service, a mob of Muslims set fire to a Catholic church in Ujung Pandang (now again known as Makassar) in South Sulawesi, allegedly in answer to the attacks on mosques in Kupang.

19 January 1999 was the start of the first period of cruel and bloody conflicts in Ambon. Many Muslims saw it as "an attack on Muslims, who were celebrating the end of Ramadan." The riots started with a Christian *preman* or undisciplined youth who did not pay a ticket for a car hired from a Muslim driver or owner. Immediately after the fight between these two, some central districts of Ambon were full of rumours "that now the great war between Christians and Muslims had started." Shops were pillaged and houses burnt.

This is not the place to give a detailed description of the many local conflicts between Muslims and Christians of Indonesia that occurred in the years between 1992 and 2002.[7] Most of the conflicts were restricted to local problems and politics only, but quite a few also had an effect on national politics. Some patterns can be seen:

1) Quite a few conflicts were caused by recent transmigrations. This was the case with the BBM, the Buginese, Butonese and Makassarese from South Sulawesi who had migrated to Ambon from the 1950s on and had disturbed the balance between Muslims and Christians in the capital of the Moluccas. These people had taken the lowest jobs in Ambon and had thus become a threat to the unemployed of Ambon, especially when the economy deteriorated after mid-1997. Much more serious was the migration of Madurese to West and South Kalimantan. They came into conflict with the mostly Christian Dayak but also with fellow Muslim Malay people. The Madurese were sent to 'empty districts' where areas of land were not used, at least according to the local bureaucracy. In fact, they occupied land that was used by Dayak people for shifting cultivation every ten to twenty years. Due to the arrival of these migrants but even more because of the deforestation by the great new palm oil plantations, even in this sparsely populated island fertile land became difficult to find.

2) Several of the conflicts were related to local or national elections. In April 2000 a very atrocious cycle of violence started in Poso, a coastal town in Central Sulawesi. There had previously been limited conflicts. In December 1998 a Christian school and several churches were burnt down, but in 1999 reconciliation was the major concern. From mid-2000 onwards many Christians from the inland village of Tentena joined the fighting, where also Muslims from the Central Sulawesi town of Palu were active. The cause of the problem was the election of the

---

[7] More elaborate overviews can be found in Kees van Dijk, *A Country in Despair: Indonesia between 1997 and 2000* (Leiden: KITLV, 2001); Freek Colombijn and J. Thomas Lindblad (eds.), *Roots of Violence in Indonesia* (Leiden: KITLV, 2002); Murni Djamal (ed.), *Communal Conflicts in Contemporary Indonesia* (Jakarta: Language and Culture Centre of the Syarif Hidayatullah Islamic University, 2002).

district head (*bupati*) in December 1998, where neither the Christian Herman Parimo nor his major Muslim rival, Arif Patangga, were successful. The Christians who came to fight here wore black clothes, like *ninjas*, but had put red cloths on their heads, since red was also the 'Christian colour' (over against 'Muslim white') in the Moluccas. The fighting in the last weeks of May and early June 1999 took at least 120 lives (during the election campaigns), with many houses burnt down. The basic reason for the conflict seems to be that there was a gentlemen's agreement that in this region, after a period with a Muslim as head of the district, a Christian would be elected, because the coastal northern region is Muslim, while the mountainous inland region has a majority Christian population. This rule was not observed in late 1998 because the *bupati* wanted to his own son to succeed him. This was the beginning of a clash that continued in 2005.

In Ambon there was an increase of local conflicts during the period preceding the elections of 7 June 1999. The Moluccas were the strongest province for Mrs. Megawati Sukarnoputri, the main opposition candidate running against the ruling president B.J. Habibie. The first goal of this violence (a new outburst after the start of January 1999 had calmed down somewhat in March and April 1999) was to destabilise this opposition stronghold. The Moluccas account for only for 0.7% of the total population of the nation. If we look at the national impact of the Moluccan tragedy, we have to take this small percentage into consideration. Finally, the Moluccas are not that important for national politics, but problems in that region could weaken the position of the central government.

3) Social factors certainly play a role in interreligious conflicts and may be translated into religious terminology. In Ambon the Christians traditionally held strong positions in the bureaucracy, because during the colonial period (until 1950) it was the Christian 50% who received better education and therefore were appointed teachers and government officials rather than the 'other half' of the Moluccas, the Muslim 50% (approximately). The animosity between Muslims and Christians was certainly more heated due to this imbalance in the bureaucracy. The Muslim governor, Akib Latuconsina, appointed in 1992 as the first local Muslim governor of the Moluccas, implemented a strong and consistent policy of appointing Muslims to most vacancies in order to restore the imbalance.

It was not only in the bureaucracy that there was a rivalry. In Jakarta many of the gambling houses and a major part of prostitution were controlled by the Moluccan mafia, divided into 'Christian' and a 'Muslim' families as already mentioned above. In November 1998 there was a war in the gambling and prostitution area of Jakarta, Ketapang, where the 'Muslim mafia' could chase away their 'Christian' rivals. It was exactly the return of some 300 defeated youngsters from Jakarta in December 1998 that caused the rumours about a coming war between Muslims and Christian that started on 19 January 1999 in Ambon.

4) There are some vigorously expressed 'religious' arguments in the complicated web of Christian-Muslim clashes of the late 1990s and the beginning of the 21st century in Indonesia. The most discussed is the theory of 'Christianization.'

Christians were said to have a master plan to conquer or at least destabilize Indonesia, starting from the east. The first step in this strategy was the separation of East Timor from Indonesia through the disastrous referendum of 30 August 1999, under the auspices of the United Nations. The next step would be support for the separatist OPM, *Organisasi Papua Merdeka* that was fighting for an independent West Papua. Virtually all members of OPM were Christians.

On Christmas 1999 several Christian villages of North Halmahera attacked their Muslim neighbours in a war that has been called "fire without smoke," meaning that this 'pre-emptive strike' was based on rumours that were not founded on fact.[8] The Christian-Muslim strife in Ambon and other places was, since the 'bloody Christmas' of 1999, also put in the perspective of the worldwide rivalry between Islam and Christianity. Seemingly emerging from nothing, a new Muslim militia, *Laskar Jihad*, organized a meeting for about 100,000 protesters against the Halmahera killings in the Senayan stadium in Jakarta on 6 April 2000.

After this major protest some 2000 *Laskar Jihad* members went to a training camp in Bogor, 80 kilometers south of Jakarta. Shops on major streets in Jakarta, Yogyakarta and Surabaya offered the opportunity to sign contracts for joining the *Laskar Jihad*. On 17 April 2000 the training camp moved to Kaliurang, a mountain resort north of Yogyakarta in Central Java. During the next two weeks several thousand *Laskar Jihad* members went to the Moluccas. The Minister of Religion asked the police to disband this militia, "which he said had questionable intentions as Maluku had entered a reconciliation and rehabilitation stage." Javanese military and police commanders declared later that they could not stop the *Laskar Jihad* members from entering ships going to the Moluccas "because they were not carrying any weapons." The official position of the *Laskar Jihad* leaders was that their members went to "help Muslims in the islands with holy books, not swords and machetes." *Laskar Jihad* carried out a devastating series of attacks in the Moluccas. In June 2000 most of the Christian sections of the town of Ambon, including the State University (Pattimura University) and the Christian University were totally destroyed. Apparently, they received military support from generals in the army who were afraid that the combination of Christianity and separatism would destroy the unity of the country. Only after the Bali bombing of 12 October 2002 did *Laskar Jihad* disband.

5) The motivations discussed above can be summarised as protests against the West and against efforts for the Christianization of Indonesia. There are also radical Muslim actions in favour of a stronger Islamic character for the country. This is partly seen in the call for the introduction of the Islamic law or *shari'a*. After the fall of President Suharto there was a strong plea for decentralization, regional autonomy and diversity. Muslim political leaders in stronger Islamic regions (West Java, especially the new province of Banten, West Sumatra, and the province of Aceh in North Sumatra) translated this as a new call for the introduction of Islamic

---

[8] Patricia Spyer, "Fire without Smoke and Other Phantoms of Ambon's Violence: Media Effects, Agency, and the Work of Imagination," *Indonesia* 74 (October 2002): 21-36.

law. This was implemented most firmly in Aceh beginning in 2001. Critics say that the central government found it much cheaper to grant the rebellious province of Aceh the right to implement Islamic law than to give it a just remuneration for the oil and gas that contributed so much to the national treasury. Therefore, the link with the national rise of religious sentiments should be scrutinized as well.

This Islamic fervour also gave rise to a number of radical and militant Muslim groups who attacked nightclubs, restaurants serving alcohol or were open in the month of Ramadan. Critics claim that their methods looked like those of gangsters: if restaurants paid enough money they would be 'spared' if they were not too open about their activities to the outside world. Thus, even in this case there was a mixture of religious enthusiasm and common crime and greed.[9]

Conclusion

We started this book with four chapters that described a supposed and even strengthened gap between the religions in the colonial period. Differences in doctrine were emphasized; marriages between religions were forbidden. One could describe the situation in various regions during the colonial period as one of *apartheid*. The legal development since the 1970s also led in this direction, as a continuation of this policy. We have seen above how in 1974 a new marriage law started a development that finally formulated a formal ban on religiously mixed marriages. In 1981 the common celebration of Christmas and other religious holidays was forbidden. There were even government decrees forbidding people from attending any ceremony of another religion, including the marriage and burial ceremonies of friends who were members of different religions. The new law on education of 2003 stipulated that children have to follow obligatory religious classes in their own religion. So, it was no longer possible that Muslim children in Christian schools could follow Christian religious classes. The new personal law of that same year regulated that adoption is only possible along identical religious lines. These are all regulations that should prevent religious conflicts. They certainly do not stimulate frequent interreligious contacts.

Whatever we should think about the genuine religious motivations of the many different developments described in this chapter, they all have been directed towards a more tense relationship between the religious communities. There were numerous Muslim and Christian initiatives to strengthen the interreligious harmony that dominated the first four decades of the Indonesian Republic between 1945-1990. Moderate religious leaders of goodwill were quite powerless in an atmosphere of growing tensions and violence. The colonial legacy partly continued and partly changed drastically in independent Indonesia.

A continuation of colonial policy was the difficult relationship between religion and politics. The official strategy was the separation of the two, or more precisely

---

[9] For the rise of radical Muslim groups see Jamhari, "Mapping Radical Islam in Indonesia," *Studia Islamika* 10/3 (2003): 1-28 and Jajang Jahroni, "Defending the Majesty of Islam: Indonesia's Front Pembela Islam," *Studia Islamika* 11/2 (2004): 187-253.

the domination of religion by politics. Religion was not supposed to play a role in politics. But it continued to be a major concern for political leaders. Religious leaders tried to control, to manipulate and to use religion. From the Muslim side, religious leaders tried to make Islam more and more visible in society. Christians hoped for more opportunities for individual conversions. In the dynamics of Indonesian society for the whole period, the relations between the Muslim majority and the 9% Christian minority remained the most important and deciding factor.

Bibliography

[A number of books and articles that are mentioned only once in the footnotes are not included in this bibliography]

Abbreviations:

ANRI = Arsip National Republik Indonesia, Jakarta.
ARA = Algemeen Rijksarchief (National Archives) The Hague
BM = Bijdragen tot de Taal-, Land- en Volkenkunde van Nederlandsch Indië ('s-Gravenhage and Leiden)
Bt. = Besluit van de Gouverneur-Generaal (Decision of the Governor-General, ANRI)
MGS = Missive van de Gouvernements-Secretaris (ANRI)
MNZG = Mededeelingen vanwege het Nederlandsche Zendelinggenootschap
Mr = Mailrapport (ARA)
TBG = *Tijdschrift voor Indische Taal ; Land- en Volkenkunde,* published by the Batavian Society for Arts and Sciences

Abdurrachman, 1986
"Jong Islamieten Bond: 1925-1942." *Organisasi Kaum Muda Islam di Jawa pada Masa Akhir Penjajahan Belanda.* Ed. H. Syamsuddin Abdullab. Yogyakarta: LAIN Susan Kalijaga.
Abdus Salam Arief, 1988
Nuruddin al-Raniry Bustanu-lsalatin Bab VI fasal 2. Master's Thesis. Yogyakarta: LAIN Susan Kalijaga.
Adriani, N., 1931
Verzamelde Geschriften. Haarlem: Bohn.
Alatas, Syed Hussein, 1977
The Myth of the Lazy Native. London: Frank Cass.
Al-Attas, Syed Muhammad Naquib, 1986
A Commentary on the Hujjat al-Siddiq of Nur al-Din al-Raniri. Kuala Lumpur: Ministry of Culture of Malaysia.
Alfian, 1969
Islamic Modernism in Indonesian Politics: The Muhammadiyah Movement During the Dutch Colonial Period (1912-1942). Madison: Univ. Microfilms.
Algadri, H., 1964
Politik Belanda terhadap Islam dan Keturunan Arab. Jakarta: Sinar Harapan.
Andrea, lohannes, 1646
Confusio Sectae Mahometanae. Tr. into Latin by Iohannes Lauterbach, with a preface by G. Voetius. Traiecti ad Rhenum.

Arasaratnam, S., 1976
"De VOC in Ceylon en Coromandel in de 17de en 18de eeuw." *De VOC in Azie.* Ed. M.A.P Meilink-Roelofs. Bussum: Uniebock. Pp. 14-63.
-------, 1978
F. Valentijn's Description of Cape of the Good Hope. Hakluyt Society Series II, Vol. 149. London: Hakluyt Society.
Aritonang, Jan, 2004
Sejarah Perjumpaan Kristen dan Islam di Indonesia. Jakarta: BPK Gunung Mulia.
Atho Mudzhar, Mohammad, 1993
Fatwa-Fatwa Majelis Ulama Indonesia. Jakarta: INIS.

Baldaeus, P., 1917 (rpt.)
Afgoderye der Oost-Indische Heydenen. Ed. AJ. de Jong. 's-Gravenhage: Martinus Nijhoff.
Bank, J., 1983
Katholieken en de Indonesische Revolutie. Baarn: Ambo.
Bachtiar, Hasrja W., 1978
"Raden Saleh: Aristocrat, Painter and Scientist." *Papers of the Dutch-Indonesian Historical Conference.* Leiden: BIS.
Behrend, T.E., 1987
The Serat Jatiswara: Structure and Change in a Javanese Poem, 1600-1930. Diss. Canbera: ANU.
Benda, H.J., 1958
The Crescent and the Rising Sun. The Hague: Van Hoeve.
Bigalke, T., 1984
"Government and Mission in the Torajan World of Makale-Rantepao." *Indonesia* 38:85-112.
Bilderdijk, W., 1795 (1806 rpt.)
Treurzang van Ibn Doreid in Neerdititsche dichtmaat overgebracht. 's-Gravenhage.
Bitterli, Urs, 1986
Alte Welt - neue Welt. Formen des europaisch-uberseeischen Kulturkontakts vom 15. bis zum 18. Jahrhunden. Munich: C.H. Beck.
Blumberger, J.T. Petrus, 1931
De nationalistische beweging in Nederlandsch Indië. Haarlem: Tjeenk Willink.
Boland, B.J., 1971
The Struggle of Islam in Modem Indonesia. The Hague: Martinus Nijhoff.
------- and **I. Farjon,** 1983
Islam in Indonesia: A Bibliographical Survey 1600-1942 with Post-1945 Addenda. Leiden: KITLV.
Boon, P., 1987
Een Westfriese zeeman als slaaf in Barbarije. Verslag van de belevenissen van Jan Comelisz Dekker in Marokko, 1715-1743. Schoorl: Pirola.

Brugman, J. and F. **Schroder,** 1979
Arabic Studies in the Netherlands. Leiden: Brill.
Brugmans, LJ., 1938
Geschiedenis van het onderwijs in Nederlandsch-Indië. Groningen: Wolters.
Bijlefeld, W.A., 1959
De islam als na-christelijke religie. The Hague: Van Keulen.

Camps, A., 1990
Het derde oog. Van een theologie in Azie naar een Aziatische theologie. Farewell Lecture. Nijmegen: Catholic University of Nijmegen.
Castles, L., 1972
The Political Life of a Sumatran Residency: Tapanuli 1915-1940. Diss. New Haven, CT: Yale University.
Chaudhuri, K.N., 1985
Trade and Civilisation in the Indian Ocean: An Economic History from the Rise of Islam to 1750. Cambridge: Cambridge University Press.
Colenbrander, H.T., 1919-1934
Jan Pietersz. Coen, Bescheiden omtrent zijn bedrijf in India. Vol. I-VI. 's Gravenhage: Martinus Nijhoff.
Colombijn, Freek and **J. Thomas Lindblad (eds.),** 2002
Roots of Violence in Indonesia. Leiden: KITLV.
Coolhaas, W.P., 1943-1944
"Over karakter en daden van J.Pz. Coen." *Bijdragen voor Vaderlandsche Geschiedenis en Oudheidkunde.* VIII 4:201-37; VIII 5:60-74.
-------, 1980
A Critical Survey of Studies on Dutch Colonial History. 2nd ed. Ed. GJ. Schutte. The Hague: Martinus Nijhoff.
"Corpus Diplomaticum Neerlando-Indicum: 1907-1955." *Verzameling van politieke contracten en verdere verdragen door de Nederlanders in het Oosten gesloten.* Ed. J.E. Heeres. 's-Gravenhage: KITLV.
Cribb, Robert (ed.), 1990
The Indonesian Killings: Studies from Java and Bali. Layton Vic.: Monash University, Centre of Southeast Asian Studies.

Daniel, Norman, 1960 (1980 rpt.)
Islam and the West: The Making of an Image. Edinburgh: Edinburgh University Press.
-------, 1966
Islam, Europe and Empire. Edinburgh: Edinburgh University Press.
Das Gupta, A., 1976
"De VOC en Suratte in de 17de en 18de eeuw." *De VOC in Azie.* Ed. M.A.P. Meilink-Roelofs. Bussum: Unieboek. Pp. 64-84.
"De VOC en de Malabarkust in de 18de eeuw." *De VOC in Azie.* Ed. M.A.P. Meilink-Roelofs. Bussum: Unieboek. Pp.100-06.

De Bruijn, J. and G. Puchinger, 1985
Briefwisseling Kuyper-Idenburg. Franeker: Wever.

De Graaf, H.J., 1978
"De Regenten van Semarang ten tijde van de VOC, 1682-1809." *BKI* 134: 296-309.

-------, 1956
De Vijf Gezantschapsreizen van Rijklof van Goens. 's-Gravenhage: Martinus Nijhoff.

De Graaff, N., 1930
Reisen. Ed. J.C.M. Warnsinck. Linschoten Vereniging 33. 's-Gravenhage: Linschoten Vereniging.

De Groot, H., 1844
Bewijs van de ware godsdienst, met overige Nederduitsche Gedichten. Ed. Jeronimo de Vries. Amsterdam.

De Hoop, L., 1984
Ethicus in een Koloniaal Conflict. Een studie naar G.AJ. Hazeu in de onderwijs- en bestuursverhoudingen Nederlands-Indie 1900-1920. Master's Thesis. Groningen: University of Groningen, Faculty of History.

De Houtman, F., 1880
Cort Verhael vant' gene wedervaren is ... tot Atchein. Gouda.

De Jong, C.A.M., 1990
Kompas 1965-1985, een algemene krant met een katholieke achtergrond binnen het religies pluralisme van Indonesië. Kampen: Kok.

De Lind van Wijngaarden, J.D., 1891
Antonius Walaeus. Leiden: G. Los.

Djamal, Murni (ed.), 2002
Communal Conflicts in Contemporary Indonesia. Jakarta: Language and Culture Centre of the Syarif Hidayatullah Islamic University.

Dobbin, C., 1983
Islamic Revivalism in a Changing Society. Copenhagen: Curzon Press.

Drewes, G.W.J., 1954.
Een Javaanse primbon uit de zestiende eeuw. Opnieuw uitgegeven en vertaald. Leiden: Brill.

-------, 1978
An Early Javanese Code of Muslim Ethics. Leiden: KIT1V.

------- and **L.F. Brakel,** 1986
The Poems of Hamzah Fansuri. Leiden: KITLV.

Enklaar, L, 1981
Kom over en Help Ons! Twaalf opstellen over de Nederlandse zending in de negentiende eeuw. 's-Gravenhage: Boekencentrum.

Eykman, H.J., 1934
De bijzondere toelating van artikel 177 van de Wet op de Staatsinrichting van Ned. Indië. Diss. Utrecht: University of Utrecht.

Federspiel, H.M., 1970
Persatuan Islam: Islamic Reform in Twentieth Century Indonesia. Ithaca,
NY: Cornell University Press.

Fisch, J., 1986
*Hollands Ruhm in Asien, Franqois Yalentyns Vision des niederldndischen
Imperiums im IS Jahrhundert.* Stuttgart: Steiner.

Fokkens, F., 1877
"De Priesterschool te Tegalsari." *TBG* 24: 318-36.

Freijburg, G., 1901
"Rapport." *TBG* 43: 331-48.

Geertz, C., 1973
"Internal Conversion in Contemporary Bali." *The Interpretation of Cultures: Selected Essays by Clifford Geertz.* New York: Basic Books. Pp.
170-92.

Geleynssen de Jongh, W., 1929
Remonstrantie. Ed. W. Caland. 's-Gravenhage: Martinus Nijhoff.

Goldziher, I., 1967
Muslim Studies. Vol. I. London: Allen and Unwin.

Hardenberg, H., 1950
*Tussen zeerovers en christenslaven. Noordafrikaanse reisjournalen
ingeleid en toegelicht.* Leiden: Stenfert Kroese.

Harthoorn, S.E., 1864
Oude grieven en nieuwe bewijzen ten aanzien van de evangelische zending.
Haarlem: Kruseman.

--------, 1865
*De toestand en de behoeften van het onderwijs bij de volken van Neerlands
Oost-Indië.* Haarlem: Kruseman.

--------, 1873
De grondlegging van Batavia. 2nd ed. Vol. MI. Batavia: Ernst en Co.

--------, 1875
*Het inlandsche karakter en de Nederlandsche invloed, eene toespraak aan
zijne leerlingen.* Batavia: Ernst en Co.

Hasjmy, A., 1971
Hikajat Prang Sabi mendjiwai perang Aceh lawan Belanda. Banda Aceh:
Pustaka Faraby.

-------, 1978
Peranan Islam dalam Perang Aceh. Jakarta: Bulan Bintang.

Heurnius, Justus, 1618
De legatione evangelica ad Indos capessenda admonitio. Lugduni Batavorum.

Hoekstra, G., 1989
Barend Schuurman. Zijn persoon en werk als zendingstheoloog op Java.
Master's Thesis. Heverlee: Theological Faculty at Heverlee.

Holle, K.F., 1886
"Mededeelingen over de devotie der Naqsjbendijah in den Nederlandsch-Indischen Archipel." *TBG* 31: 67-81.

Hourani, A., 1962
Arabic Thought in the Liberal Age 1789-1939. London.

Izutsu, T., 1966
Ethico-religious Concepts in the Qur'an. Montreal: McGill University Press.

s'Jacob, H.K., 1976
"De VOC en de Malabarkust in de 18de eeuw." *De VOC in Azie.* Ed. M.A.P Meilink-Roelofs. Bussum: Unieboek. Pp. 85-99.

Jacobs, H., 1971
A Treatise on the Moluccas (c. 1544): Probably the Preliminary Version of Antonio Galvao's lost Histbria das Moluccas. Rome: Jesuit Historical Institute.

Jahroni, Jajang, 2004.
"Defending the Majesty of Islam: Indonesia's Front Pembela Islam." *Studia Islamika* 11/2: 187-253.

Jamhari, 2003
"Mapping Radical Islam in Indonesia." *Studia Islamika* 10/3: 1-28.

Jaquet, F., 1936
"Mutiny en Hadji-ordonnantie: ervaringen met 19e eeuwse bronnen." *BKI* 136: 283-312.

-------, 1983
Sources of the History of Asia and Oceania in the Netherlands. Vol. II. Munich: Saur.

------- (ed.), 1987
Kartini. Brieven aan Mevrouw R.M. Abendanon-Mandri en haar echtgenoot met andere documenten. Leiden: KTTLV.

Johns, A.H., 1984
"Islam in the Malay World." *Islam in Asia.* Vol. II. Ed. R. Israeli and A. Johns. Jerusalem: The Magnes Press. Pp. 115-61.

Jones, R, 1979
"Ten Conversion Myths from Indonesia." *Conversion to Islam.* Ed. N. Levtzion. New York: Holmes and Meier. Pp. 129-58.

Jongeling, M.C., 1966
Het Zendingsconsulaat, 1906-1942. Arnhem: Van Loghum Slaterus.

Juynboll, T.W., 1903
Handleiding tot de kennis van de mohammedaansche wet, volgens de leer der sjafi'itische school. Leiden: Brill.

Juynboll, W.M.C., 1931
Zeventiende-eeuwsche beoefenaars van hetArabisch in Nederland. Utrecht: Kemink en Zoon.

Kartodirdjo, S., 1966
The Peasants' Revolt of Banten in 1888. 's-Gravenhage: Martinus Nijhoff.

Kern, RA., 1938
"De Verbreiding van den Islam, I." *Geschiedenis van Nederlandsch-Indië.* Ed. G. Stapel. Amsterdam: Joost van den Vondel. Pp. 299-365.

Kernkamp, W.J.A., 1946
"Regeering en Islam." *Daar werd wat groots verricht* .... 2nd. ed. Ed. W. van Helsdingen. Amsterdam: Elsevier.

Keuning, J. (ed.), 1938-1949
De tweede schipvaart der Nederlanders naar Oost-Indië onder Jacob van Neck en Wijbrant Warwijck, 1598-1600. Vol. I-V. 's-Gravenhage: Martinus Nijhoff.

Knaap, GJ., 1987
Kruidnagelen en Christenen. De Verenigde Oost-Indische Compagnie en de bevolking van Ambon, 1656-1696. Dordrecht: Foris.

Koolen, G.M.J.M., 1967
De Colleges van de Compagnie. Master's Thesis. Nijmegen: Catholic University of Nijmegen, Theological Faculty.

Kraemer, H., 1921
Een Javaansche primbon uit de zestiende eeuw; inleiding, vertaling en aantekeningen. Leiden: Trap.

-------, 1938
De Islam als godsdienstig en als zendingsprobleem. 's-Gravenhage: Boekencentrum.

Kritzeck, J., 1964
Peter the Venerable and Islam. Princeton: Princeton University Press.

Kruijf, E.F., 1894
Geschiedenis van het Nederlandsche Zendelinggenootschap en zijne Zendingsposten. Groningen: Wolters.

Kumar, A., 1976
Surapati: Man and Legend. Leiden: Brill.

Kwantes, RC., 1978
De ontwikkeling van de nationalistische beweging in Nederlandsch-Indië. Bronnenpublicatie. 2nd Part medio 1923-1928. Groningen: Wolters Noordhoff.

La Chapelle, H.M., 1899
"Nota betreffende het Tenggergebied." *TBG* 41: 32-54.

Lach, Donald F., 1968
Southeast Asia in the Eyes of Europe. Chicago: University of Chicago Press.

Lancaster, Sir James, 1877
The Voyages of Sir James Lancaster to the East Indies. Ed. C.R. Markham. London: Hakluyt Society.

Levtzion, N. (ed.), 1979
Conversion to Islam. New York: Holmes and Meier.

Lian, The and **Paul W. Van Der Veur,** 1973
The Verhandelingen van het Bataviaasch Genootschap: An Annotated Content Analysis. Papers in International Studies. Athens, Ohio: Ohio State University.

Lion Cachet, F., 1896
Een jaar op reis in dienst der zending. Amsterdam: Wormser.

Lombard, Denys, 1970
Le "Spraeck ende Woord-Boek" de Frederick de Houtman. Paris: Ecole Française d'Extreme-Orient.

Marshall, P.J., 1988
"British Asessments of the Dutch in Asia in the Age of Raffles." *Itinerario* 12: 1-16.

Meilink-Roelofs, M.A.P. (ed.), 1976
De VOC in Azie. Bussum: Unieboek.

Michel, T., 1984
A Muslim Theologians's Response to Christianity: Ibn Taimiyya's Al-lawab al'Sahih. New York: Caravan Books.

Mooij, J., 1927-1931
Bouwstoffen voor de Geschiedenis der Protestantsche Kerk in Nederlandsch-Indië. Vol. I-III. Weltevreden: Landsdrukkerij.

Muskens, M.P.M., 1969
Indonesië. Een strijd om nationale identiteit: nationalisten, islamieten, katholieken. Bussum: Paul Brand.

Nakamura, M., 1983
The Crescent Arises over the Banyan Tree: A Study of the Muhammadiyah Movement in a Central Javanese Town. Yogyakarta: Gadjah Mada University Press.

Natsir, N., 1969
Islam dan Kristen di Indonesia. Bandung: Diponegoro.

Nieuwenhuys, R., 1978
Oost-Indische Spiegel. 3rd ed. Amsterdam: Querido.

Olthof, W.L. (ed.), 1987 (rpt.)
Babad Tanah Djawi. Javaanse Rijkskroniek. Vol. I-II. Leiden: HITLV.

Parrinder, G., 1982 (rpt.)
Jesus in the Qur'an. London: Sheldon, 1965.
Partonadi, Sutarman S., 1988
Sadrach's Community and its Contextual Roots: A Nineteenth Century Javanese Expression of Christianity. Amsterdam: Rodopi.
Peacock, J., 1978
Purifying the Faith: The Muhammadiyah Movement in Indonesian Islam.
Menlo Park: Cummings.
-------, 1978
Muslim Puritans: Reformist Psychology in Southeast Asian Islam.
Berkeley: University of California Press.
Pigeaud, T., 1927
"Alexander, Sakender en Senopati." *Djawa* 7: 231-361.
-------, 1933
De Serat 7jabolang en de Serat 7jentini. Batavia: TBG.
Pires, Tomfs, 1944
Suma Oriental. Ed. and Tr. A. Cortesao. London: Hakluyt Society.
Poensen, C., 1886
Brieven over den Islam uit de binnenlanden van Java. Leiden: Brill.
Poeze, H., 1988
Politiek politioneele overzichten van Nederlandsch-Indië. Vol. III (1931-1934). Leiden: KITLV.

Raffles, T.S., 1930
Memoirs of the Life and Public Serivices with Some of the Correspondence of T. S. Raffles. London: John Murray.
-------, 1817 (1978 rpt.)
The History of Java. Kuala Lumpur: Oxford University.
Ras, JJ., 1986
"The Babad Tanah Jawi and its Reliability." *Cultural Context and Textual Interpretation.* Ed. C. Grijns en S. Robson. Leiden: KITLV. Pp. 246-73.
-------, 1987 (rpt.)
"Betekenis en functie van de Babad Tanah Jawi." *Babad Tanah Djawi. Javaanse Rijkskroniek.* Vol. I-II. Ed. W.L. Olthof. Leiden: KITLV. Pp. IX-LIV.
Reimers, E., 1932
Memoirs of Rykloff van Goens, Governor of Ceylon: Selections from the Dutch Records of the Ceylon Government. Vol. 3. Colombo: Government Press.
Ricklefs, M.C., 1979
"Six Centuries of Islamization in Java." *Conversion to Islam.* Ed. N. Levtzion. New York: Holmes and Meier. Pp. 110-28.

Ridder de Stuers, HJJ.L., 1849-1850
De vestiging en uitbreiding der Nederlanders ter Westkust van Sumatra.
Vol. I-II. Amsterdam: Van Kampen.

Rinkes, D.A., 1909
*Abdoerraoef van Singkel, bijdrage tot de kennis van de mystiek op Sumatra
en Java.* Heerenveen: Hepkema.

Roessingh, M.P.H., 1982
Sources of the History of Asia and Oceania in the Netherlands. Vol. I.
Munich: Saur.

Roff, W., 1987
"Islamic Movements: One or Many?" *Islam and the Political Economy of
Meaning.* Ed. W. Roff. London: Croom Helm. Pp. 13-30.

Rogerius, A., 1915
De Open-deure tot het verborgen heydendom. Ed. W. Caland. Lindschoten
Vereniging 10. 's-Gravenhage: Lindschoten Vereniging.

Rouffaer, G.P. and **J.W. Ijzerman,** 1915
*De eerste schipvaart der Nederlanders naar Oost-Indië onder Cornelis de
Houtman.* Lindschoten Vereniging 7, 25, 32. 's-Gravenhage: Linschoten
Vereniging.

Rusli Karim, M., 1985
Dinamika Islam di Indonesia, suatu tinjauan sosial dan politik. Yogyakarta: Hanindita.

Schuurman, B.M., 1933
Mystik und Glaube, im Zusammenhang mit der Mission auf Java. The
Hague: Martinus Nijhoff.

-------, 1931
Over alle Bergen. 's-Gravenhage: Daamen.

Serton, P., 1971
François Valentyn's Description of the Cape of Good Hope. Cape Town:
Van Riebeeck Society.

Simon, G., 1909
Der Islam wie ich ihn kennen lemte auf Sumatra. Barmen: RMG.

-------, 1910
*Islam und Christentum im Kampf um die Eroberung der animistischen
Heidenwelt; Beobachtungen aus der Mohammedanermissions in Nieder-
ländisch-Indien.* Berlin: Warneck.

-------, 1912
Mohammedaansche propaganda en christelijke zending in onze Oost. Tr.
G. Smit. Utrecht: Ruys.

Situmorang, S. and **A. Teeuw,** 1952
Sedjarah Melaju menurut terbitan Abdullah. Amsterdam: Djambatan.

Skinner, C., 1963
Sja'ir Perang Mengkasar. 's-Gravenhage: Martinus Nijhoff.

Slomp, J., 1984
"Luther en de Wortels van het anti-Islamisme." *Begrip* 68: 1-18.
-------, 1988
"Kraemer en de dialoog met moslims." *Wereld en Zending* 17: 222-27.
Smith, W.C., 1962 (1964 rpt.)
The Meaning and End of Religion. New York: Mentor Books.
-------, 1967
Questions of Religious Truth. London: SCM Press.
Snouck Hurgronje, C., 1893-1894
De Atjehers. Vol. I-II. Batavia: Landsdrukkerij.
--------, 1911
Nederland en de Islam. Leiden: Brill.
-------, 1923-1924
Verspreide Geschriften. Vol. I-VI. Leiden: Brill.
-------, 1957-1965
Ambtelijke Adviezen. Vol. I-III. 's-Gravenhage: Martinus Nijhoff.
Soebardi, 1971
"Santri-religious Elements as Reflected in the Book of Tjentini." *BKI* 127: 331-49.
Southern, R.W., 1962
Western Views of Islam in the Middle Ages. Cambridge, MS: Harvard University Press.
Spindler, M.R., 1988
Hendrik Kraemer. Bibliografie en Archief. Leiden: HMO.
Spyer, Patricia, 2002
"Fire without Smoke and Other Phantoms of Ambon's Violence: Media Effects, Agency, and the Work of Imagination." *Indonesia* 74 (October): 21-36.
Steenbrink, K.A., 1972
"Het Indonesisch Godsdienstministerie en de godsdiensten." *Wereld en Zending* 1: 174-79.
-------, 1974
Pesantren, Madrasah, Sekolah: recente ontwikkelingen in indonesisch islamonderricht. Meppel: Krips Repro.
-------, 1988
Kitab Suci atau Kertas Toilet? Nuruddin ar-Raniri dan Agama Kristen. Yogyakarta: IAIN Sunan Kalijaga.
-------, 1990
"Pancasila, Entwicklungen innerhalb der civil religion Indonesiens." *Zeitschrift für Missions- und Religionswissenschaft* 74: 124-41.
-------, 1993
"Indonesian Politics and a Muslim Theology of Religions: 1965-1990." *Islam and Christian-Muslim Relations* 4: 223-46.

-------, 2000
"Patterns of Muslim-Christian Dialogue in Indonesia, 1965-1998." J. Waardenburg (ed.). *Muslim-Christian Perceptions of Dialogue Today.* Louvain: Peeters. Pp. 81-112.
Suminto, HA, 1985
Politik Islam Pemerintah Hindia Belanda. Jakarta: LP3ES.
Sutherland, H., 1982
"Mestizos as Middleman? Ethnicity and Access in Colonial Macassar." *Papers of the Dutch Indonesian Historical Conference in Lage Yuursche, The Netherlands, June 1980.* Ed. G. Schutte and H. Sutherland. Leiden: BIS.
Swellengrebel, L. (ed.), 1984
Bali: Studies in Life, Thought and Ritual. Leiden: KITLV.

Tanja, V., 1982
Himpunan Mahasiswa Islam. Jakarta: Sinar Harapan.
Taylor, J.G., 1988
Smeltkroes Batavia. Groningen: Wolters-Noordhoff.
Teeuw, A. and **D.K. Wyatt,** 1970-1971
Hikayat Patani. Leiden: KITLV.
Ten Berge, JJ., 1931
"'De Koran' en 'Evangelie en Koran'." *Studien, Tijdschrift voor Godsdienst, Wetenschap en Letteren* 60: 58-278; 285-307.
Termorshuizen, G., 1988
P. A. Daum, Journalist en Romancier van Tempo Doeloe. Amsterdam: Nijgh and Van Ditmar.
-------, 1990
P. A. Daum: Ik ben journalist ex professo. Amsterdam: Nijgh en Van Ditmar.
Tibawi, A.L., 1972
Islamic Education. London: Luzac and Co.

Unger, W.S., 1948
De Oudste Reizen van de Zeeuwen naar Oost Indië 1598-1604. Linschoten Vereeniging 60. 's-Gravenhage: Martinus Nijhoff.

Valentijn, F., 1724-1726
Oud en Nieuw Oost-Indiën. Vol. I-VIII. Dordrecht.
Van Baal, J., 1939
"De bevolking van Zuid-Nieuw-Guinea onder nederlandsch Bestuur: 36 jaren." *TBG* 79: 309-414.
-------, 1989 rpt.
Ontglipt verleden. Vol. I-II. Franeker: Wever.

Van Butselaar, J., 1988
"Tambaram revisited. De betekenis van de wereldzendingsconferentie van 1938 kritisch bekeken." *Wereld en Zending* 17:207-12.

Van den Berg, L.W.C., 1886
Le Hadhramout et les colonies Arabes dans lArchipel Indien. Batavia: Landsdrukkerij.

Van der Chijs, JA, 1865
Verslag van het Inlandsch Onderwijs. Batavia: Landsdrukkerij.

Van Dijk, Kees, 2001
A Country in Despair: Indonesia between 1997 and 2000. Leiden: KITLV.

Van Goor, J., 1978
Jan Kompenie as Schoolmaster. Diss. Utrecht: University of Utrecht.

-------, 1982
Kooplieden, predikanten en bestuurders overzee. Beeldvorming en plaatsbepaling in een andere wereld. Utrecht: HES.

Van Koningsveld, P., SJ, 1978
"Het Raadsel van de Islam." *N7T* 32: 270-82.

-------, 1988
Snouck Hurgronje en de Islam. Leiden: Documentatie-centrum Islam-Christendom.

Van Leeuwen, A.T., 1947
Ghazali als apologeet van de Islam. Diss. Leiden.

Van Linschoten, J.H., 1910
Itinerario; voyage ofte schipvaert van ... naar Oost ofte Portugaels Indien, 1579-1592. Ed. H. Kern, 's-Gravenhage: Linschoten Vereniging.

Van Nieuwenhuijze, C.A.O., 1945
Samsu'l Din van Pasai; bijdrage tot de kennis der Sumatraansche mystiek. Leiden: Brill.

-------, 1949
Mens en Vrijheid in Indonesië. The Hague: Van Hoeve.

Van Ophuisen, A.H., 1907
De Huwelijksordonnantie en hare uitvoering. Diss. Leiden.

Van Randwijck, S.C. Graaf, 1981
Handelen en Denken in Dienst der Zending. Oegstgeest 1897-1942. Vol. III. 's-Gravenhage: Boekencentrum.

Van Ronkel, P.S., 1919
"Zeventiende-eeuwsche wijsheid over het Maleisch." *Koloniaal 7ijdschrift* 8: 296-304.

Van Rijckevorsel, L., 1952
Pastoor F. van Lith, S.J.. De stichter van de missie in Midden Java, 1863-1926. Nijmegen: Claverbond.

Van de Velde, JJ., 1932
"Godsdienstige rechtspraak in het Gouvernement Atjeh en Onderhoorigheden." *Koloniaal 7ijdschrift* 21: 504-15.

Van der Wal, S.L., 1963
Het onderwijsbeleid in Nederlands-Indie, 1900-1940, een bronnenpub-likatie. Groningen: Wolters.

-------, 1967
De Opkomst van de Nationalistische Beweging in Nederlands Indie, een bronnenpublikatie. Groningen: Wolters.

Voetius, Gisbertus, 1648-1655
Selectae Disputationes Theologicae. Vol. I-II. Ultrajecti.

-------, 1663-1676
Politica Ecclesiastica. Vol. I-IV. Ultrajecti.

Voorhoeve, P., 1955
Twee Maleise geschriften van Nuruddin ar Raniri in facsimile uitgegeven met aantekeningen. Leiden: Brill.

Vredenbregt, J., 1962
"The Haddj: Some of its Features and Functions in Indonesia." *BKI* 118: 91-154.

Walaeus, A., 1647
Opera Omnia. Lugduni Batavorum: A. Wyngaerden.

Wap, J.J.F., 1862
Het Gezantschap van den Sultan van Achin, 1602, aan Prins Maurits van Nassau. Rotterdam.

Wawer, W., 1974
Muslime und Christen in der Republik Indonesia. Wiesbaden: Franz Steiner.

Wertheim, W.F., 1978
Indonesië van Yorstenrijk tot Neokolonie. Meppel: Boom.

Wijnmalen, T.C.L., 1869
Hugo de Groot als Verdediger des Christendoms Beschouwd. Utrecht: Dannenfelser.

Woelders, M.O., 1975
Het Sultanaat Palembang 1811-1825. 's-Gravenhage: Martinus Nijhoff.

Zoetmulder, P.J., 1935
Pantheisme en Monisme in de Javaansche Soeloek-litteratuur. Nijmegen: Berkhout.

Index

'Abduh, M. 134, 135
Abdul Muis 96
Abdulgani, Ruslan 146
Abdurrahman Wahid 148-49
Abel 48
Abraham 34, 48, 109, 129
Achin 12, 14, 15, 29-31, 35, 51, 64,
Adam 33, 48
Adat 74, 98, 135
Aden 21
Adultery 62, 77
Advisor for Native Affairs (Adviseur voor inlandsche zaken) 77, 78, 90, 93, 94
Africa 38, 51, 104
Agus Salim, H. 111, 134, 137
Ahmad Dahlan 136
Ahmad Rijaluddin 130
Ahmadiyah 137, 138
Akib Latuconsina 151
Alamsyah Ratu Perwiranegara 147
Albuquerque 25
Alexander the Great 131
Ali, Haji Abdul Mukti 147
Ambon 39, 41, 63, 67, 149-53
Ameer Ali 138
Anabaptism 53, 55
Arabic (language) 11, 17, 30, 37
Arabs 37, 39, 47, 72,74,102, 128
Arianism 24, 52
Ar-Raniri, Nuruddin 51,128
Arswendo Atmowiloto 148-49
Ascension 127
Asia 59, 61, 65, 88
Averroes 52

Babad Suropati 130

Babad Tanah Jawi 126, 127
Bacon, John 20
Bali 110
Banda 32, 61, 63, 64
Bandung 78, 81-84, 94, 119, 136
Banten 58, 68, 153
Banyumas 17, 18
Baptism 14, 65, 69, 106, 116
Baronius 57
Barth, K 102, 113
Batak 93, 107, 108, 144
Batavia 20, 37, 40, 49, 55, 76, 81
Batavian Society of Arts and Sciences 59, 76
Beel, L.J.M. 121
Benda, H.J. 88
Bengal 36, 71, 130
Bible 30, 47, 68, 86,105, 111, 117, 143
  1 Cor. 11:26 47
  1 Cor. 15:24 47
  2 Cor. 5:10 47
  Matt. 28:20 47
  Matt. 3:17 14, 16
  John 17:3 51
  Luke 1:32 47
  Luke 12:11 13
Borneo 40
British 12, 16, 22, 31, 55, 57, 73, 82, 135, 137, 138
Brugmans, I.J. 85
Buddhism 42, 59, 102, 125
Buitenzorg 105, 109
Bulgaria 52
Busbequius 49
Bustanus-Salatin 128

Calvinism 14, 26, 51, 76, 115, 136

Catholicism 18, 26, 51, 55, 66, 98
Ceribon 64
China 27, 55, 118
Chinese 57, 68-70, 72, 92, 103, 144
Cianjur 81-83, 94
Cilegon 132
Circumcision 14, 26, 34, 40, 99
Civil religion 146
Coen, J.P. 60-67, 96
Colombo 22, 66
Communism 142-43, 145
Compagnie van Verre 11
Counsellor for Missions (*Zendingsconsul*) 108-10
Cordoba 19, 52
Covenant 14, 35, 50, 69
Crusades 19, 35

Dachlan, K.H.M. 144
Daniel, Norman 19, 20, 55
Darul Islam 141-42
Daum, PA. 77,82
David 13, 30, 38, 112
Davies, John 29, 30
De Graaff, N. 35, 36
De Groot, Hugo 43-46, 50, 57
De Houtman, F. 11, 12, 29
De Jonge, B.C. 50, 64, 92, 121
Death penalty 62
Delft 102
Demak 126
Dili 149
Dingemans, L.F. 136
Divorce 48, 72, 90, 103, 138
Djajadiningrat, H. 89, 96
Du Bus de Gisignies, L.P.J. 121

Elmacinus 52
Epilepsy 53
Erpenius 54, 57
Ethical politics 85, 92, 96, 133
Europe 23
Eve 33

Fachruddin, H. 136
Fasting 40, 51, 53, 80, 133
Flores 115
Fock, D. 136
Fort de Cock 134
Francis of Assisi 53
Funeral 27, 32, 35

Gajo 93
Galvao, Antonio 28
Ganges 36
Gereformeerd 16, 18, 104
Germany 49, 54, 109
Giri 126
Goa 25, 26
Golius 54
Gramedia 149
Greece 52
Gujarat 21, 51, 128, 129

Habibie, Baharuddin Yusuf 149-51
Hagar 30
Haji 78-80, 95, 111, 112, 134
Hamzah Fansuri 128
Harmoko 148
Harthoorn, S.E. 99-102
Harun Hadiwijono 147
Haryono Anwar 144
Hative Besar 149
Hazeu, G.A.J. 76, 77, 91-97, 107
Headhunting 103, 107
Heaven 14, 26, 33, 45, 47, 51, 57
Hebrew 51
Hervormd 16
Het Licht 112, 137,138
Heurnius, J. 49
Hila 39
Hinduism 27, 34, 35, 42, 34, 59,
Hindus 26
Holle, K.F. 59, 76-81, 83-86, 92
Holy Spirit 14

Holy war 19, 81, 128-30
Homosexuality 29
Hoornbeek, J. 55, 57
Hungary 52
Ibrahim, K.H. 30, 93, 94, 136
ICMI, the *Ikatan Cendekiawan Muslim Indonesia* 148
Idenburg, A.W.F. 94, 95, 99, 109
Idols 56, 126
Independent Moluccan Republic (*Republik Maluku Selatan* or RMS) 141
India 20-23, 25, 26, 31, 34-36, 38
Indian Ocean 21, 22, 125
Indisch Vaderland 82
Indonesian Council of Churches 145
Inheritance 22, 72
Inquisition 28, 53
Iran 27
Irian Jaya 18
Isaac 48
Iskandar Tsani 35
Islamic State 140, 146
Islamization 27
Istanbul 21

Jacob 22, 30, 31, 48, 67
Jaelani Naro 143
Japan 55
Java 17, 18, 24, 27, 29, 37, 38, 40
Javabode, De 81, 82
Jember 17
Jeroboam 47
Jesus, Christ 13, 14, 33, 36, 38, 41
Jews 26, 27, 39, 45-47, 55, 129
Johannes Andrea 49, 50, 53
John of Segovia 20
Jong Islamieten Bond 111, 112
Jong Java 111, 114

Jongeling, M.C. 88, 98, 108, 109
Judaism 41, 50, 55
Juynboll, T.W. 21, 49, 138

Kediri 17, 102
Keuchenius, L.W.C. 87, 88
Kompas 149
Koran 16, 17, 19, 26, 39, 41, 26, 39, 46-48, 50-54, 56, 57, 68, 79, 84-86, 117-19, 125, 129, 131, 134, 137, 143, 145
Kraemer, H. 57, 99, 102, 111-15, 121, 134, 136, 138
Kris 12, 15, 101, 126
Kupang 150
Kuyper, A. 109

Lammens, H. 118
Langgar 17, 86
Laskar Jihad 152-53
Lebanon 145
Leiden 21, 43, 46, 49, 51, 88, 89,
Lion Cachet, F. 104-06, 116
Locher-Scholten, E. 92
Lombok 18
Ludovicus Vivem 49
Lulofs, C. 94
Luther, Martin 24, 53

Macassar/Makassar 20, 38, 144, 150
Madagascar 11, 21
Madura 17, 18, 100, 101
Magnis Suseno, F. 147
Mahasiswa Muslim Maluku (Moluccan Muslim Students) 150
Majapahit 126
Majelis Ulama Indonesia (MUI) 145, 147
Makassar Affair 144
Malabar 66, 67, 124, 125
Malacca 25, 27, 125, 128
Malang 99, 114

Malay (language)   13, 29, 30,
    33, 37, 38, 56, 57, 78, 83,
    86, 91, 92, 98, 107, 114,
    118, 119, 124, 127, 128,
    130, 131
Malaysia 21, 124
Maldives 11
Malikul Adil 125
Manichaeism 52
Marind Anim 18
Marriage 48, 69, 72, 91, 103,
    116
marriage law 144, 153
Marsil Ficinus 52
Mary 14, 33, 112, 118
Masjumi 112, 142-43
Mataram 37, 60, 69
Maurice, Prince 16
Mecca 51, 53, 56, 59, 72, 74,
    79, 148
Medina 132
Megawati Sukarnoputri 151
Messiah 45, 46, 118
Middelburg 31, 46, 64
Milton Matuanakota 150
Minahasa 86
Minangkabau 93, 134, 135
Ministry of Religion 144
Mintaredja H. 143
Mission 18, 21, 24, 31, 43, 79,
    86
Modjowarno 99
Moesa, R.M. 38
Mogul empire 21
Moluccas 21, 24, 28, 31, 34,
    38, 39, 28, 52, 60, 61, 63,
    65, 67, 76, 86, 141, 150-53
Mongeer 36
Monitor 148
Moor 13, 15, 26, 51, 63-65
Morocco 140, 147
Moses 13, 38, 47, 48
Mosque 12, 26, 30, 34, 70, 72
Muhammad 13, 16, 19,28, 33,
    34, 38, 39, 41, 46-48, 50-

53, 56, 59, 100, 102, 105,
    112, 118, 119, 124, 125,
    127, 132, 135-37
Muhammadiyah 120,134-36
Muhammadiyah 146
Munawir Syadzali M.A. 147
Muntilan 115, 118
Muskens, M.P.M. 123
Muslim Indonesia (Indonesian
    Organization of Muslim In-
    tellectuals) 148

Naires 27
NASAKOM ideology 142
Natsir, M. 119-21, 134
New Guinea 11, 17, 18
Nicholas of Cusa 20
Nortier, W. 99, 102
North Halmahera 152
Nunes, S. 12

Ongky Pieters 150
OPM (Organisasi Papua Mer-
    deka) 152
Ottoman 21, 24, 21

P4 (Pedoman Penghayatan dan
    Pengamalan Pancasila) 144
Padri 74, 75
Panarukan 29
Pancasila 140-43, 146-48
Pantheism 115, 121
Papist 18
Papua 18
Parimo, Herman 151
Parmusi (Partai Muslimin Indo-
    nesia) 143
Partonadi, S. 106
Pasai 28, 125
Pasuruan 149
Patangga, Arif 151
Paul 40, 76, 86, 129
Paulo, Antonij 37, 38
Pembela Islam 119
Pemuda Pancasila 150
Penghulu 78, 80, 81, 83, 90, 91

People's Council 110, 111, 119
Persatuan Islam 119, 120, 134
Persia 21, 25, 67
Pesantren 80, 85, 86, 101, 106,
Peter the Venerable 33
Philippines 21, 125
Pijper, G.F. 91
Pires 27
Pires, Tomé 27, 28
PMP (*Pendidikan Moral Pancasila*) 146
PNI (*Partai National di Indonesia*) 142
Poensen, C. 102-05, 116
Policy of association 92
Polo, Marco 21
Polygamy 103, 138
Pope 54, 80
Portuguese 12, 14, 15, 22, 25-30
Poso 151
PPP (*Partai Persatuan Pembangunan*) 143
Priest 39, 71, 72, 80, 89, 118, 120
Propaganda Fide 46, 53
PRRI-Permesta revolt 143
Ptirwokerto 18, 80
Purworejo 105, 106

Radermacher, J.C.M. 59
Raffles, Sir Thomas Stamford 59
Red Sea 21, 44, 105
Reformed 16, 18, 46, 55, 66, 67
Regent 73, 79, 80, 82, 94, 95, 101
Reification 140, 141
Relandus, Adrianus 43, 54-57, 103
Renegade 13, 31, 64, 135
Resident 17, 75, 78, 79, 81-84
Ridderkerk 144
Rinkes, D.A. 95, 133

Romantics 58
Rotterdam 104
Ruterus 71

Sabbath 51
Sadrach 105, 106, 116-18
Safawid Shah Abbas I 21
Safawides 27
Sale, G. 57, 68, 95
Samsurijal 111
Samudra 124, 125
Santri 80, 85, 99, 112,
Saracen 41, 51
Sarekat Islam 93, 95, 96, 120, 133
Scharp, J. 43, 57, 58
Schuurman, B. 113-16, 121
Secularization 102, 103, 117
Seda, F. 122
Segaf, M. al- 81, 83
Sejarah Melayu 124
Seminarium Indicum 43,46
Serat Baron Sakender 131
Serat Centini 127
Shah Ismael 27
Shahrastani 129
Shamsuddin as-Samatrani 128
Shariah 141, 145, 148
Shi'ite 27, 39, 54
Simatupang, Tahi Bonar (1920-90) 141, 144-45
Simon, G. 93, 106-08
Singapore 79, 124, 130
Situbondo 149
Smith, W.C. 112
Snouck Hurgronje C. 59, 77, 84
Soegijopranoto, Mgr. Albertus 141
Solomon 47
South Africa 38, 104
Southern, R.W. 13, 19, 20, 22
Spanish 29, 49, 53, 55
Sri Lanka 22, 24, 34, 38, 42, 38
Suharto 145

Sukarno 140-43, 146
Sulawesi 38, 109
Sultan Iskandar Tsani 35
Sulu 21
Sumatra 21, 38, 67, 74, 75, 93
Sumbawa 68
Sumenep 73
Sunni 39, 54
Surabaya 64
Surakarta 127, 133
Surat 21
Surinam 140
Synod of Dort 46, 66

Tambaram 113
Tarekat 17, 80, 84
Ten Berge, J.J. 118-21, 134,
137
Tengger 93
Ternate 29, 52, 60
Tentena 151
Thailand (Siam) 27, 52, 125
Theosophy 111
Thomas Christians 66
Tidore 29, 68
Transmigrations 150
Tuban 28
Turkey 140
Turks 18, 27, 35, 53, 54, 62

Unger, W.S. 11, 29
Uthman bin Yahya al Alawi 84
Utrecht 44, 49, 53, 55, 72, 98

Valentijn, Rev. Francois 32,
38-41
Van Baal, J. 11, 16-18
Van Butselaar, J. 113
Van den Berg, L.W.C. 59, 84,
90

Van der Capellen, G.A. 85
Van der Chijs, J.A. 86, 87
Van Goens, Rijkloff 22, 37
Van Haren, Onno Zwier 43, 58
Van Leeuwen, A.T. 149
Van Limburg Stirum, O.J.H. 93
Van Linschoten, Jan Huygen
25-27
Van Lith, F. 115-18
Van Neck, Jacob 31, 33, 34
Van Randwijck, S.C. 99, 109,
110
Van Ronkel, P.S. 56, 57
Vedic scripture 143
Venus 51, 56
Voetius, Gisbertus 41, 43, 49-
55
Vork 26, 33, 55, 126

Waalwijk 144
Wailete 149
Walaeus, Antonius 43, 46, 47,
49
Warwijck, W. 31, 34
Weber, Max 147
Wertheim, W.F. 74
Wibisono, J. 138
Willekens, P.J. 120
Wine 33, 48, 55, 81
Wiranatakusuma 94
Wiranto, General 150
Wiwoho 137
World Council of Churches
(WCC) 145

Yogyakarta 37,111, 116, 127,
131, 135-37, 140, 152

Zoetmulder, P.J. 115, 121